The American Byron

The American Byron

HOMOSEXUALITY AND THE FALL
OF FITZ-GREENE HALLECK

John W. M. Hallock

The University of Wisconsin Press

Illustrations

The American Byron

Introduction

And when the death-note of my bugle has sounded,
And memorial tears are embalming my name,
By young hearts like his may the grave be surrounded
Where I sleep my last sleep in the sunbeams of fame.
Fitz-Greene Halleck, "Young America"

T
HE SUN beamed brightly at three o'clock on Tuesday afternoon,
May 15, 1877, as William Cullen Bryant introduced the president
of the United States to an audience of fifty thousand men, women,
and children.[1] At a private luncheon before the ceremony, President and
Mrs. Hayes had been presented with a miniature of the twelve-thousand-
dollar monument that was about to be unveiled in New York's Central
Park. President Jackson had dined twice with the man honored on this
day, President Lincoln had complimented him, and John Quincy Adams
had alluded to one of his poems in a speech delivered to the House of
Representatives in 1836. In addition to nurturing political relationships
in the United States with the likes of Daniel Webster, Henry Clay, and
John C. Calhoun, the venerated poet had been a personal friend of such
foreign dignitaries as Joseph Bonaparte and British government minister
Charles Richard Vaughan, who had thrown a grand dinner just to honor
him. The poet had also impressed other major authors of his time who
almost unanimously ranked him their superior. He was a favorite of
Charles Dickens and William Thackeray as well as of the American literary giants, Bryant, James Fenimore Cooper, Washington Irving, and Edgar Allan Poe. As military bands played on the day of the unveiling, artists
and politicians rubbed elbows with polished etiquette.

The illustrious poet had once joked about being carved in stone along
with the green umbrella that had become his trademark accessory. In fact,
he had told a friend who had helped to plan the statue that "the likeness
would not strike" without the umbrella and that he hoped another ad-

3

mirer of his work had obtained "a sculptor cunning enough in carving stone umbrellas."[2] But it was without an umbrella that his figure would have to withstand the torrents of praise showered upon him that day. Even so, the fine weather and smooth collaboration of the elite could not prevent controversy from overshadowing the auspicious occasion commemorating America's earliest homosexual poet, Fitz-Greene Halleck.

President Hayes, who had taken office only two months earlier, unknowingly sparked the controversy when he yanked a sheet painted with the national colors off of the stone figure of the man he called "the favored of all the early American poets."[3] While favorable portraits of Halleck had been painted by America's leading artists (including Brown, Elliott, Hicks, Inman, Jarvis, Morse, Rogers, and Waldo), the statue by J. Wilson MacDonald, who had recently created Irving's memorial bust, was sharply criticized. *Harper's Weekly* declared it "a very poor work of art,"[4] and Bayard Taylor complained:

It is not a fortunate specimen of our native art. The posture is ungraceful, the face over-conscious to the verge of ostentation, and the general character of the figure is so theatrical that few of those who knew the poet will immediately recognize him.[5]

Taylor denounced the effeminate depiction of his friend and had commented elsewhere on Halleck's unease with his looks and age. William Allen Butler, another poet, also commented on Halleck's "habitual self-depreciation."[6] Indeed, Halleck joked that no paintings of himself had caused him or "any one else to violate the second commandment" and complained that he was the ugliest of the numerous men in the famed group portrait of Washington Irving and his literary friends.[7] He declined to be photographed for *Putnam's Magazine,* asking instead to be illustrated "not as I am but as I ought to be"—words echoed in his initial refusal to be photographed by M. B. Brady: "I much prefer that you should remember me as I have been, not as I am."[8] Often relieved when admirers managed to get outdated pictures of him rather than images that conveyed the ravages of time, Halleck displayed a self-conscious neurosis about his appearance that proved utterly modern. He would have been pleased to see that the statue depicted a youthful Halleck, in spite of its flamboyant pose.

In addition to the alleged misrepresentation of Halleck's person, the occasion was dampened by the absence of certain key figures. Ralph Waldo Emerson, Henry Wadsworth Longfellow, and former president Ulysses S. Grant had sent notes expressing their regrets.[9] Even worse, John Greenleaf Whittier, who had written a fourteen-stanza poem for the ceremony, was too ill to attend. General James Grant Wilson, Halleck's literary executor and first biographer, read Whittier's elegy.

The statue was placed in the "Poet's Corner of America," strangely nicknamed since it had previously included only the English and Scottish figures of William Shakespeare, Robert Burns, and Sir Walter Scott. Halleck remains the only American among the writers honored on what is now referred to as Literary Walk. Though New York City mayor Smith Ely graciously responded to remarks by the country's president, he was clearly annoyed by the trampling of the mall, which motivated him to create an ordinance prohibiting future parades in Central Park.[10]

With much pomp, a Rhode Island granite monument had already been dedicated to Halleck in 1869 near his birthplace and grave site in Guilford, Connecticut. Several thousand people had arrived by special trains from New Haven on the anniversary of his birthday.[11] A two-thousand-dollar, eighteen-foot obelisk, surrounded by clippings of the Melrose Abbey ivy given to Washington Irving by Sir Walter Scott, had been dedicated in the oval center of Alderbrook Cemetery. The event had featured military bands and a keynote speech by Bayard Taylor. Oliver Wendell Holmes had planned to participate, but Wilson had delivered Holmes's elegiac lines in the ailing poet's absence.

Both the monument and the statue were forged to immortalize Halleck, who had the dual distinction of being "the first American poet to whom a public monument was ever erected in this country, and the first to have a full bronze statue in the New World."[12] Both representations indubitably failed their purpose. In 1980, the *New York Times* complained that more famous authors (such as Irving and Cooper) are not represented on the Mall and deprecatingly described Halleck's statue: "Halleck's teacup fingers, pursed lips and negligently strewn books suggest a literary prig . . . now forgotten."[13] In 1993, a centerfold of the statue and famous walk appeared in the May *National Geographic*, which only identified Halleck in a caption. A 1997 photograph and explanation of the statue's presence appeared in the *New York Times Magazine*, which accused Halleck of "schmoozing" his way into stone.[14] But friends and admirers at the time were vocal about Halleck's asocial propensity and horror of being publicly "called out," and despite recent appearances in popular magazines, he remains thoroughly unsung. Further, the reasons for his anonymity today are themselves obscure.

Nineteenth-century American readers would be perplexed by the current neglect of Halleck. Poe, whose reviews were so notoriously harsh that he was nicknamed the Tomahawk Critic, wrote that a passage of "Alnwick Castle" was "the noblest to be found in Halleck, and I would be at a loss to discover its parallel in all American poetry."[15] While the *National Magazine* noted that this critique was a rare example of "when Poe *did* praise anything," by 1843 Poe had concluded, "No name in the American poetical world is more firmly established than that of Fitz-

Greene Halleck." [16] Twenty-six years later, Bryant held that Halleck "furnishes a standing and ever-ready allusion to all who would speak of American literature, and is familiar in the mouths of hundreds who would be seriously puzzled if asked to name any other American poet." [17] Edith Wharton certainly felt that Halleck's name needed no explanation in *The Age of Innocence* (chapter 12) and ranked his notoriety alongside that of Irving in her 1917 novel, *Summer.*

Although Halleck was endorsed as the national poet of America by the *New York Times* on January 30, 1864, this reputation was lost by 1930, when a *New York Times* critic realized that "few outside a very small circle of close students of literary history in this country could identify off-hand the name of Fitz-Greene Halleck." [18] His radical fall from fame demonstrates the politics of decanonization, just as his decanonization negates his significant contributions to American verse and sexual ideology. Halleck's love for another man contributed to the dismantling of the platonic framework of Romantic idealism.

Fitz-Greene Halleck was born in 1790 and remained in rural Connecticut throughout his adolescence, when he began writing verse with same-sex love themes. He was alienated by the puritanical community's tenacious repression of aesthetic and romantic impulses. His poetry increasingly empathized with the plight of Native Americans, slaves, women, and heretics as he came to perceive his own position as an outcast. When business took him to New York City at age eighteen, he determined to reside there, and he would call Greenwich Village home for the next forty years.

Nourished by New York's urban sophistication, Halleck rose rapidly. He was elected poet laureate of the Ugly Club, a fraternity of the city's best-looking men, and joined the Bread and Cheese Lunch (ca. 1824–1830) along with James K. Paulding, Gulian C. Verplank, Richard H. Dana, Bryant, and Cooper. Halleck was increasingly courted by New York's most elite social circles. Privately, he had begun a series of erratic romances with foreign men, but these did not eclipse his persistent doubt that he would ever find his ideal partner.

Halleck's search for a soul mate was delayed by the War of 1812 when he served in the Iron Grays, a metropolitan military unit consisting of wealthy boys. By his mid-twenties, his muse finally materialized in the figure of Joseph Rodman Drake, a young doctor and the most desirable man in town. Halleck was physically and emotionally drawn to Drake, but the powerful attraction was not completely mutual. The two men did collaborate, however, on a series of comic social commentaries. An overnight sensation, their Croaker poems initiated a form of social dialogue unprecedented in American periodicals. In the spring of 1819, more than thirty-five of these satirical Pindaric odes appeared anonymously in the

New York Evening Post and later in the *National Advocate*. This venture of "Croaker" (Drake) and "Croaker Jr." (Halleck) awoke Halleck's poetic strength and permanently linked him with Drake.

Within three months, the Croakers catapulted Halleck to fame. Halleck's enormously popular *Fanny* (1819) followed and was the first noteworthy American mock-epic. The unmarried woman satirized in the poem was modeled on Drake. This profitable work elevated Halleck to the status of the only other American writer Irving's publisher would print, and first editions quickly became exceedingly valuable.[19] *Fanny* railed against wedlock just as ardently as Halleck had protested Drake's sudden 1816 marriage to a wealthy socialite. Halleck grew despondent in this competition for Drake's affection and pulled away. But Drake's effort to include Halleck as a family member and his poems written to Halleck (during the Drakes' honeymoon) proved irresistible bait and rekindled the friendship. The contest between Halleck and Drake's wife did not last long, for the physician could not cure himself of consumption; Drake died in 1820. Situated in what became Joseph Rodman Drake Park, his stone is engraved with Halleck's quatrain beginning, "Green be the turf above thee," which opens what became a classic American elegy still recited on the radio as late as the 1950s.[20] The poem protests Halleck's diminished role at the funeral and reiterates his belief that marriage had consumed Drake's spirit. Halleck lived a long life, but never loved again.

Halleck attempted to eulogize Drake in a series of sporadic poems and translations. Although none of the attempts seemed adequate, he did develop several strategies for expressing his homosexual longings and grief. Metaphorical crime, antinationalism, and silence came to represent his misunderstood feelings for Drake, who was nicknamed the American Keats. (Indeed, Drake and Keats had their birth year, age of death, study of medicine, and fatal consumption in common.) Soon after the burial, Halleck's spoofs on marriage and his political antagonism increasingly undermined federalist conventions of love and freedom, and his themes and satires grew so irreverent that he became known as the American Byron.

Halleck was contracted to edit anonymously the first complete edition of Lord Byron's works and letters; it appeared in 1832. Halleck's text contained many suppressed letters and boldly incorporated bisexual aspects of Byron's life. As in the case of his coauthorship with Drake, Halleck's allegiance to Byron was simultaneously artistic and erotic. Although Halleck and Byron never met, Halleck burst into tears upon the news of Byron's death in an uncharacteristic display of emotion that startled friends.

Halleck objected to cultural conformity and defended his eccentric friends with renewed fervor following the deaths of Drake and Byron. He also defied the social expectations of marriage and fatherhood. Instead, he revised national history in the countercultural lines of "Connecticut" (a deconstruction of Puritan tyranny), "Red Jacket" (a sarcastic tribute to the Native American), and "Wyoming" (a satire of Thomas Campbell's "Gertrude"). His 1822 European tour was patterned on Drake's honeymoon trip and seemed cathartic. Halleck returned a serious poet. International topics wooed a larger audience. "Alnwick Castle," "Burns," and "Marco Bozzaris" were written on the heels of this literal and psychological journey. These and other poems were included in a collection of Halleck's poetry published in 1827. "Marco Bozzaris" defended Greek liberation and became known as America's eminent lyric poem, frequently recited at academic graduations and political conventions.

Halleck was astounded by the success of his poetry and wore the role of national poet uncomfortably. Perhaps in an effort to shun this burden, he published "The Field of the Grounded Arms" in 1828. Devoid of rhyme, its innovative form was a daring attack on convention that would not be launched again until Whitman's experimental *Leaves of Grass* decades later. Halleck's entirely unrhymed poem "greatly puzzled the reviewers,"[21] and a critical debate ensued in which his personal character came under attack. Halleck found his inheritance of the Byronic myth too invasive and retreated from society.

Pursued by aristocratic women, professionally solicited by men of letters, and often the center of the most prominent sphere in New York, Halleck found refuge in the fast-paced world of New York's wealthiest entrepreneur, John Jacob Astor. In 1832, Halleck was installed as Astor's right-hand man. Astor named him an original trustee of the Astor Library, but Halleck was cheated of a large pension at the time of the millionaire's death in 1842, in spite of Samuel F. B. Morse's canvas of Halleck that still decks the portrait room's east wall of the New York Public Library. Halleck was forced by finances to retire to Guilford, where his verse became an affront to the conservatism brought on by an ensuing national crisis.

Convinced that civil war would blur the democratic vision he had glimpsed in urban New York, Halleck grew debilitated. Homophobic criticism began to insinuate that his verse was unhealthy. While Poe commented that *bonhomie* was the leading feature of Halleck's poetry "and, indeed, of his whole moral nature,"[22] an incendiary article of the *Southern Literary Messenger*'s Moral and Mental Portrait Series (1842) further isolated the already reclusive poet with its sexually suspicious terminology. The reviewer, who had previously had hostile dealings with Halleck, accused his subject of "unnatural transition" and "unnatural similes," adding, "the alliteration and antithesis, if effective, are unnatural."[23] Naturally, Halleck took cover.

A decade of virtual poetic silence followed. Back in Guilford, drinking heavily, Halleck finally produced an addition to "Connecticut" in 1852. A bitter denunciation of American Puritanism, the poem provided a sharp contrast to the pleasant transcendental meandering of its 1826 version. The inherent irony of civil war was not lost on Halleck, whose "Connecticut" blasted the American forefathers' legacy of intolerance and hypocrisy. Civil war is an oxymoron, and the idea of one nation divided against itself particularly reinforced Halleck's view that the American government threatened the very rights that it had guaranteed. What some read as his "disgust for things modern and American"[24] was not antiquarianism at all, rather his fear that national evolution was proving retrogressive. Halleck took a sarcastic political stance declaring himself a Loyalist and refusing to write about a failed democracy that pitted brother against brother. His verse mingled democracy and anarchy as his sexual imagery continued to blur love and crime.

From the outset, Halleck refused invitations to write on the national conflict, asking instead, "Is this Southern, this sin-born war of ours, worthy of a poet's consecration?"[25] At the end of the Civil War, he emerged from his self-imposed literary exile. In a letter written that year, N. P. Willis asked the rhetorical question, "How is it that Fitz-Greene Halleck has never let himself be known to audiences?"[26] Halleck answered the inquiry with his last major poem, "Young America" (1864). Produced at the age of seventy-four, "Young America" appeared in the *New York Ledger,* ending the literary silence that had left his readership mystified. The poem was at once a jaded critique of marriage and a pederastic boy-worship reminiscent of classical homosexuality. It joined the rest of Halleck's work which "violates many of the fundamental rules of taste and art."[27] It also coincided with the new sexual literacy of medical, psychological, and social sciences that left "inverts" or "the third sex" standing naked before the unblinking eye of a modern society. Halleck had succeeded in a fiercely heterosexist market only because it had been sexually blind. Already by the middle of the nineteenth century, the techniques that he had employed were no longer viable. Silent signifiers replaced the Byronic "negative" Romanticism and overt protestation of earlier works.

Silence as a practice and as a metaphor came easily to Halleck who had suffered from partial deafness since the age of two. The hearing loss was traceable to a prank two drunken soldiers had played on Halleck. Planning to startle the toddler, the men discharged their guns near his left ear. The assault resulted in a number of public embarrassments and ultimately an almost total loss of hearing in the years following an unsuccessful and excruciating remedy Halleck underwent when he was thirty years old. In addition to corresponding to his physical disability, soundless symbols were perfectly suited to the suppressed existence of American homosexuals driven underground. The resulting nuance of poetry which no longer spoke but which only gestured to the reader produced content rich in irony that both disgusted and delighted his audience. The muted emotion of Halleck's work became an international landmark of gay representation. Dropping his mask for a moment in 1861, he scolded a crony who failed to decode his last letter by quoting the motto: "one true use of language is, not to express, but to conceal our thoughts."[28]

In 1859, Halleck replied to a potential biographer with characteristic modesty and comic guardedness:

I have published very little, and that little almost always anonymously, and have ever been but an amateur in the literary orchestra, playing only upon a pocket flute, and never aspiring, even in a dream, to the dignity of the bâton, the double bass, or the oboe. My every-day pursuits in life have been quite opposite to those of authors; and if, among them, there is one who deems me worthy of a biography from his pen and a place in the future, he must be a very clever fellow himself to make out of my "Life and Adventures" any other than an exceedingly dull and unsalable book![29]

If bravado can compensate for one's inadequacies, then Halleck's humility can be said to hide his accomplishments. This pocket flute player resounded in Whitman's unrhymed emancipation of the poetic body from its previous constraints. Equally significant, Halleck's love for Drake inspired Bayard Taylor to challenge the conventional heterosexual novel with his homosexual romance *Joseph and His Friend,* published shortly after Halleck's death. A ghostly figure in his last years, the white-bearded Halleck haunted New York's streets through 1867 and revitalized his interest in the next generation of young male poets who paused to flatter him.

As a central influence in the Americanization of poetic form and as a founding father of a subculture in panic, Halleck occupies a complicated position in cultural history. Although no poet had received such tribute in American history, in the second half of his life Halleck's voice became a hollow song devoid of democratic hope. He dwelled alone as Drake's survivor and felt increasingly frightened as the veil of homosexual allusion was lifted from his lines.

Halleck escaped the exiles suffered by Byron and Oscar Wilde and avoided the desperate denial of homosexuality such as that Whitman made to John Addington Symonds in 1890 when he claimed six illegitimate children. Rather, Halleck had recognized that the physical desire for male companionship had to be balanced with a prudent respect for the social limits of homoerotic expression. Perhaps less self-aware (or more careful) than his contemporaries, he still faced serious opposition. In the patriotic atmosphere of Reconstruction, he was accused of converting to Catholicism, displaying excessive wealth, and indulging in sloth and decadence. All of these accusations had sodomitical implications for his hometown detractors.

Poetry and love, like nation and self, formed a complex relationship for Halleck, whose determination to free his culture was only matched by its ultimate mastery of his singular form and content. Absorbed in Halleck's literary experimentation, an enthusiastic readership had unknowingly suffered the infusion of same-sex passions into the poetics of American Romance. Biography can readily be reconstructed by modern scholars to out Halleck by reexamining his sexual identity in light of postmodern precepts. The more valuable study, however, lies in unraveling the frustration apparent in his prose and verse. As a man living in an era lacking homosexual constructs, he vacillated between embracing heterosexual paradigms and confessing his lack of emotional identification with them. The central struggle decipherable in his poetry is remarkably modern. Gay writers today still struggle to define their place in American society and in so doing reveal an irreconcilable tension: they simultaneously aspire to emulate and to resist the heterosexual institutions that legitimize relationships in the culture.

Halleck's previous popularity was enhanced by his condemnation of the emerging political machinery of the federalist period and by his elevation of same-sex friendship. He was often "proclaimed as the literary savior of America" by reason of his radical break from past form and his controversial lampoons.[30] As such, he remains a significant figure in the development of American verse as a prophet of the poetic and sexual revolution of which Walt Whitman was the messiah.

Mortified by titles like Gary Schmidgall's *Walt Whitman: A Gay Life,* the dominant camp of gay studies, social constructionists, believes that early nineteenth-century homosexuality is an impossible category since homosexuality did not become formally conceptualized until late in the century. Given this historical framework, then, one must ask: What's a gay man like Halleck doing in the nineteenth century? The rhetorical question is threefold.

As a colloquial expression, the question ponders the psychosocial presence of a homosexual figure in pre-Stonewall America. It appears that Fitz-Greene Halleck's sexuality was developing during the 1790s when "gay," "queer," and "friend of Christopher Marlowe" did not allude to homosexual orientation. In fact, no words at that time clearly communicated homosexual love. "Sodomy," "buggery," and "pederasty" were not only criminal acts but terms of coercive sex which also included heterosexual behaviors. Therefore, Halleck would not have seen himself as a "sodomite," that is, as a rapist. Nonsexual terms such as "friend," "bachelor," and "comrade" were generally not employed as codes for homosexual men by the general public. Literary allusions to Jonathan and David,

Introduction

Arabian Tales, or Turkish baths were more often innocent historical or literary references than homosexual signs laden with double meaning. Yet in the midst of this apparently neutral language, there are symbols of deliberate same-sex romance—such as the mythological Calamus or the color green, then red, then eventually lavender.

Rictor Norton's *The Myth of the Modern Homosexual* argues that "the American experience is largely irrelevant" in examining the birth of homosexual culture, providing an essentialist counterattack to constructionist essays like Jonathan Katz's "The Early-Nineteenth-Century Organization of Love." Social constructionist essays, for example, David M. Halperin's "Sex before Sexuality," and essentialist counterarguments, such as John Boswell's "Revolutions, Universals, and Sexual Categories," can only agree that it is unproductive to speculate about the physical sex acts of an earlier subject. Given the general divisiveness, the very use of the word "homosexual" in this cultural biography may be convenient but illegitimate. How, then, can one answer the critical question: Was there any such creature as a gay man cruising nineteenth-century America?

According to radical social constructionists, who rely heavily upon Foucault's demonstration of evolutionary sexual identifications, the answer is no. Constructionists do not deny that homosexuality is omnipresent but insist that interpretations of this behavior (i.e., as initiation/fertility rite or spiritual transportation) constitute a social rather than individual function. True constructionists argue that there was no such thing as homosexuality in early America and, accordingly, no such thing as homophobia. That would be a hard sell to those colonists executed for bedding other men.

At the other theoretical extreme, pure essentialists affirm that the self-defined homosexual person has and will exist in any time and place, whether or not the language and society acknowledge that presence. This predetermined state might include universally inherent traits such as cross-gender tendencies or aesthetic capabilities. The rift of public opinion is evident in *Newsweek*'s front-page question for August 1998, "Gay for Life?" In admittedly oversimplified terms, the new theoretical debate is an abstraction and a complication of the older scientific discussion on homosexuality: chromosomes or choice, innate or learned, nature or nurture. Between these extremes, and more complex than either, I propose a con-sential or consensual theory of homosexuality. Of course, consensual homosexuality excludes male rape and conditional cases of male-male contact, as in prison. However, con-sential (constructed + essential) sexuality represents a larger paradigm that incorporates the extremes of purely biological sexual orientation and external sexual composition.

Con-sential homosexuality suggests that a mutual agreement, either conscious or subconscious, positive or negative, emerges between an indi-

12

vidual outside of the sexual norm and his culture. A space, jointly created by the self and other, takes shape in which an essentially homosexual person agrees (consents) to express this difference by conforming to the arbitrary social boundaries established to define him. Not limited to sexual identity, con-sential dynamics also take place regarding race, gender, and other social distinctions. This interpersonal relationship explains both the varieties of gay subcultures, often binary poles where two cultures clash, as well as the common tension between expression and repression, individual protest and public policing. Self-recognition and/or cultural regulation of the homosexual individual may result in a celebrated, elevated position (usually in Eastern and aboriginal communities) or in criminal or fatal catastrophe (as often seen in Western and Christian societies). Homosexuality is the metaphorical seed (essentialism), culture the rich or poor soil (social climate), and expression of sexuality in a given time and place is the resulting plant that may be thwarted and thorny, lush and blooming, or pruned somewhere in between. This dynamic is also reciprocal: a hearty seed can loosen the hardest soil. Thus, essentially gay members can shape themselves to social confines or cultivate new forms that the existing culture may tolerate. For instance, Halleck did not find himself in puritanical models of nonconsensual sodomy, and yet he consented to utilize the criminal motif as the central symbol in writing about his love for another man—which in turn promoted a homosexual literary tradition accepted by the mainstream. Although this book generally applies "sodomite," "homosexual," and "gay" with regard to the era under discussion, the employment of these terms is potentially misleading since the reader cannot fully disregard the connotation bound to each word.

Second, the question, "What's a gay man like Halleck doing in the nineteenth century?" functions at a sexual level which is quite literal. What were homosexual men doing with one another in the nineteenth century? Fellatio, anal intercourse, and mutual masturbation between men represent the majority of applications of sodomy law in early American texts predating the term "homosexual," which did not appear in any American document before 1890 and was not in common use until more than thirty years after that.[31] In 1850, Melville wrote that Hawthorne had "dropped germinous seeds into my soul" and had "shot his strong New England roots into the hot soil of my soul." Was his review expressing genteel love or did he just want to get plowed? Did he even know himself? Similarly, Halleck chose to clothe his sentiments for Drake in sexually charged metaphors as well as modified marriage (same-sex holy union). Melville's scatological figurativeness has more in common with the homosexual pattern of an earlier American period than his own.

Colonial literature suggests that anal intercourse was the preferred application of male sodomy, whereas letters of American Romanticism suggest that fellatio and mutual masturbation had become the homosexual experiences of choice. Since most of the recorded male-male acts of colonial America and early Federalism are court cases for nonconsensual sodomy or male rape between men of significant economic or age differences, it is not surprising that anal intercourse, also known as Greek sex, prevailed in these violent power struggles. Masturbation and fellatio would be harder to force. Ideology may have reinforced the physical preference for anal intercourse in that classical culture, which depicted anal rather than oral pederasty, was more influential in earlier American literature.

Fellatio, like mutual masturbation, implies consent. Curiously, fellatio and mutual masturbation appear in American documents more commonly from the advent of the new democracy. Both acts suggest an egalitarian model of homosexuality; evidently, same-sex relations of the nineteenth century were increasingly held between men of common age, class, and education. Halleck himself moved from adolescent associations with foreign men beneath his social status to his adult infatuations with coworkers and particularly with Drake, who almost perfectly matched Halleck's age, income, and professional standing.

Just as one does not consciously consider one's parents as sexual beings, our culture is notably squeamish about the sex lives of our collective forefathers. The psychological need to desexualize the past does not diminish the intellectual probability that sexual relations in earlier American history were ardently pursued in all known and sundry varieties. Our comfort level with nineteenth-century homoeroticism is high because the term effectively (and ironically) negates homosexual activity and actuality. The visualization of sucking and fucking by nineteenth-century men strikes most Americans as incongruous with the age. But the recent scholarship of Patricia Cline Cohen on a New York prostitute murdered in 1836 and Janet Farrell Brodie on abortion in nineteenth-century America clearly demonstrate that Halleck's heterosexual neighbors were sexually active and knowledgeable. There is reason to believe that homosexual activity was equally lurid and present. While a soldier was executed for engaging in same-sex activity in 1660s New Amsterdam, same-sex unions in the homosocial New York of the 1840s and 1850s "might well have been taken as an extension of existing norms rather than a flagrant transgression of them."[32] While constructionists may argue that moderns invented sexual orientation, they certainly did not invent sex.

The third layer of rhetoric in the question, What's a gay man like Halleck doing in the nineteenth century? ponders the value of visiting past sexualities. For one thing, this study of Halleck provides a measure of our present progress (or lack thereof) regarding American masculinities. For example, the masculine types of the past (dandies, fops, rakes, aesthetics, athletes, and actors) have respective modern equivalents that additionally define sexuality (queens, fags, jocks, bottoms, butches, and actors). Such rigid sexual categories suggest that Americans have grown less comfortable with the ambiguity of male sexual genres. The reader may experience some small sense of Halleck's psychological discomfort in an era lacking the extraordinary labels and dichotomies that, however artificially, soothe the modern sensibility.

Gay academics appear equally distressed outside of absolute ideas. This angst can lead to premature interpretations of the past based upon insufficient data. With every new leaf of archival material rediscovered, I am more convinced that we have failed to excavate enough material on past consensual homosexuality to espouse many theories about it. Nineteenth-century scholars have particularly narrowed their focus on Whitman, as though he is a fair representation of an immensely complex and varied American society. In fact, Whitman's pederastic gaze was conspicuously aimed at boys who were almost exclusively blue-collar youths of inferior education (preferably illiterate). Whitman, unlike his predecessor Halleck who sought an egalitarian and committed connection, represents a gay throwback to the ancient Greek model.

The past is crucial for understanding our current mistakes in framing sexuality and its history. As African Americans and feminists know, public voices and private silences have perpetuated American myths for centuries. Panting beneath heterosexual and homosexual sex, there is often love, but—as critics, scholars, and theorists—we never seem to know what to make of it. Most academics argue their way through the genderfied purgatory of nineteenth-century American sexuality, while only a few invoke its emotional content. Halleck's internal turmoil was not cerebral. He openly expressed physical disdain for women; his "central emotional direction"[33] was toward men, to whom he was intensely attracted. Alongside these fundamental observations regarding his feelings of love, Halleck simultaneously denied that he could be "in" love with a man.

Though shrouded by a century of neglect, Halleck's writing reveals more than an anomaly that contradicts historical assumptions about sex and art in nineteenth-century America. Just as the statue suggests that his poetry was of special significance in his time, his decanonization tells us a great deal about America since the *New York Tribune*'s assessment a decade after Halleck's death:

To-day, for the first time, an American author will receive the honor of a commemorative statue. Busts, shafts, or tablets have been erected to others of the guild of letters, but Fitz-Greene Halleck is the first to be monumentally treated as the equal of statesmen, divines, and inventors. . . . no reader of to-day can fairly estimate the service he rendered, without intimate knowledge of that earlier day when each of his poems was at once a surprise and a prophecy.[34]

Halleck's lines contained emotional contradictions and communal conflicts that have yet to be fully appreciated.

The discrepancy between Halleck's cultural autonomy and professed nationalism was related to his disruption of conventional romance. Unable to conform to the American dream, he favored the amorphous metaphor. Perhaps a complete disclosure of earlier homosexual aesthetics is not possible, but Halleck's expression of his love for a dashing young doctor was not entirely turned to stone with him.

1

Shepherds of Sodomy

There are some three thousand of them, all well to do and
industrious, not a pauper among them, and all can read and
write—*not that they ever do either.*

Fitz-Greene Halleck on the residents of Guilford

ITZ-GREENE HALLECK was not like the other little boys in his
hometown. His sense of difference led him to distance himself from
Guilford whenever questioned about his birthplace. While still a
teenager, he stole away to New York, which provided psychological asylum for the next forty years. He produced almost no poetry during the
first and last twenty years of his life that were spent in the Connecticut
village. James Grant Wilson's life of Halleck (1869) is reinforced by Nelson Frederick Adkins's biography (1930), which shows that Halleck grew
more and more estranged from the town. An insulated coastal community, Guilford preserved its puritanical ideology well into the nineteenth
century. The hamlet, a half-century after it had banished Halleck, exported its granite to New York for the Statue of Liberty's base. For Halleck, exile to liberal New York proved a happy alternative to the town's
propensity for persecuting homosexual activity. Had Halleck been born
in an earlier generation, he would have witnessed a sodomy trial resulting
in the execution of Guilford's own founding father.

The adolescent Halleck was at a complete loss in rural New England,
where he was unable to discover himself in available sexual representations. Although largely subverted, histories of classical pederasty and of
British and Native American homosexual institutions were circulated
throughout Halleck's lifetime. Out of tune with small-town morality,
these three models all had positive aspects: Greek pederasty accompanied
great learning; British mollies threw grand balls and were socially celebrated for a time; and aboriginal berdaches were mystical healers who were

often elevated by same-sex marriage to chieftains. Access to these three models of homosexuality were limited, yet they were manifest throughout the nineteenth century.

Allusions to Greek pederasty abounded in literature of the period, and the North American berdache was cited by Karl Ulrichs in his 1860 argument for homosexual emancipation and by Edward Carpenter. A catalog of British Renaissance homosexuality was published by Havelock Ellis before the turn of the century. But the positive attributes of same-sex love had already been expunged in most rural American communities. The Greek model of man-boy love had become a literary allusion to the worship of the male form rather than the union of philosopher and pupil within a courtship tradition.[1] The British mollies were ultimately repressed by campaigns and executions in England.[2] These lusty artists of high camp had named themselves, and "molly" or "molly cull" popularly replaced "sodomite" in England by 1710.[3] Molly was probably derived from the Latin word for "soft" (hence "mollycoddled"), and culls were criminal assistants or a crook's lover; hence, some men born a century before Halleck referred to themselves as "molly-bitches." While veering away from the effeminate self-identification of mollies, Halleck relentlessly evoked their criminal metaphors. Mollies created a notorious homosexual subculture in eighteenth-century London; four-fifths of these men never married but took "husbands."[4] As opposed to the sacred same-sex marriage ceremonies of medieval Europe,[5] "married" mollies gave male partners female names, inverted gendered pronouns, engaged in transvestism, and bore doll-babies, often after considerable labor and followed by mock baptisms.[6] Unlike the pseudomarriages of mollies, the berdache or *winkte* figure prevalent in numerous North American tribes was encouraged to actually wed a same-sex partner.

A sixteenth-century account of Florida natives who married other men and a Russian explorer's nineteenth-century description of same-sex marriage in southern Alaska demonstrate the duration and geographical breadth of North American holy unions.[7] "Berdache" may have been a European application of *bardag*, a Persian term for a boy courtesan, or might have derived from "bardash," translated from the French as "a boy kept for unnatural purposes."[8] These tribal members were essentially tested and recognized as homosexual in early childhood and retained the prerogative of cross-dressing for the duration of their lives. Berdaches have been documented in well over a hundred different North American tribes, which uniformly accorded high honors to these men whom colonists regarded as "sodomites by profession."[9] While early European documents assumed tribal contempt for the berdache, later nineteenth-century reports realized that berdaches were "never ridiculed or despised by the men . . . but are, on the contrary, respected as saints or beings in some degree inspired."[10] Along with platonic Greeks and incarcerated mollies, berdaches were largely quelled by colonists who reinterpreted the berdache's tribal privilege as punishment.

For the American berdache, trouble came with the first arrival of Europeans. Christopher Columbus's physician gave testimony to the prevalence of homosexual behavior among the aboriginals, which was used to justify the eradication of Native American culture.[11] English settlers, in turn, solidly repressed berdachism in North America, although a score of nineteenth-century texts reveal a lack of sexual assimilation.[12] Included among accounts from the 1850s, the army's surgeon general conducted medical exams to confirm that berdaches possessed normal male genitalia.[13] As late as 1886, newspapers humorously reported the White House visit of a berdache to President and Mrs. Cleveland, who were caught off guard by the revelation of their guest's true sex.[14]

Halleck was attracted to slightly younger men and engaged in campy humor, but he did not aspire to pederasty or to the flippant rites of mollies. Chances are that he had studied enough classical material to glean passages on pederasty, but he was probably never directly made aware of the molly subculture in London. It is also unlikely that he was acquainted with berdachism—the model of homosexual love most fitting his own romantic inclination to find a soul mate.

Prevailing sexual conceptions in Guilford were intrinsically negative. Some familiarity with the puritanical paradigm is necessary for understanding Halleck's point of view and varied attempts to reestablish mutual and nurturing same-sex ethics. The colonial American version of homosexual desire divorced such activity from its previously recognized benefits of intellectual, social, and spiritual growth between consensual partners as seen in Greek, molly, and berdache traditions. Halleck determined that Guilford was even prudish regarding heterosexual activity and complained, "They fined a man . . . for *kissing his wife on Sunday!*"[15]

New England provided a reconfiguration of same-sex love as a violent sex crime that frayed the social fabric. Early American sodomy laws were enacted against any sex that was not procreative; however, such laws were applied almost exclusively to homosexuality, less occasionally to bestiality. Colonists related sodomy to aboriginal conflicts, depopulation, depressed economy, physical hardships, political dependence, religious strife, and second-generation dispersal. Same-sex activity (at least the accusation of it) became an ideal scapegoat because it was able to deflect a wide array of cultural problems not faced by Old World Puritan counterparts.

American Puritans had applied new same-sex constructs to Indian sexuality, natural catastrophes, and British depravity since their arrival in the New World. A strong New England earthquake in 1638 and droughts of the early 1640s were reinterpreted as divine judgment and linked by the superstitious to the destruction of Sodom.[16] In addition to the apocalyptic weather, British corruption gave New Englanders cause to look over their shoulders. American Puritans not only linked aristocracy to sodomy but also believed that the general populace of England had become particularly hospitable to mollies and their kind.[17]

Eighteenth-century London's gay scene was thriving and boasted numerous clubs known as molly houses, largely ignored by law enforcement.[18] Homoerotic literature littered the city's shelves, such as Michael Drayton's *Piers Gaveston,* Thomas Heywood's *Jupiter and Ganimede,* Richard Barnfield's *Sonnets,* Christopher Marlowe's *Hero and Leander,* and John Wilmot's poem, "Love a woman? You're an ass!"[19] Francis Bacon's love affairs with male servants "were unapologetically public,"[20] and sodomitical scenes appeared in stage productions of Aphra Behn's *The Amorous Prince* (1671) and John Vanbrugh's *The Relapse* (1696) back home in England. Roger Thompson points out that Puritans argued that the British theater's use of boys in female roles encouraged the audience to experiment with sodomy. Hence, the New World's sacred politic was married to sexual and literary policing.

Colonialists prescribed capital punishment for sodomy for well over a century, enacting new legislation from 1610 (Halleck's ancestors arrived in 1640) until 1732 (after the birth of Halleck's paternal grandparents).[21] Thomas Jefferson's 1777 "liberal" proposal to reduce sodomitical punishment from death to mere castration was not ratified.[22] While a 1672 Connecticut law eliminated the death penalty for rape victims or consensual sodomy performed by those under age fifteen in favor of lesser punishments, Connecticut state law officially condoned killing homosexuals until Halleck was in his thirties. Despite previous attempts by British Puritans and Spanish explorers to squelch same-sex institutions, American sodomy did not become a social crisis until the 1640s when a rash of sodomy trials spread throughout the colonies.

William Bradford's *Of Plymouth Plantation* reported an epidemic of same-sex lovemaking in 1642: "Sodomy and buggery (things fearful to name) have broke forth in this land."[23] His alarmist account illustrates the development of American-style homophobia that enhanced and modified Dutch and English prerogatives. Contrary to the great American myth, the *Mayflower*'s Pilgrims did not flee England under threat of religious persecution. They sailed from Leyden, Holland, where their economic opportunities had been restricted, where assimilationism had threatened their identity, and where sodomy was a capital offense. The Dutch citizenry followed and settled New York, which consequently employed Dutch Roman Law ensuring sodomitical executions on both sides of the Atlantic.[24] Dutch treatment of homosexual relations paralleled English persecution.

Act 26 Henry VIII, 6 (1533) was the first civic law requiring death for sodomy and officially remained on the English statute book until 1967.[25] Stuart England appeared more sexually tolerant, meshing charges of "religious heresy, political offenses, or violating social-class distinctions" with charges of sodomy.[26] Jacobean sodomy laws were generally not enforced due to rumors of the king's own homosexuality.[27] Two sodomy executions between 1630 and 1640 were apparent exceptions.[28] Puritans, who believed they were God's elect, utilized a strict code of conduct to rationalize their migration. Bradford's peers referred to him as their Moses, and Halleck's "Psalm CXXXVII" (1821) was certainly in keeping with the colonial association between American Pilgrims in the New World and the plight of Jews seeking freedom of worship in the Promised Land. Halleck's motive for using the song, however, appears to be his identification with its narrator: a musician forced to sing in the midst of enemies. Halleck may have lived in federalist America, but he was still fighting colonial law.

Bradford had been caught up in the endeavor to preserve his colony's piety upon which sodomy "might cast a blemish and stain upon them in the eyes of [the Eurocentric] world."[29] Biblical argument, as well as an exaggerated concern for appearances, usurped British civil law as Puritan fathers increased the pressure on sodomites. John Cotton's 1636 legal code against sodomy relied upon the English civil code, but Massachusetts Bay colonists chose Nathaniel Ward's legislation that invoked Scripture as its authority and set the pattern for all subsequent sodomy laws.[30] Ward's Buggery Law upheld capital punishment with religious authority until 1805. Halleck had already turned fifteen.

The Puritans' strict endeavor to create a morally cohesive community added to Bradford's amazement that severe punishment "could not suppress" sodomy. Instead, others were seduced by its powerful allure. Bradford believed that the "inquisition" of sodomites may have had the reverse effect by bringing sodomy "into the light" and making it "conspicuous." As an enforcer of sanctioned sexuality, the governor helped redefine sodomy as contagious, alien, and primarily homosexual. Bradford established the sodomite as a contagion when he observed "how one wicked person may infect the many." He further stressed that the sodomite was, literally, a foreign creature. In one case, Bradford noted that the convicted man "had long used [sodomy] in old England: and this youth last spoken of said he was taught it by another that had heard of such things in England"; in another case, the governor blamed traders for transporting sodomites to America: "By this means the country became pestered with many unworthy persons."[31] Bradford had company in his regard of the sodomite as illegal alien.

In 1629, "five beastly Sodomitical boys" aboard the *Talbot*, a ship transporting the second major party of Puritans to the New World, were sent back "to be punished in old England as the crime deserved," which for boys over fourteen was by hanging.[32] Sodomites were still regarded as essentially English in Ben Franklin's "Edict by the King of Prussia," which threatened to send America's sodomites back to England. Bradford also helped to reconstruct the sodomite as theoretically foreign. The homosexual was distinguished from his heterosexual counterpart who was also guilty of sex crimes. Bradford categorized the "incontinency between persons unmarried" and fornication among married couples as separate from "that which is worse, even sodomy and buggery."[33] The governor and other colonial legislators successfully forged an American sodomite whom all New Englanders could regard as a literal and philosophical enemy.

Sodomy had been an act that any man who wandered too far from the straight and narrow might commit. In modern terms, Puritans believed all men were potentially bisexual.[34] In fact, the earliest Puritans feared all sins of the flesh without much regard to the object's gender. However, by the end of the 1640s, same-sex partners were identified as more than men tempted by sodomy—they were the new breed of sodomites. Therefore, Halleck would be seen as a type, separated from the rest of humanity. As such, he would become a dandy who spurned the sacred duties to family, country, and God.

Like cold war McCarthyism, the sexual hysteria created by seventeenth-century American leaders served to divert public fears. Civic ills could be purged. Same-sex intercourse, seemingly running against nature, represented disorder to the puritan mind in which symptom and disease were inseparable. Today's zealots who envision AIDS as God's verdict against sexual emancipation echo forefathers who saw sin as the cause of divine retribution. The public consequence of private conduct evolved rapidly concerning homosexual relations until execution was the order of the day. Even more than putting himself at risk of contracting disease in the 1990s, a man seeking a homosexual experience in puritan New England had to contemplate whether his partner was literally one to die for. Colonists involved in same-sex affairs who avoided being burned, strangled, or drowned employed the closet motto of Silence = Life. Chances are that there was probably no more sodomy in 1642 (proportionate to the population) than at any other time in history. The American outbreak of sodomitical persecution was not random but part of an ideological program.

Bradford's 1642 observation of increased sexual deviancy in Massachusetts coincided with the listing of sodomy as a capital crime by the General Court of Connecticut in 1642. Sodomitical accusations in both colonies were furtive responses to three colonial crises: the onset of intergenerational friction, the 1642 Puritan uprising back in England, and the renewed threat of depopulation. Samuel Danforth's "The Cry of Sodom

Enquired Into" (1674) emphasized sodomites' lack of obedience to parents and joined other seventeenth-century writings intended to silence the restless youth who did not value their parents' mission.[35] The likes of such an intergenerational campaign would not be so clearly exemplified again until the advent of Nazi propaganda, which also fused religion, sexuality, and control of the younger generation in an effort to achieve social purity. With young Puritans turning from the parent mission and others joining the revolt, so many returned to England that procreative sex in the New World became a practical concern. *Mayflower* Pilgrims may have felt hope as two babies were born en route to America and upon the Great Puritan Migration of 350 people in 1629, but migration reversed itself so greatly that by the early 1640s more people abandoned New England than arrived from the mother country.[36] Bradford was well aware that the Pequot War threatened Connecticut's population by 1637, although his antisodomy proposal required penetration for prosecution.[37] The need for biological reproduction grew obvious to the colonists. Colonial law was swift to respond.

The responses varied only in degree. John Rayner argued that nonpenetration and nonemissive contact were capital crimes against the family and posterity. Charles Chauncy not only sided with Rayner but also made sodomy analogous to abortion. Chauncy reasoned sodomy was "equivalent to killing the man who could have been born" of the seminal emission; therefore, all stages of homosexual behavior were capital for affecting "the whole of human nature."[38] The Puritans' meticulous hierarchy of sodomitical crimes reveals deep angst about the dwindling population of agricultural New England. Legislation categorized sodomy as masturbational, anal, oral, voluntary, forced, nonemissive, orgasmic, penetrative, and nonpenetrative. The variety of penalties for same-sex activity was further cataloged based upon the age, class, gender, and race of the accused parties. In part the result of a breeding campaign, the American homosexual was born—if only to be killed.

As in America, a puzzling and abrupt shift of homosexual typology took place in seventeenth-century Britain, which gradually transformed the rake (who was masculine, older, and penetratively active with both adolescent boys and women) into the molly.[39] The *Women-Hater's Lamentation* (1707) illustrated the new breed of homosexual couple that emerged: of equal age and class, anally reciprocative, practicing transvestism, and fluent in camp.[40] Unlike the new British sodomite, however, the new American homosexual was anything but comical. The sexual sinner was transformed from a victim of Satanic derailment into the Devil himself. The resulting personality expressed itself in Michael Wigglesworth's private prose (1631–1705). The tone of his journal, which blurs spiritual illness with individual sexuality, echoes sections of his "Day of Doom" with its lyrical raving against sodomy. Wigglesworth confided in Doctor John Alcock and John Rogers who suggested that Wigglesworth find a cure for homosexual lust in clean bowels and marriage. Praying for "a circumcized heart" not only failed to relieve him of wet dreams about male students but also aggravated his revulsion for the cravings he experienced.[41] Within twenty-four hours, the prescribed marriage also backfired.[42]

Sodomy had moved from spiritual catastrophe to social disease, but it was still thought to bring Holy retribution upon the entire colony. Guilford appeased an angry God with the trial of a town father.

In 1646, William Plaine (or Plane), who seven years earlier had founded the town, was executed. Plaine was the only person from Halleck's hometown ever to be executed. Plaine, "being a married man, had committed sodomy with two persons in England" prior to having "corrupted a great part of the youth of Guilford by masturbation . . . above a hundred times."[43] Plaine did not appear to have been coercive, and the tone of resistance in his testimony showed no remorse for challenging either sexual propriety or theological authority. John Winthrop, himself an author of homoerotic correspondence in the Jonathan and David vein, accused Plaine of implanting young men with "the seeds of atheism," not to mention his biological seed. While sexual accusations against Plaine appear sound, "the term *sodomites* was used to condemn those who held unorthodox theological beliefs" as well.[44] Even those not charged with sodomy who objected to the political inducement of colonial sodomy trials faced dire consequences by 1624.[45] In contradictory terms, the married Plaine was also guilty of "frustrating the ordinance of marriage and hindering the generation of mankind."[46]

In deceptively simple rhetoric, religious objection to sodomy was again fused with concerns for metaphysical deviation ("atheism"), depopulation ("hindering the generation of mankind"), second-generation dispersal (having "corrupted a great part of the youth"), and English depravity (having "committed sodomy with two persons in England"). Bradford's notation that Plaine had repeatedly committed sodomy in England before founding Guilford effectively removed the sin from the New Jerusalem established on American soil. Whether the social climate of England had indeed grown more tolerant or William Brown simply had extraordinary courage, Brown protested blatantly during his own sodomy trial in 1726: "I think there is no crime in making what use I please of my own body."[47] New England did not tolerate such insolent testimony.

Although more than a century had elapsed since Plaine's execution, Halleck found his town still heavily influenced by the past. Similarly, twentieth-century gay men would find religion denying their civil rights, despite the separation of church and state guaranteed by the Bill of Rights, which was not fully ratified until after Halleck's birth.

The genocidal policies of Halleck's heritage inevitably led to his discomfort with Guilford's faithful. He was reared on texts by the Puritan bigwigs: Bradford, Samuel Danforth, Jonathan Edwards, Cotton Mather, Thomas Shepard, Michael Wigglesworth, and John Winthrop. Halleck's formal education would have included a curriculum largely based upon these writers who distorted pre-Columbian homosexual precepts. Late colonial Guilford heavily resisted the moral moderation visible on the horizon of Federalism. In *A Modern History of New Haven and Eastern New Haven County,* Everett Gleason Hill attests, "Never was there a settlement formed of more rigid Puritans" than Guilford.[48] Despite being ostracized, Halleck succeeded in his art while still residing there. He moved same-sex love from Puritan crime toward a poetic ideal, just as colonial rebellion was being redressed as patriotism. His sense of being a felon incognito was reflected in the crime-love motif so common in his writings. Perhaps not grasping the full measure of his own words, Halleck risked a great deal by articulating his love for another man. Perhaps he could not help himself; he was born into an era lusting freedom.

Halleck was born in 1790. By then, the tension between nationalism and homosexual expression was evident. In 1790, the first election was held for a U.S. president and the first U.S. Copyright Act was passed, but 1790 was also the year in which several private letters were penned between two Bostonian men hoping to found "a permanent friendship" in one home and in "one our bed."[49] Perhaps because Guilford's town records have no official report of Halleck's birth there, many miscalculations of his age were made during his lifetime; for instance, Poe shaved more than five years off of Halleck's age.[50] Halleck's ancestry was more certain, dating to the Pilgrim era when Peter Hallock, one of thirteen Puritan leaders who left England in 1638, landed at Hallock's Neck, Southold, Long Island, in 1640.[51] It appears that the Indians resold Peter's land when he returned to England to fetch his wife. The Puritan legacy was quickly challenged by Hallock's eldest son, disinherited for marrying a Quaker. Fitz-Greene Halleck retained a diluted sense of this prejudice against the Society of Friends, once quipping, "[Quakers] are the most dangerous of dishonest men. They will never cheat you, not they; but, by the help of plain, friendly, and apparently sincere manners, they will manage so that you will cheat yourself."[52] Halleck found humor in his ancestors' rigorous morality as well and maintained a pet joke regarding Joshua 11:17 and 12:7, which mention Mount Halak.[53] He was, however, more proud that his family had incurred Guilford's disapproval. Halleck's great-great-grandfather, John Eliot, a divine who preached to Native Americans, stood accused of opposing the Puritan agenda.

Nicknamed the Apostle to the Indians, Eliot recorded his life in the wilderness among Native Americans and also preached against wigs.[54]

His second son, Joseph, was a popular preacher in the Guilford pastorate he served for thirty years. John Eliot has been accused by his biographer, Convers Francis, of having "indulged the rhyming vein for his own amusement," an offense to Puritans who forbade secular poetry.[55] With Richard Mather, Eliot cowrote the *Bay Psalm Book,* justified as holy poetry, which contained paraphrased Psalms set to hymn tunes. It became the standard text for generations of Calvinists and was in its ninth edition by 1698.

Eliot also translated the Bible into native tongues. This action smeared the clean line drawn between the Christian colonizers and the heathens they vanquished. His first translation appeared in 1663 and was the first Bible produced in the United States. Editions followed in 1680, 1685, and 1691, the latter being a revision written with John Cotton. Halleck appears to have inherited this family interest in coauthorship and translation in his own literary career.

Settlers differed in their opinions of the natives as inherently evil offspring of fallen man or as one of the ten lost tribes of Israel. Eliot's tract, *Jews in America, or Probabilities, that those Indians are Judaical,* argued the godliness of the natives. Although Eliot has been portrayed as a part of the Puritanical effort to control Indians,[56] his self-proclaimed mission in effect contradicted goals of communal purity and threatened profitable land deals that had discouraged Puritans from extending religious conversion and literacy to Indians. In short, Eliot's peers objected to his inclusive ideology. Eliot died in 1690, exactly a century before Halleck's birth, but Bryant believed that Halleck inherited Eliot's spirit of nonconformity.[57]

A much closer influence on Halleck was his father. Israel Hallock came to Guilford as a tailor but was better known as a local comic who figuratively kept people in stitches. Still, Israel alienated townsmen by professing his loyalty to the British crown and by making known his love of dancing. Dancing, a frivolity disallowed by Puritans, had gotten Thomas Morton, "Lord of Misrule," exiled to England for leading male prancers "frisking together like so many fairies, or furies; and [even] worse practices . . . beastly practices."[58] Halleck would antagonize fellow Americans by emulating his father's unpopular positions. Fitz-Greene's sarcastic declaration of loyalty to the British monarchy lasted through the Civil War, and his chief charity was the theater. Israel Hallock was acutely aware that his own love of fine arts was best kept under wraps and literally smuggled music into his home. In addition to hosting a French musician for a year, Israel was entertained by a family friend who snuck a violin under his cloak in order to screen the instrument from "the lynx-eyes" of Guilford's pious townsmen.[59]

Halleck's view that the small town housed even smaller minds but that the Hallock family was an exception was constantly reinforced. "Inspired by his self-educated parents," Halleck praised his mother's "particular fondness" of poetry.[60] Fitz-Greene's cousin, Barnabas Hallock, was also a notable poet, but that was nothing to boast about in Guilford. Adkins explains, "Hemmed in geographically, the village [built on a peninsula] naturally underwent mental and moral restraint. Early prejudices remained." He adds that other nineteenth-century New England communities had relaxed while "much of the old bigotry and intolerance remained and found expression in the daily life" of Guilford.[61] Halleck's retirement years in his hometown demonstrate that even forty years later little had changed since he had left the town of his schooling.[62]

Like Henry James, who felt "a strenuous conflict between his American Puritanism and his intellectual curiosity,"[63] Halleck was a voracious reader and an academic prodigy. He attended public school between the ages of six (when he was already reading Thomas Campbell's poetry) and fifteen. Although Halleck was the teacher's favorite, he was fed "pabulum" for an "intellectual diet" according to one wry nineteenth-century critic.[64] The town library was located over Andrew Eliot's store, where Halleck would live his adolescent years as an apprentice. The library housed about four hundred volumes, mostly sermons and theology; consequently, Halleck recalled, "I fastened like a tiger upon every romance and collection of poetry that I could lay my hands on."[65] (His mother forbade him candles for study only after he had set his room on fire one night reading until midnight.) Both Halleck and his father claimed to have read every book in the town's library.[66] The son's literary interests provided imaginary flights from Guilford where Romantic literature, along with music and sexuality, was largely forbidden. Halleck found poetry liberating and began writing it at a young age.

James Grant Wilson states that "The Tempest" is Halleck's earliest published poem. Written at fourteen, it did not appear in *Hours at Home* until sixty-four years later. Other poems, however, were produced even earlier. Wilson dates "Evening" to Halleck's twelfth year and believes that his "A View of the United States," "The History of New England," and "The Fortunate Family" were written before age ten. Nelson Frederick Adkins and others disagree, dating these works to the age of thirteen. At thirteen, Halleck also wrote a poem to his sister, Maria, dated May 20, 1803. Although Poe felt Halleck's juvenile poetry had "been kept very judiciously from the public eye," Bryant disagreed.[67] Halleck's final collected edition contained seven poems composed before leaving Guilford in 1811. "Memory" and "Lines, Written on a Blank Leaf in Ossian's Poems" were written in 1810 and appeared in the *Connecticut Herald* in 1811. The *Herald* had already published Halleck's "Ode to Good Humor" several months earlier. Halleck's futile struggle to identify with heroes of conventional romance is evident in these early works. Exemplars of justice provided the necessary inspiration, and the juvenilia consistently hails freedom fighters. His relatively early "The Pilgrims," also known as "The Pilgrim Fathers," written in 1814 but not published until 1869, grants the Puritans an impulse toward independence but credits the Bunker Hill army for attempting intellectual freedom: "But 'twas that battle's bugle-blast / That bade the march of mind begin."[68]

Halleck also set historical fiction to rhyme in "The History of New England" and "A View of the United States," the latter of which was based on events of 1798 when French and American navies were engaged. "The History of New England" is a standard tribute to the American Revolution and "A View of the United States" further extolls revolutionaries. Halleck commemorated America's nonconformists at a time when his own dissent was being detected. His variance from expected gender roles did not go unnoticed, and his juvenile verse betrayed confusion regarding sexual difference in a chauvinistic culture. Halleck would certainly ape rigid gender distinctions (criticizing Elizabeth Barrett Browning as too masculine and Tennyson too feminine) but then undermined his own gender identification with effeminate phraseology such as in an apologetic response to a male reader in 1856: "Mine is not the Autograph of . . . a poetess. I therefore cannot add as you ask, one more to your collection, but 'such as I have give unto thee.'"[69]

From about the age of fourteen, Halleck permanently altered the spelling of his surname from Hallock. He offered no explanation to his friend Wilson and perplexed others by the act.[70] From this period onward, the budding poet was ostracized by peers who found him effeminate, hypersensitive, and withdrawn. A solitary figure, Halleck preferred fishing and playing marbles by himself. Wilson faithfully records Halleck's dislike of "the rough sports and adventures in which most boys find delight" and notes that the young Halleck "preferred to wander alone."[71] At fifteen, he moved into his cousin's store where he kept books in a "dainty feminine hand" for the next six years.[72] Socially awkward, Halleck's initiation as a Son of Guilford[73] was remarkably painful by all accounts. He recorded his distress in poems like "Invocation to Sleep,"[74] which sought release.

The first-person narrator in "Invocation to Sleep" walks in solitude along a shore, conjuring Halleck's beloved pastime. Hoping for "gay"[75] visions from the "oblivious" and "opiate" qualities of Sleep, the speaker craves "sweet relief" that "shuts the springs of grief." The poem, rather morose for such an early composition, also provides a premier example of Halleck's crime motif. Slumber, personified as a magician who "dissolves the pris'ner's chain," gives temporary joy to the downtrodden. Sleep's refuge proves "the choicest gift of Heaven" by removing the speaker from his present life. He embraces unconsciousness: "in thy Arms my song and sorrows end." The emotional surrender underlines a strong inclination toward escapism. In addition to Guilford's athletes, Halleck hoped to evade the town's girls. He took the role of the prey escaping the huntresses' flirtations.[76]

Halleck explored romantic conventions in verses to females written at about age fifteen. When one young lady named Laura sent him a lock of her hair, he responded with five stanzas of clichés. In another poem, his metaphors of crime and emotional repression dominate. "Dear Sarah" ponders an admirer's scorn "though I know not my crime." When Eliza Capland's crime of borrowing Eliza Burr's handkerchief was atoned for by a note and white violet, Halleck volunteered his poetic services to Burr and wrote in feminine narration that the flower was "a cement of our mutual love" that will "bid me think of you." The romantic language used to describe two girls' "flame divine" of friendship would reappear in his first serious homosexual love poems, "Lamentation of David" and "Epistle to Carlos Menie." One significant adolescent poem, "Rubus, No. 2. To Miss * * *," asked the curious question, "What is that passion—can you guess, / Which I can feel, but can't express?"[77]

While the lines above went unanswered, another poem guessed Halleck's emotion. "The Fortunate Family" is a prototype of gay fantasy literature that surfaced much later in the century. For instance, Henry James's "The Pupil" would showcase a protagonist who wins parental permission to go off and form a new family with his male tutor. Indeed, Michael Moon argues that the youngster "literally dies from the intensity of his emotional response to finally being released from his unhappy family to go make the home of his dreams."[78] Fred Kaplan gives a homoerotic reading of "The Pupil" and notes that the sexual theme of James's "Master Eustace" still pushed "against the boundaries of puritanical American propriety" as late as 1871.[79] "The Pupil" could have borrowed its central plot from Halleck's "The Fortunate Family."

"The Fortunate Family" was influenced by Wordsworth's *Ballads* and foreshadowed Halleck's deliverance from his hometown. The tetrameter couplets involve four siblings; the two sisters seem to represent Halleck's only sibling, Maria, and her alter ego, whereas the two brothers suggest his own inner conflict. Maria Halleck, who was two years older than Fitz-Greene, emulated his name change, wrote envious letters after he had moved to New York, and like her famous brother, never married. In "The Fortunate Family," the two sisters have no avenue of escape except for marriage. The brothers each scheme on their own to leave their town. The tension lies in the legitimacy of their separate departures.

The first son is named Dick, a name that may have doubled as slang for an erect penis since the seventeenth century.[80] He is an effeminate child, described as being like his mother, who follows social protocol when a traveling couple wishes to adopt him, pleading "'O, father! pray,

pray let me go / And live with him—oh, don't say no!'" Curiously, Halleck used the singular male pronoun, inconsistent with the plural antecedent for the foster couple, husband *and* wife. The request is to ride off with a strange man. As in a real marriage contract at that time, only the father's permission is needed. The blissful Dick gains his father's "consent," a word further suggesting a metaphorical same-sex marriage.

The surrogate family travels away from the town, leaving Dick's brother, Bill, to declare:

> . . . that now he would not stay,
> And said he did not think it fair
> That he should stay and Dick go there.
> Determined not to stay at home,
> He took his clothes and off did come.
> He reached a ship, to his great joy,
> And got on board as cabin-boy.
> Where we shall leave him for to see
> What happened to the family.[81]

In an abrupt change in tone, the poem informs the reader that upon discovering what Bill has done, "his mother round the house did run, / Screaming, yelling * * *." Here, the unfinished poem ends. The careful meter and rhyme of the poem suggest a polished draft, making the ending appear intentionally unresolved. The fraternity of "The Fortunate Family" mimicked Halleck's own situation; he fervently loved his family but was determined to flee Guilford with or without their consent.

Like modern gays, each brother redefines family for himself. The hometown, rather than the poem's pastoral region and "happy pair" of birth parents, is unsatisfactory. Dick leaves with his parents' blessing and understanding. Left behind, Bill steals away to a ship. His attraction to the male world of sailing suggests that he has chosen to inhabit a homosocial realm with all of its apparent dangers.

Bradford's "Anno Dom: 1646 [A Noted Pirate in Plymouth]" vaguely complained of "80 lusty men" who visited the colony; however, the relationship between piracy and homosexuality was anything but ambiguous. British drama was portraying pirates as presumed sodomites as early as 1713, and literary critics have explored homosexual relations on the high seas in Smollett, Melville, and Whitman.[82] Reconstructionists are proving that "sex with another male was the ordinary and acceptable way of engaging in erotic pleasure" for buccaneers.[83] Recent works exploring same-sex love and seafaring especially note the acceptable sexuality of "considerable affection between captains and their cabin-boys." The *matelot* tradition assigned captured youths to officers, and homosexual unions, *matelotage,* among mates could result in promotions for captives.[84] Terry Boughner claims seventeenth-century piracy culture "is the only known example of a predominantly homosexual community . . . with little or no interference from the rest of the society"; however, even members of that community did not go untried, and one Virginia shipmaster was hung for sodomy with a crew member,[85] just as the fictionalized captain in Charles Johnson's homophobic *Middle Passage* receives poetic justice for raping a cabin boy. The homoerotic reading of the climax of "The Fortunate Family" is reinforced by the mother's hysteria upon Bill's departure, which was not evident upon Dick's. Though perfectly calm regarding the first son's adoption, Bill's mother is driven berserk by the unspoken perils of life for her son as a cabin boy. By the age of thirteen, Halleck's family values had transported the orthodox adventure genre into the realm of homosexual emancipation literature.

Halleck also found same-sex applications for Scripture during his adolescence. He used Christian arguments in verse to support his position against slavery shortly before the importation of slaves to the United States was officially banned in 1807. With more immediate self-interest, he ignored Sodom and Gomorrah and concentrated on Jonathan and David, whose story "has long been a source of inspiration for Western homoerotic art and literature, and has been construed as the one episode in the Judeo-Christian scriptures which affirms . . . [a] homosexual relationship."[86] The biblical pair have been called upon for centuries to both conceal and expose same-sex desires. Robert K. Martin explains that Halleck's "Lamentation of David over Saul and Jonathan" (ca. 1805) was sanctioned by its subtitle, "paraphrased from 2 Samuel i 1–19," and was a striking choice out of all available Bible stories.[87] Martin also proposes that Halleck embellishes David's feelings, choosing the story solely for its emotional content. The poem also foreshadowed Joseph Drake's death, asking,

> Is my loved companion gone
> And left me friendless and alone?
>
> A wound that time can never heal.
> A mutual flame our bosoms fired,
> A mutual love our breasts inspired,
> Our pleasures and our cares the same;
> We felt sweet friendship's hallowed flame,
> . . . Affection twined our souls around[88]

The poem elevates platonic love above the superficial love of women, a tactic Halleck would repeat in his mature lines to Drake. The premonitory parallel between the passionate biblical friendship and Halleck's love for Drake has not been missed by twentieth-century critics such as Everett Gleason Hill: "Whether [Halleck] was David or Jonathan, that was the nature of his friendship for Joseph Rodman Drake, for whom his love surpassed the love of woman."[89] Only four of Halleck's boyhood poems are biblically based; two are concerned with David and two with Job.

Feeling stuck as a clerk in Guilford, Halleck's biblical usage focused on a same-sex relationship and the epitome of a man whose trials are tests of patience. "Versification of Job, 14th Chapter" is based upon an Old Testament section wherein a victimized hero awaits a new life. Halleck, however, did not have long to wait before New York alleviated his lamentations.

Still, not all memories of Guilford were bitter ones. The town was also the setting of his first same-sex love. At nineteen, Halleck became infatuated with Carlos Menie, a handsome young Cuban whose father had sent him from Havana to Guilford for a year to study English. While Menie's physical description comes from Adkins, the more progressive account of Halleck's affection for him comes from Wilson. Adkins entirely dismisses the intense friendship and retreats to more comfortable territory: Halleck's trite responses to Guilford's young ladies. Adkins excludes entirely from his analysis of Halleck's early verse the poems to the Cuban, "Lamentation of David over Saul and Jonathan" and "The Fortunate Family," which he only mentions as "a tissue of banalities."

Wilson says Halleck's attractive Cuban visitor was intimate with the poet and publishes one of an unspecified number of untitled poems sent to Menie after his departure.[90] Eighteen quatrains follow in which "days and months have rolled away" since "the parting tear," yet Halleck recalls Menie's "pleasing form" and traces "every gesture" of his body, confessing:

> Oft in the stillness of the night,
> When slumbers close mine eyes,
> Your image bursts upon my sight;
> I gaze in glad-surprise!

The epistle asserts that time has not effaced the pleasing body mapped out in the speaker's memory. He follows fancy as "her wild, romantic flights unfold / Events of former days" when the two young men's smiles "caressed" one another. The pensive narrator questions Menie's emotional fidelity and wonders if thoughts can "a rapturous charm impart" before three climactic quatrains:

> Ah, yes! that gentle heart I know,
> At friendship's touch it beats;
> I feel the sympathetic glow,
> My breast the throb repeats.
>
> Then let us cherish well the flame
> Of friendship and of love;

Let peaceful virtue be our aim,
  Our hopes be placed above.

There, in affliction, may we find
  A refuge ever nigh;
May time our friendly union bind,
  And years cement the tie.

Like Halleck's other homoerotic juvenile poetry ("The Fortunate Family" and "Lamentation of David over Saul and Jonathan"), the Menie poem does not appear in any collection of Halleck's poetry. Except for the one preserved by Wilson, the other epistles to Menie appear to be either lost or destroyed. Along with the hallowed flame from his "Lamentation of David over Saul and Jonathan," the "cement" phrase recycles Halleck's lines for Eliza Burr and Eliza Capland. Apparently, Halleck borrowed his prime phrases from earlier works to achieve his strongest love poem to that date. The physical idealization of Menie, however, is tempered.

Robert K. Martin suggests that Halleck carefully shifts to platonic ideals in the middle stanza:

There [is] a deliberate check upon the emotions . . . one can observe in Halleck's lines the first traces of what would later be called the Uranian attitude: the assumption that love between men was purer and more spiritual than heterosexual love.[91]

Yet Menie's touch and his sympathy with the speaker's heart present more than the platonic in the hope that friendship and love will be possible in the refuge of heaven. Friendship by itself is, after all, conceivable in the here and now. Likewise, a sympathetic heart is only necessary if the reciprocal emotion is beyond the norm.

Halleck's poetry and prose directly refer to Milton,[92] and the poem to Menie echoes the Puritan Milton's sonnet to his deceased wife ("Mee Thought I Saw . . ."). But Halleck's poem also presents elements of a wet dream. As though distressed by a nocturnal emission, the narrator wakes suddenly as Carlos's image "bursts" upon him, reenacting a passionate embrace. The connotation of "gaze," "touch," "glow," "breast," "throb," and "flame" follow a logical sequence of sexual attraction, physical contact, nudity, rising heat, and orgasm. The speaker discovers his mate and dreams of an eternal bond that supplies new power to fend off present afflictions. Affliction here signifies self-affliction (the "self-abuse" of masturbation or the self-inflicted wound of suicide prevalent in Halleck's later poetry) and social afflictions of physical separation and homophobia that prevent a same-sex union sealing Halleck's love. The seminal overtones of wet cement are bound as well to the ending's phallic language:

Mary Ann Hardy's 1842 miniature of Fitz-Greene Halleck on ivory. Probably based on earlier portraits, it was produced in the year that Halleck broke his long poetic silence with the radical second half of "Connecticut." (Collection of the New-York Historical Society.) Earlier portraits of Halleck include two by Nathaniel Rogers, who produced an 1811 portrait of Halleck under the guidance of Mysterious Brown, a British artist residing in New York at the time, and a miniature of Halleck in 1820. The 1811 miniature was presented by Halleck to his parents as his enlistment in the War of 1812 grew closer. John Wesley Jarvis also painted a youthful Halleck in a group picture of American poets (ca. 1820–1825).

Carlos, adieu! within my heart
Your memory firm shall dwell;
Till, pierced by death's unerring dart,
I bid the world farewell!

Stiff memory is penetrated by a metaphoric dart, akin to Cupid's arrow. "Firm" and "pierced" suggest erection and insertion just as death provides a conventional poetic allusion to orgasm, *la petite mort*. The youthful Halleck's French was so good he boasted that he had "been often taken, or rather mistaken, for a Frenchman by Frenchmen themselves," and others claimed that Halleck read and spoke French fluently.[93] This factor, as well as the introduction of "adieu" into the stanza, invites a French reading of the imagery. Metaphors aside, the lines clearly conveyed the void created by Menie's absence: "in my hours of lonely thought / I muse and think of you."

Halleck also mused on Menie in "Soft as the Falling Dews of Night" (composed in 1809–1810), which corresponded with his anguished separation. Ironically, Wilson published the poem posthumously in the *Independent* on Sadie Hawkins Day, 1872, during the twenty-four hours in which women could forego sexual modesty and openly pursue single men. "Soft as the Falling Dews of Night" thanks a woman (possibly Halleck's sister and lifelong confidant) for her "tear of pity" and "sympathetic sigh" as she tries to "teach me to blunt Affection's dart." The dart conjures up the preserved epistle to Menie, which was apparently copied before Halleck sent the original across the Gulf of Mexico.

"Trifles 'Light as Air!'"[94] a series of light-hearted epistolary verses that may have disguised Halleck's attempt to work through feelings for Menie, was completed just before Halleck left Guilford. In 1878, *Harper's New Monthly* made an unsubstantiated claim that the poem was cowritten with an unidentified, beautiful socialite who adopted a pseudonym and was a friend of Halleck, "for it never progressed farther than friendship."[95] The only reliable information offered is that Halleck loved pseudonyms, some of which remain unintelligible.[96] Antonio, an appropriately ethnic name for Carlos, and Margaret are nicknames taken on by the couple in "Trifles 'Light as Air!'" A British pamphlet, *Hints to the Public* (1811), explained that Margaret was a term for mollies or "Mary-Annes" close to the time when Halleck wrote this poem.[97]

Antonio asks what "concealed intention" and "secret anguish" the letters he has received signify, beseeching, "I must beg you to disclose, / In plainer language all thy woes." If the poem is indeed autobiographical, Menie may have confronted Halleck about the meaning of his poems during their correspondence, now lost. The woman, representing Halleck who consistently took the female role for himself, initially denies that the problem is love until she realizes that she may never meet her consummate man:

> Too soon the rose, the lily, fades
> And lo! the Land of *Cross Old Maids* . . .
> From this lone state, ye powers, defend me!
> But ah! take care what *lad* you send me!

The lone state from which the speaker seeks deliverance may have referred to psychological unrest or, more literally, to the state of Connecticut, and the capitalization and italics of *Cross Old Maids* phonetically suggests Carlos Menie's encoded name. If this code were intentional, the land referred to is Cuba. With the platonic affection of a brother, Antonio tells Margaret that suitors will commit suicide or go insane if she rejects them and urges her not "to discover / The sense or *nonsense* of your lover; For of *our sex* this truth I know, *Perfection dwells not here below.*" Antonio's implication that all the good men are taken is provocative. He tells his friend to take the first man to "pop the question" and advises her to let the suitor linger for one day, during which Antonio will visit, weather permitting.

"Trifles 'Light as Air!'" provides the earliest example of Halleck's attempts to trivialize marriage and to minimize his own feelings by poking fun at romantic disappointments, such as his unreciprocated devotion to Menie. One can observe that Halleck often "reflects an inability to reconcile the real and the ideal, and he frequently undercuts a serious statement with frivolity."[98] But there was a practical side to Halleck, too. It is no coincidence that his first love object was a foreigner.

Early Americans were conditioned by colonial accounts to see homosexuality as foreign. Confident that debauchery resided across the English Channel, English Puritans drew moral boundaries along national borders. The belief that sexual immorality originated in the heathen East and had spread throughout the rest of Europe fit neatly into the Puritans' religious typology. British society as a whole boasted "sterner sexual morality than the French, above all, with respect to homosexuality" and saw the growing tolerance of sodomy in Italy and France as proof of Protestantism's superior morality.[99] In fact, France had decriminalized homosexual acts between consenting adults in 1791, a year after Halleck's birth, and even today, French remains synonymous with fellatio in the gay vernacular.

Prose works depicting the French as homosexual were carried over from England to American audiences. In 1703, a man invited his British acquaintance to join him "in Paris with two or three pretty smiling unthinking fellows that know nothing and do everything."[100] By 1748, a "Frenchified" Captain Whiffle in Tobias Smollett's novel *The Adventures of Roderick Random* swished in his pink satin and was rumored to engage in a vice not fit to be named with the ship's surgeon; a bit later, Earl Strutwell, who is full of French phrases, argued at length that homosexuality was natural and historic: "The most celebrated poets have not scrupled to avow it." Although it was a French lawyer and politician who attacked American lesbianism a decade after Halleck's birth,[101] the association between France and homosexuality did not wane. When sexual corruption reached London, Puritans went "flying from the depravations of Europe, to the American strand."[102]

The established moral map remained intact two hundred years later when Byron recommended Turkish baths for their "sherbert and sodomy."[103] Of Britain's carnal exiles, Byron and Shelley chose Italy, whereas Wilde found France especially hospitable. In the United States, Halleck's search for same-sex love took him to New York City. Only within the wider limits of this multicultural mecca could the Puritans' view of coercive sodomy be challenged. Communal contamination was transformed into mutual companionship.

Moral lines had already been drawn between wholesome country living and decadent urban existence. In going to America where "the deer were tamer and more plentiful than prostitutes in London," the Puritans also left a city infested with male prostitution.[104] Lydia Maria Child, who had once met a berdache, wrote a story in 1863, "Willie Wharton," which cautions the title character against becoming a city fop. As Camille Paglia argues the "development of a sexual underworld may be intrinsic to urbanization as a worldwide phenomenon," and as David F. Greenberg believes that American homosexual subcultures could not form until nineteenth-century urbanization,[105] New York did in fact offer Halleck sexual sanctuary.

New York had eliminated sodomy as a capital offense when Halleck was only six years old, but Connecticut would not drop the death penalty for sodomy for another twenty-six years. (Truth being stranger than fiction, Edward Hyde [New York's governor from 1702–1708] habitually appeared in his wife's clothes in public.)[106] Both Halleck's contemporaries and twentieth-century critics have highlighted the impact that New York had on him. During his first trip on behalf of his cousin's store at age eighteen, Halleck discovered a life much to his liking in Manhattan, which would soon provide him with "life's richest experience and life's sweetest friends."[107] Others have noted that "the sidewalks of New York seemed the Vale of Tempe to his muse" and that New York offered "a freer moral and intellectual atmosphere . . . that clashed harshly with the restraint and bigotry imposed by" Guilford.[108] "A veritable oasis" to Halleck, the city fostered "his freedom from moralizing cant,"[109] and Halleck immediately recognized the rising masonry as his paradise. A raw confidence accompanied his resolve to move there. During his interim back in Guilford, Halleck taught bookkeeping in an evening school he opened so that he could indulge his passion for buying contemporary poetry and romance novels. He also risked submitting poetry to local publishers. "The Indian Warrior," his first published poem, appeared in a New Haven paper in January 1810.

The editorial preface to "The Indian Warrior" referred to its author as "an obscure, uneducated country boy" whose work showed "uncultivated genius."[110] Halleck signed the poem "A Connecticut Farmer's Boy," but the editor declared, "We are informed that the following verses are really the production of a Connecticut Farmer's boy, but we doubt it— *they are too good to be original*."[111] The poem, based on an actual burial site, was reprinted in New York (*Holt's Columbian,* August 22, 1810). After leaving home, Halleck would continue to submit poems anonymously, but never again as a New England country bumpkin. He seemed for a time to be caught between his puritanical past and a promising cosmopolitan future.

Reviewers also noticed that Halleck's twist on American romance was not attained without considerable internal conflict leading to "the partial suppression—or, at least, the imperfect development—of his aesthetic nature."[112] He seemed "half developed on the artistic side" and was accused of running either hot or cold.[113] The intellectual schizophrenia resulting from the lessons of his hometown confronting the world outside of it left him in a state between "the flippancy and conventionalism of modern society and the baldness of Puritanic worship [that he found] repulsive."[114] In spite of these comments and George S. Hillard's comparison of Halleck to two poets rolled into one, "analogous to that of the Siamese twins,"[115] Halleck had managed to form an identity—he was an outsider.

Halleck learned to associate his sexuality with otherness to the point of changing his name, seeking out foreigners, and shedding his hometown. By age twenty, he counterattacked puritanical notions of sodomy. Nurtured in a new, more open environment, he would reconstruct a same-sex model that borrowed heavily from the federalist transformation of British traitors into revolutionary heroes. Prisoners became indistinguishable from patriots in his works. Ultimately, Halleck would rewrite the Puritan as pervert. Small wonder that Guilford's citizens rejected him as an aristocrat and a libertine when he faced his return to town almost four decades later.

The unfounded rumor that Halleck had converted to Catholicism while in New York implied spiritual deficiency as well. He became a cultural reincarnation of town founder William Plaine, who had been one of the great "conceptual traitors" of Protestantism.[116] Halleck's alcoholism was further aggravated by the sodomitical allusions implied in both false accusations about Catholicism and excessive wealth. A surge of homophobic criticism would further silence him at the outset of the Civil War, just as the American sodomy trials had reached their zenith during an earlier period of civil crisis. In between these events, Halleck found himself in Manhattan. As he was finalizing plans to quit Guilford in 1810, New York surpassed Philadelphia as the largest city in America. It also exceeded his greatest expectations.

His hunch about relocating to New York paid handsomely. By his early thirties, he was transformed into the right-hand man of New York's wealthiest businessman, the nucleus of a stylish social sphere, and the nation's leading poet. The city freed his pen and marked what Bayard Taylor would call "the beginning of a new epoch in the story of our culture."[117] The unfolding era of homoerotic poetry that contradicted America's prevailing sexual ideology made Halleck a sheep in wolves' clothing back home. His attraction to foreign men persisted beyond his infatuation with Carlos Menie and beyond his formative years. Halleck's democratic vision shocked Guilford; it seemed the only line left for him to cross was to mingle with the French.

Jonathan Katz's research shows that immigrants, in general, were viewed with sexual distrust in nineteenth-century America. As late as 1880, U.S. Census reports purported an "extremely disproportionate" number of those incarcerated for homosexual crimes were foreign-born white, and Paul Nacke's "The Homosexual Market in New York" (1905) blamed homosexuality on "inferior individuals who cross the ocean." In fact, some homosexual emigrants were fleeing to America from worse persecution in European countries. One emigrant complained that the antiquated law of his native land made him "obliged to reside in America" in 1882 when he hoped, "May the time soon come when science shall educate the people [about homosexuality] . . . but before that time can come there will be many victims."[118] While all outsiders potentially carried the homosexual germ, none were believed to be as infected as the French.

At the time of Halleck's move to New York, America had just clashed with the French over the XYZ affair. Playing both sides, the French government had offered to sell protection to American ships that were taken by French pirates who were, in turn, sanctioned by France. Halleck's sexual dissension from the law of his land appropriately found its expression in taking up with a Frenchman. After finding a boarding house in New York, Halleck cohabited with a first-generation French immigrant, Eugene MacCarthy.

Although he was born to wealthy Irish parents, MacCarthy was raised as a native of Bordeaux and Halleck's letter to Maria repeatedly refers to

MacCarthy as a Frenchman. MacCarthy came to America to study business and probably met Halleck during an unpaid apprenticeship that a French agent had arranged for him. The friends converted the two-room apartment into a one-bedroom flat. Halleck divulged to his sister, "The other we call our drawing-room."[119] Having looked at accommodations in twenty houses, the two finicky men settled on Greenwich Street in Greenwich Village, separated from the male and female prostitution of the Bowery by a narrow strip of Broadway.

One critic, who never met Halleck, claimed in "New Publications: Life of Fitz-Greene Halleck" that Halleck always looked for "'the substantial beauties of the Bowery' as he called the rosy-cheeked damsels to be met with in that democratic thoroughfare." But Halleck's reference may have been to the male prostitutes there who were identified by their cosmetics. Hordes of female and male prostitutes turned tricks in New York City since at least the mid-nineteenth century; Greenwich Village was the ghetto of aberration and the Bowery had wide-spread male prostitution. Apparently, the Bowery and lower Broadway in the nineteenth century were the central cruising grounds of male hustlers who wore both rouge and eye shadow.[120] Halleck's new neighbors would not judge him or his living arrangement peculiar.

Halleck's appraisal of the young MacCarthy is characteristically generous. It is, however, for Halleck a uniquely disparaging physical description of a male. While Halleck compliments the Frenchman's fluency in Romance languages and English as well as his singing, dancing, and other musical talents, Halleck adds:

He, however, has one of the ugliest faces (though his person is handsome) that I ever met with. . . . I will now speak of him as a man. He is an agreeable companion, an obliging friend, an accomplished gentleman, and possessed of an amiable, friendly, benevolent disposition. With such qualities, I cannot but be pleased with him.[121]

Halleck's parenthetical comment suggests that he felt MacCarthy had a nice body even if his face was not worth a second glance. Like a proud bride, Halleck was pleased with his companion's intrinsic qualities. He may even have exaggerated MacCarthy's bad looks to ward off any sexual suspicion regarding their common sleeping arrangement, as bachelor roommates eventually came to have strong homosexual connotations. In addition, choosing to room with MacCarthy during an international conflict with France reflected Halleck's perception of his own sexuality as foreign, criminal, and unpatriotic. He was literally sleeping with the enemy.

Today as Guilford enters the twenty-first century, it remains cautious about embracing Halleck. In recent years, plans to dedicate a room to him in the public library were shot down because of his reputation for strong drink. The house in which Halleck died however, bears a plaque, and the Stone House Museum in Guilford, hailed as one of the oldest structures in America, still displays Halleck's coffee mill, bellows, cane, and white leather gloves. His chair can be viewed at Guilford's Thomas Griswald House Museum. But Guilford today seems no more eager to have itself associated with Halleck than it did in 1850 when he was drowning his sorrow of having to retire there in sherry.

Eluding the threat of Guilford's sexual policing, Halleck sought higher intellectual ground. One classic Puritan text that Halleck would have read was Nathaniel Morton's *New-England Memorial,* which included a eulogy to Thomas Dudley, father of Anne Bradstreet. In it the New England deputy governor is lauded because his "zeal to order appeared in contriving good laws, and faithfully executing them upon criminal offenders, heretics, and underminers of true religion. He had a piercing judgement to discover the wolf, though clothed with a sheep skin." [122] Little had changed in the culture by 1800 when the *Columbian Centinel and the Massachusetts Federalist* warned tavern dwellers of a "French beau" whose "soul seems to recoil upon itself" in the presence of women. Other men were to be on guard as he "stalks the room like a bear prowling around a sheep-fold." [123] Such prescribed morality would weigh heavily on Halleck who was defined as a criminal by both his community and himself. His same-sex eulogies would ultimately expose his heresy to a later generation of Guilford saints.

Writing his family often, but seldom visiting Guilford, Halleck candidly scoffed that the townspeople could all "read and write—*not that they ever do either.*" [124] But Guilford was literate in its own way: it had been prolific in creating sodomy legislation and had read Halleck proficiently as a sexual outlaw, an exposure he had come to realize long before his reluctant retirement there. He was probably certain of it even before the age of eighteen and made plans to reside forever in less dangerous territory because of it. The same sexual issue that had led to the execution of a town father had also driven off the town's most eminent son. Guilford once again lost one of its flock.

2

Love and War

He is, perhaps, the handsomest man in New York, . . . I felt
myself during the ceremony as committing a crime in aiding
and assisting in such a sacrifice.
                    Fitz-Greene Halleck on acting as Drake's best man

OMING from a man who would become New York's most eligible
bachelor himself, Halleck's description of Joseph Rodman Drake
as the handsomest man in New York[1] is quite striking, but perhaps even more impressive is Halleck's confidence in his sister, for whom
the portrait of Drake was drawn. While Drake's sex appeal elevated him
to an Apollo, in Halleck's words, Halleck's accessibility to him made
Drake equally desirable as a prospective husband. N. P. Willis claimed
Halleck had all the "advantages of physiognomy and manners, so winning a look," and was "so admirably formed" that he had many female
admirers. Poe agreed, adding style and grace to his physical assessment.[2]
Halleck's forehead arched intelligently, his cleft chin suggested nobility,
and his gray eyes incessantly sparkled. Even as Halleck aged, friends like
Bryant and acquaintances like Catherine Sedgwick took note of his
princely appeal. Such compliments were common, but still Halleck felt
he could not hold a candle to Drake's charms. Drake was, as Halleck
knew Apollo to be, the sun god.

Halleck could not understand the comparisons made between himself
and Drake. Such thoughts were most candidly shared with his sibling.
Maria was her brother's best friend. He frequently sought her counsel
during the emotional battles of his first years in New York, and it was she
who guided his unsure footing through the unfamiliar emotional territory
of Drake's friendship and death. According to Everett Gleason Hill, "If
Halleck had any but male love affairs, his biographers and his neighbors
alike have singularly overlooked them. His love for women seems to have

wholly satisfied itself on his sister."³ Halleck sensed that Maria understood his feelings better than he did himself.

Shortly after leaving Guilford, Halleck lamented impatiently to Maria that he would never find "among the numerous fellow-mortals I meet with, a person whose disposition and ideas are congenial with mine own, and whose friendship I might cherish as a valuable acquisition, nor do I expect to find one."⁴ Halleck felt that he was looking for a needle in a haystack in seeking one man after his own type, especially since he was not sure what kind of a man he was himself. At an age when other young men might have asked a sister's advice on selecting a female mate for marriage, Halleck was feeling terminally unique. He had apparently forgotten how easily he had fallen for a sexy Cuban visitor or how pleased he had been with a certain homely Frenchman. He would, however, discover his special mate within two years, and in finding Drake he would come to know himself.

Halleck's urban experience fostered his self-awareness. New York was centered on commercial diversity rather than social conformity. At least for the first seventy years of the nineteenth century, the city provided a relatively relaxed atmosphere for homosexuals. Halleck "felt free and gayer" in the city, telling his sister "how he really felt . . . how social and friendly" New Yorkers were in contrast to Guilford's citizens.⁵ His "striking personality" jumped "zestfully into the stimulating whirl of New York life" like an exhilarated high diver.⁶ That city of fortune and fame would soon provide Halleck with both. Swaggering down Broadway with a dashing air, Halleck's urban posture became his public image, and yet he had nearly missed making his big splash in New York's social pool altogether.

Halleck's job search extended for over a month after his May 1811 arrival in the city. Writing his father that he would leave for Richmond, Virginia, the very next day and try his luck there, he was suddenly hired by Jacob Barker, a Quaker banker on South Street. Barker's firm would become one of the brokers and banks accused of having wasted Halleck's poetic talents in what James Russell Lowell called "a world of back-offices, ledgers, and stoves."⁷ Halleck managed his employer's money meticulously, although he personally despised thrift. He punished one rich man, who was known for a daily regime of sleeping until eleven o'clock, by arriving at dawn in order to repay the six cents that the client had expressed concern about on the previous day. Yet dealing with an annoying client on occasion was a small price to pay for new friendships. By August 1811, Halleck contrasted his early years to his New York experience that opened "a source of pleasure hitherto unknown" as he began "to trace the endless variety of man, to mark the different propositions, passions, and pursuits" of his coworkers and fellow boarding-house tenants.⁸

Halleck kept his parents abreast of financial news and fed Maria's imagination with the city's social pageantry—a working world overwhelmingly constituted of single males. By the 1820s, New York's sex trade was booming, providing prostitutes galore to the commercial part of town via more than two hundred brothels by the decade's end.[9] Liberated from Guilford's censorship, Halleck could joke about its banal standards. Sounding cosmopolitan after only three months in New York, he wrote Maria about a newly arrived New Haven man who had "disposed of enough of his Connecticut principles" to see a play.[10] But Halleck was watching more than just staged dramas; he was eyeing men all around him in an effort to cast players in his own life. He was especially smitten with one of his coworkers whom he sketched for Maria.

James B——r was "a fine young fellow, very pretty-looking—I say pretty, for he has quite a boyish appearance." Perhaps moved by wishful thinking, Halleck claimed, "On my first entrance into the office, [James] appeared very anxious to form an intimacy with me; his condescending and amiable manners soon endeared him to *me,* and we vowed eternal friendship when we had hardly seen each other an hour." Despite the instant, deep bond Halleck sensed, James turned out to be a ladies' man, whom Halleck judged a fool for deciding to abandon his life in New York to take up with a country girl named Rebecca. In trying to persuade his sister of James's strange behavior, Halleck revealed his own lack of heterosexual identification: James confided "a number of pretty little things about [Rebecca], which, though, most undoubtedly, of the first importance to *him,* to *me* appeared rather non-sensical."[11] Even as other colleagues envied James's romantic flight, Halleck could not comprehend the lure of a woman. His strong sense of difference had tracked him.

Halleck's interpretation of James's eventual marriage disclosed even more about himself. In April 1812, he wrote that James had "become a candidate for offering an oblation on the alter of Hymen." Inverting gender roles, Halleck described the groom as sexually sacrificed to the bride. He would recurrently denigrate women as duplicitous and aggressive and the men who married them as passive but greedy. Shocked that James was not marrying Rebecca, whom he had so fervently pursued the previous summer, Halleck advanced this theory: "Miss Somebody," James's new fiancée, had "a fortune of 12,000 dollars, [which] obliterated the remembrance of Rebecca from [James's] mind, and induced him to make proposals of marriage. . . . So much for James B——r."[12] In these few words, Halleck negates the bride's identity ("Miss Somebody"), cancels James's sincerity toward either woman (one being obliterated for the other's fortune), emasculates the groom (who is induced to propose), and ascribes calculated exploitation to the friend he writes off ("so much for James

B——r"). Maria would trace this formula time and again in her brother's correspondence.

Less than a year later, Halleck wrote his sister that another coworker named Davis was also "induced" to marry: "He is a fortune-hunter, and has lately discovered a very handsome girl, whose father he thinks to be rich, and he accordingly is laying a train to get possession of her and her money, the latter being his real object."[13] This groom, possibly duped by a father-in-law whom he thinks to be rich, has the real motive of marrying for money, even though the bride is quite lovely. Davis is also emasculated; induced by his future wife, he lays a train down the aisle in Halleck's pun. Such cynicism appeased Halleck, who did not see himself as a sore loser in competition with his friends' brides. Halleck apparently hid his cooled affection for Davis who retained enough warmth to nickname his son Fitz. Davis's gesture would be the first of many dubious honors Halleck came to resent as others named their offspring after the man who would never be a father himself.

Single men and women emerged as aesthetic opposites in almost all of Halleck's letters to Maria. Men are beautiful, even if lacking substance. An August 3, 1811, letter describes Samuel W——s as a handsome young man who is also an airhead: "Nature, in forming him, made a blunder, for he is not quite so deep as the Red Sea, and rather empty in the garret." Only two days later, a letter compliments Catherine Foote's mind but not her face. Halleck notes that Foote's physician is very handsome, but she is so ghastly that Halleck is sure she will die soon, although she had just been out riding for several hours. The same letter describes one celebrated actress as "abominably homely and ugly" and another reputed for her great beauty as "hideous."[14] Halleck's misogyny may have stemmed from a sublimated homosexuality, but his verse reveals "a clearly defined distinction between the love of men, pure, holy, and virtuous, and the love of women, impure and destructive."[15] As "the only son of a Puritan family, Halleck's resistance to marriage was fairly unique," according to Adkins, who found this resistance "veiled in obscurity."[16] Halleck's letters, however, do lift that veil; he was simply unable to sustain any genuine interest in the female sex.

In an August 20, 1811, letter, Halleck gossips about his first boarding house and shows a disproportionate interest in its male tenants.[17] One tenant, coded as B——d, was another ladies' man who is criticized for being "well adapted to suit such a fickle, rattle-headed set of beings as the female sex in general." Halleck claims, B——s is "about twenty-two, and the handsomest man, without exception, I ever saw." L——e "has a very handsome person," P——s is "the finest young man in the house" with "a *rustic appearance*," and T——e is a "pretty-looking fellow, about twenty-one years old." The long letter also depicts a man named Lord, "a singular-looking fellow [who] constantly wears a kind of grin on his countenance, somewhere between a smile and a laugh," and who "seems inclined to pay considerable attention to me, and, as I believe he is a worthy young man, I have no objection to accepting his addresses." [18] Each of the half-dozen appraisals is grounded on physical appeal, and the decision to favor Lord is tinged with the language of courtship. The singular Lord's inclination toward Halleck suggests some unspoken but gestured attraction spawning considerable attention. At the receiving end of Lord's leering, Halleck's acceptance is dressed in the language of wooing, wherein intentions are honorable and met with no objection.

In contrast, Maria's life in Guilford was uneventful, although she had recently entertained a medical student named James E. DeKay. She sensed an eagerness in DeKay to meet her brother and provided a letter of introduction. DeKay would in turn introduce Halleck to another medical student, Joseph Rodman Drake. Most sources credit DeKay as the mutual friend who brought Halleck and Drake together; however, Maria was the catalyst, at least indirectly. DeKay would become Drake's brother-in-law and would form a foursome with Halleck and two women after Drake's death. Before Drake, however, Halleck had moved in with MacCarthy in February 1813, though the move caused Halleck anxiety regarding his reputation back in Guilford.

In the same letter telling Maria about his French roommate, he pondered old friendships:

I am led to remark that I have received no letters from any of my Guilford correspondents for a long time past, and know not how to account for their neglect and indifference towards one who is unconscious of having merited such treatment. I certainly am fallen "to dumb forgetfulness a prey" in their minds, and, as from an ignorance of my crimes to punish which they adopt this method, I feel unwilling to attribute to myself any part of the blame. [19]

The unacknowledged crimes and the personification of dumb amnesia may allude to Halleck's love that dare not speak its name. These two metaphors of criminality and silence figure centrally in his same-sex verse. Self-conscious of his fallen standing, Halleck began to balance negative metaphors with indignant vindication from the beginnings of his years in New York. His posture grew increasingly defensive. Feeling punished without cause, he is unwilling to accept blame for the neglect of others. However, his innocence may not have been as unconscious as he claimed.

This letter also focused on one particular friend's indifference and asked Maria to intercede: "Please ask George Foote, whose acquaintance I would gladly cherish, whose virtues and amiable qualities I shall ever admire, and whose friendship I shall always prize far above my other Guilford companions, what is the reason for his silence." The letter goes on to imply that Foote is angry because Halleck has failed to visit Foote's sister Harriet. Ironically, Halleck puts forth this theory even as he claims to be unaware of the offense. Apparently, a visit would have meant a great deal to Harriet Foote. Halleck would eventually replace even the one friendship above all others back home with new friends—like Daniel Embury, a coworker who became a New York bank president. Halleck closed his letters to Embury with romantic phrases such as "Adieu—mon cher ami," and "'Warm from the heart and faithful to its fires' / Affectionately yours." One letter closes by joking about tailors, such as Halleck's own father, who are "the quotient of man divided by nine."[20]

Halleck scoffed at his hometown's morality and exhibited a new sexual awareness in other letters to Guilford friends. An 1814 letter to Joel Lewis Griffing[21] remarked about a mutual acquaintance: "I am sorry that his libertinism has been made so public in G. [Guilford] as such is the great regard of the good people there for morality and virtue at least for the appearance of them." The man referred to "had to do" with three women in three weeks, one of whom was "as arrant a w——e [whore] as George St[reet] afforded." More important than displaying an awareness of urban depravity, the letter to Griffing casts new light on MacCarthy's sexuality.

Apparently, Halleck's Frenchman did not abstain from women. MacCarthy's history is sketchy and his disassociation from Halleck is not recorded. Halleck rarely mentioned him again after relocating to a new boarding house. MacCarthy, like Menie, probably did not share Halleck's exclusively same-sex orientation. Halleck's letter to Griffing reports that MacCarthy produced an illegitimate daughter with a rather loose woman who might have had intercourse with any willing body. He disparages MacCarthy's lover as "the mother of a fine girl which she does MacCarthy the honour to call his. . . . the child is as likely to be the offspring of another as himself." In a clean sweep, Halleck doubts that his roommate could have fathered the baby and shifts the quality of promiscuity onto the female. Nevertheless, MacCarthy fulfills the stereotype for Frenchmen by failing to be sexually selective.

Halleck moved away from MacCarthy shortly after his letter to Griffing and continued the search for men more like himself. The letters of his early twenties continued to code scandalous material but plainly conveyed Halleck's indulgence in tawdry rumor. His sexual naiveté was a thing of the past. Rather than being squeamish of sexual tidbits, he appears to have relished every circumstantial detail. Halleck's future letters, also animated by sexual vice, suggest that it would be fair to assume some degree of self-consciousness regarding his own desires. In fact, his astute evaluation of male beauty led him to join New York's Ugly Club (ca. 1813–1815), situated at 4 Wall Street.

MacCarthy, whom Halleck had once described as having a most ugly face, would have been ineligible for membership. The Ugly Club was a mysterious organization of the handsomest young men to be found in New York City. Meetings were frequent and open "only to those deemed the most handsome and foppish." Members signed letters under initials such as X and Z and recruited those who were "*what the ladies call rather pretty*" or the "model of manly beauty."[22] Drake's good looks made his membership inevitable, although the date of his initiation remains uncertain.

The Ugly Club was exclusive to the point of secrecy, and Halleck's private solicitation for Abraham S. Fowler to join, on the condition that his looks had not altered since Halleck had last seen him, demonstrates the typical camp of correspondence between members. Fowler was also congratulated on his qualifying "deformities" by the club's secretary whose whimsical letter speaks for all members who "anticipate the pleasure of feasting their eyes on your ugliness."[23] Though the club threw all-male balls (a feature of molly-like clubs in nineteenth-century American cities), there is no evidence it was an exclusively homosexual body.

Clubs that did cater to homosexual clientele were the Artistic Club, the Black Rabbit, the Golden Rule Pleasure Club, the Little Bucks, the Palm, Manilla Hall, and Paresis Hall. Hundreds, perhaps thousands of men attended New York City drag balls, which were well documented by the late nineteenth century. Their notoriety was recorded in *Doctor and the Devil* (1892), which described the common but "worst vice that New York holds" (male brothels using drag and camp); Charles H. Hughs's description (1893) of a large urban "drag dance"; "Fairies of New York" (1896), a depiction of American homosexuals; and an "Investigation of the City of New York" (1899), which decried the drag balls of "male harlots."[24] Fraternities were also in vogue, although they usually had philanthropic service as their founding principle. In *Secret Ritual and Manhood in Victorian America*, Mark C. Carnes argues that men joined clubs to escape a society increasingly dominated by women. Halleck would also join the Free Masons around 1850.

Halleck was elected the Ugly Club's poet laureate in October 1814. His lines invited virginal bachelors to sign up:

> Ye, who ne'er basked in "Ladye's bower,"
> Whose lips were ne'er by Beauty kiss'd,
> For you it comes—the welcome hour!
> List! list!—O list![25]

The club's public advertisement offers to young men a welcomed option of male companionship over heterosexual passion or basking in a woman's private chambers.

For Halleck, the period during which the Ugly Club existed was a time of love and war. *Holt's Columbian,* which published Halleck's attempt at Ugly Club recruitment, had already published his anonymous poems asking American men to join the impending war with Britain. One of these untitled poems was Halleck's first New York publication and was accompanied by editorial doubts about its originality (intended as a compliment) on December 22, 1813. Its narrator objects to war even though he exalts the warrior: "Blame not the bard, that with humane aversion, / He shuddering turns, as the battle-storm lours." Halleck was not merely being philosophical, he leaned heavily toward pacifism. *Holt's Columbian* also published "Lines," which was decidedly pro war, as the British had gained proximity to New York.[26]

Halleck served as a sergeant in the Connecticut state militia at the age of nineteen, but military discipline had not built his character. Two poems written in 1814 expose Halleck's disguised responses to love and war. "To Margaret"[27] was reminiscent of the epistolary "Trifles 'Light as Air!'" to Menie and reinforced Uranian ideals. The superficial heroine pursues a poet who, in turn, refuses the "fruitless toil" of writing for one whose "passion could not be sincere— / Love claims a purer test of feeling." A higher, platonic relationship with another male is expressly preferred to the shallow adoration by women, who had seduced James B———r, Davis, and MacCarthy. Asking Margaret to "love the Man, and not the Poet," the verse concludes that, unlike Lord, she is unworthy.

The first part of "Young America," a poem completed fifty years later, also coincided with Halleck's split from MacCarthy and his introduction to Drake. Both men were blue-eyed and musically gifted, so the depressive fragment may have referred to either disrupted friendship. "Life's best music" becomes the empty "winter wind" as the melodramatic speaker declares, "I would shun, if that could be, the light of young blue eyes; / They bring back hours I would forget, and painful memories." The speaker believes that he has successfully masked his isolation and a heart heavy with "griefs it veils from all" as "thoughts of agony" drive him to tears over a lost love. In the end, a rebound occurs: "When I can free my prisoned thoughts, and wing them where I will. / And then thy smiles come o'er my heart, like sunbeams on the sea, / And I can feel as once I felt, when all was well with me."[28] Written to a female subject, the poem is an example of gender encoding, a technique that Halleck would eventually drop. The early segment incorporates the criminal secrecy ("prisoned thoughts") that dominates his homosexual verse. Its emotional content also recalls Menie whose memory serves as a surge of warm waves washing over the poet's repressed and distant joys. "Young America" also used international war as a metaphor for internal conflicts, including a reluctance to serve the United States.

Halleck was in one of the worst possible professions for the events of 1812. At twenty-two, he was gravely affected by the war. His boss was completely caught up in the political storm and delegated the business to his nephew, Thomas Barker, and Halleck. Their company, Halleck & Barker, would not survive the Embargo Act that clogged the economic ports of trade-reliant New York. On April 14, 1812, Halleck wrote Maria a simile on the new legislation that "flew like wildfire through the mercantile part of the city."[29] Ten days later, he described to his father the Embargo Act's effect on both the Republican and Federalist parties. The remainder of Jacob Barker's business would crumble.

The War of 1812 foreshadowed the Civil War. The North could not compete with the price of British goods and resented the South's profitable trade with England. Outraged by British attacks on American ships and the capture of American seamen to fight the French in the Napoleonic Wars, American "War-Hawks" demanded that England give up Canada, which they envisioned as a part of the continental expansion known as America's Manifest Destiny. New England actually considered withdrawing from the union at that time. Halleck's sympathies remained with the North. As the war escalated, so did his alarm, and he forewarned Maria in early February 1813 that the British might "attack the city and batter it to atoms."[30] Fear spurred an unexpected visit to Guilford before Halleck enlisted in the army. He gave his parents an ivory miniature portrait by a student of Mysterious Brown in case they might not see him again.

Long Island experienced British occupation in the fall of 1814 when it was rumored that Sir George Prevost was preparing to attack Manhattan. Halleck responded by joining the Iron Grays, an army of 112 of New York's wealthiest young gentlemen. He wrote Maria on December 28, 1814, that most of the troops arrived for marching parades "in their coaches and curricles" and complained that the eight-dollar monthly pay did not match what was "spent in *feasting each other* $5 per day regularly, besides extra 'wine and women' bills for dinners and dancing."[31] With candor normally reserved for his sister's eyes, he confessed his true feelings to Dan Embury. The flirtatious tone of Halleck's earlier correspondence with Embury was replaced with serious rhetoric on the war. Halleck's September 1814 letter admitted wavering loyalty. "Can you believe it?" he asks, "I am a soldier—a *gentleman common soldier*," who found "a faint spark of patriotism yet unextinguished" beneath the dying embers of his civil duty.[32]

Washington Irving noted the Grays were encamped in the Greenwich area (their winter quarters were in the Battery) and his memoirs included a reference to Halleck's stories about the corps's "very fussy" major.[33] Halleck's ode to the Iron Grays (October 1814) was allegedly shared in solemn secrecy with a peer who then recited the poem, which was published in *Holt's Columbian* under the cryptic pen name Y.H.S. The lofty tribute compares the Grays with the classical "Spartan band," demonstrating Halleck's familiarity with ancient Greek history and possibly with the Spartans' widespread practice of pederasty. Halleck also refers to the Grays in a Croaker poem and in *Fanny*. The army proved a good hunting ground for a man as long as no fighting ensued. None did.

Word of the Treaty of Ghent, which declared peace Christmas Eve 1814, did not reach New York City until February 11, 1815. Halleck was attending a concert at the City Hotel that Saturday night when shouts of joy drew the audience outside to join an impromptu Broadway parade of tens of thousands. Halleck was more relieved than the average citizen. Despite his jovial anecdotes—such as the Grays' mutiny for cleaner straw[34]—he had found his military obligation repugnant overall. He wrote a great deal in praise of the soldier but also hoped to bind the "blood-dripping fingers of War."[35]

In the closing days of 1814, Halleck sought solace with Maria. He grumbled about the cold, boring, and sleepless winter, realizing that "with it has fled my martial spirit, and disinterestedness, and patriotism," and finally confessed that his participation was psychologically forced:

Other motives actuated me at the moment, not quite so consistent with honor and patriotic feeling, but conformable to true worldly wisdom and a regard for the opinion of others. I was conscious that the dictates of duty were in favor of defending one's country, one's fireside, wife, children, etc., in the hour of danger. By volunteering, in a moment of peril and alarm, to die for their defense, I have discharged that duty, and stand acquitted not only at the bar of my own conscience (if there is any such thing in the case), but also at that of the world's opinion, and am now resolved to volunteer no more.[36]

Halleck had felt pressured to conform in order to avert public criticism but paid a high personal price to be in step with America's civic and family values. Having discharged his duty, he finds his conscience is relieved not because he has served, as his parenthetical aside indicates, but because he has passed an important male cultural initiation. Afraid not to answer the dictates mandating the defense of wife and children, he marched for marriage and fatherhood. But his sarcasm inverts an honorable discharge by transforming it into a dishonorable charge against American values. The family values at his society's core are almost facetiously bundled under "etc." In the criminal metaphor common to his homoerotic verse, he is acquitted at the bar of a global court that equates patriotism with manhood. The Federalist military had replaced Puritan forefathers as sexual police who arrested and exiled America's sodomites. Maria could hardly have been surprised to hear her brother conclude that he would not make "the flinty couch of war my bed."

The federal government in its military arm had taken over colonial law, and even today gays must still contend with its revised code of conduct. Courts-martial replaced Puritan trials as the chief mode of purging homosexuals and provided the social ceremony of sodomitical cleansing. Just two years before Halleck's birth, George Washington reported the discharge of a lieutenant who had attempted sodomy on another soldier and was to be "drummed out of Camp . . . by all the Drummers and Fifers in the Army never to return; The Drummers and Fifers to attend on the Grand Parade."[37] Replacing the scaffold erected for public executions, military assemblies and bands constructed the new American theater for homosexual disgrace.

Ironically, Halleck's famous poems, "Marco Bozzaris," "The Field of the Grounded Arms," and "On the Death of Lieut. William Howard Allen of the American Navy," caused the *New York Times* to declare, "Halleck should be called upon by the nation to write lyrics for the army" by the end of the Civil War.[38] His satirical Croaker "The Militia of the City" stressed the relationship between masculinity and the military and accused New York governor DeWitt Clinton of producing an effeminate generation of soldiers. Clinton's "young nurslings of fame, / With their sashes of crimson and collars of flame; / Their cocked hats enchanting—their buttons divine," step "through the streets to their battle-drums prancing." Wearing "more hues than the rainbow," these soldiers frighten "cartmen, pigs, and old women."[39]

In contradictory terms, the service defended the family while disrupting venerable marital relations. Suspending domestic life, the military forced men to choose between staying home or temporarily leaving their families. In "Young America," "the joy of soldier life" and "wild war-music of the manlier song" are juxtaposed to the young hero's decision to marry a rich wife rather than join the troops. Embodying prophetic images of the rainbow flag that has come to symbolize gay liberation and solidarity, two stanzas tangle militaristic and matrimonial imagery:

> Memories of our sires of old,
> Who, oppression-driven,
> High their rainbow flag unrolled
> To the sun and sky of heaven.
> Memories of the true and brave,
> Who, at Honor's bidding,
> Stepped, their Country's life to save,
> To war as to their wedding.[40]

Allan Berube's *Coming Out under Fire* addresses such military contradictions, for example, the endorsed drag shows versus homosexual expulsion, but Halleck, more than a century earlier, remarked on the homoerotica of the army in a letter concerning an anecdote about Perth Amboy. "I delight in recollecting" the account that had "long been a favorite of mine," wrote Halleck, of Amboy and "his comrades" and the "'*as one man*' kiss of affection with which they greeted kneeling their 'Mother Land' [being] the only instance of kissing by *Platoons* within my memory." Halleck's deliberate emphases on "as one man" and "platoons" suggest that the soldiers may have been kissing not only American soil but one another. His next sentence may have been intended to clarify: "There was more woman in their great Leader and Teacher, General Arnold, than we are willing to believe."[41]

The army of the early nineteenth century essentially shared the current palatable but ambiguous policy of mutual denial (don't ask, don't tell) since only nonconsensual or publicized sodomy could result in court-martial. But the sexual policies of the democracy's military still negated the homosexual soldier's service. Having sprouted a beard that would rival Whitman's, Halleck often joked, "I grew this long beard and painted it white to avoid the draft" during the Civil War,[42] but the War of 1812 had been no laughing matter for Halleck. His sense of cultural obligation to march and to marry was only heightened after the initial relief that moving to New York had provided. Whittier's elegiac poem to Halleck would call New York "O, city of his love!"[43] That love could have alluded to his urban freedom or to his feeling for Joseph Drake. Even given the city's need to be defended, it remained the place to be because a handsome young doctor had taken up residence there.

For the first time in Halleck's life, there existed the potential for an equal partnership with another American. At twenty-three, Halleck fell under "the spell which awoke his true powers."[44] It was cast by Drake. Earlier in 1813, Halleck had written Maria, "I abhor the sound of a flute, and ever shall,"[45] but that changed when the instrument was touched by Drake's breath. In addition to praising Drake as an accomplished flutist and Shakespearean orator, Halleck's first letter to Maria about his new friend gushed, "I owe to his acquaintance many a pleasant hour, he has become endeared to me, and I must apologize for dwelling so long upon a picture, the details of which are so uninteresting to one who has not seen the original." As if holding up a line of art students studying the Mona Lisa, Halleck apologizes for the paragraphs describing Drake.[46] His own words indicate that a lengthy physical description preceded and he was now guilty of James B——r's annoying habit of chattering about Rebecca, who was only of high interest to her lover. The letter shifts suddenly to old news about MacCarthy, who had returned to America ill and whose ugliness had "that advantage over time," although his "sandy locks" were beginning to gray. MacCarthy's "heart still warm and affectionate" led to a genial reunion. The sudden introduction of his ex-roommate amid the depiction of Drake's superior looks may reveal a sense of disloyalty to the old in favor of the new.

Halleck dwelled upon Drake's image as he had fawned over Menie's form, even though Halleck was nearly as attractive as Drake. Charles P. Clinch compared the two men and declared, "Drake was the handsomest man in New York."[47] Halleck had finally "met a man after his own heart" whose poetical mind corresponded to his physical beauty.[48]

Accounts of the Halleck-Drake meeting in the spring of 1813 are varied but universally idealized. Speculating that it was a spectacular sunset or sudden rainbow that ignited discussion about Thomas Campbell between the two young men, biographical materials have variously placed their initial introduction at the Ugly Club, via a formal intervention by James DeKay on another occasion, through an accidental encounter during a summer afternoon on a muddy pathway in New York's Battery Park, or in a mixture of circumstance on a boat excursion on New York Bay. Perhaps Drake overheard Halleck wish aloud "to lounge upon the rainbow" and read Campbell "and from that moment took Halleck to his heart."[49] Or maybe the wish was Drake's, the response Halleck's who "grasped [Drake's] arm cordially, and said 'We must know each other.'"[50] The rainbow may have been seen during a September ride down the bay, or possibly when the two men first went sailing together.[51] Perhaps DeKay simply invited both friends over in that winter of 1812–1813.[52] Adkins wrote that whatever the account of the meeting, Halleck "discovered in the sensitive and poetic Drake the true companion for which he longed."[53] Both early and late critics described the immediate friendship, which had been delayed nearly three years by the War of 1812, as "romantic."[54] Others called the connection "sweet companionship," adding that the poets aspired to a "romantic youthful friendship, not common."[55]

The "frozen summer" of 1816 in the eastern United States, due to volcanic dust from eruptions in the East Indies, proved an emotional ride of extreme gain and loss for Halleck. The spring presented him with the warmest friendship he would ever know. He had met the intellectual, social, and emotional companion whom he had feared he would never find only two years earlier. Halleck (who recited) and Drake (who sang) entertained visitors and engaged in dynamic poetical debates with one another. They also took numerous overnight fishing trips. Halleck delighted in spinning anecdotes about these private excursions, such as the day Drake lost a fish but accidentally hooked another by the tail. Upon Drake's exclamation that he had caught a fish, Halleck retorted, "No, no, Joe. I should say that he caught himself."[56] Above all else, Halleck treasured these outdoor sleep-overs.

It was probably on a hiking trip that Halleck proposed Drake's most famous project, "The Culprit Fay." Drake argued against Halleck's and Cooper's positions that Scotland possessed superior rivers to America and set off to prove his point with verse. "The Culprit Fay" (1816), a fairy tale, was consequently set in the Hudson River Valley. Allegedly written in three days, the 600-line poem was recently considered by Gorton Carruth to be a milestone in American verse. If not great poetry, it is certainly singular in American Romance literature. Even more unique in American poetry was Drake's collaboration with Halleck.

The two men appeared inseparable,[57] but their flowering intimacy was to be interrupted by Drake's marriage. If the military had kept Halleck from Drake's side, this more powerful force would surely separate them and turn Halleck's hot hopes cold by summer's end. He was defeated again by his most constant adversary, marriage. Within a year of finding Drake, Halleck had to give him away.

Several aspects of Halleck's homosexual construction are evident in his description of Drake as a groom. Halleck told Maria that Drake was

the handsomest man in New York—a face like an angel, a form like an Apollo, and, as I well knew that his person was the true index of his mind, I felt myself during the ceremony as committing a crime in aiding and assisting in such a sacrifice.[58]

The account worships Drake's physical beauty as divine, comprised of an angelic face and godly body, and as a reflection of his internal beauty. Halleck's praise of Drake's mind appears to temper the homoerotic description of the handsomest man Halleck had ever seen, a title that had previously fallen on B——s of Halleck's first boarding house. Even more contradictory, Halleck feels dishonored as Drake's best man and expresses as much in metaphors of committing a crime and assisting in a sacrifice. The criminal motif is hardly appropriate for the occasion, and the sacrifice seems to describe Halleck's own painful separation rather than Drake's self-immolation in marriage.

In 1930, Percy Hutchison portrayed Halleck as "always 'bachelor-minded'" and noted that when Drake became engaged "Fitz-Greene was not a little irritated." "Bachelor" was a euphemism for homosexual by the time of Hutchison's portrait, and the code word was even applied to lesbians.[59] Many critics emphasize that Halleck lived and died a bachelor and note his early resignation to be a "very gay bachelor."[60] However, his mood was anything but gay, as ironic as that may be for the best man at a wedding. Typical of Halleck, his duress was expressed in jest and in earnest.

More than "reluctant" to perform his "lukewarm" service as best man,[61] Halleck was embittered. The same letter that praised Drake also denigrated him, telling Maria that "as [Drake's] wife's father is rich, I imagine he will write [verse] no more. He was poor, as poets, of course, always are, and offered himself a sacrifice at the shrine of Hymen to shun the 'pains and penalties' of poverty. I officiated as groomsman, though much against my will."[62] His angry sense of abandonment led him to emasculate Drake, who now joined the likes of James B——r and Davis as a virginal offering ultimately seduced by his own fortune-seeking. Halleck left no room for doubt that Drake's motivation was purely monetary and predicted that Drake's poetic abilities would be seriously compromised. Having defamed Drake, Halleck asserts his belated protest by stating that he served against his will. The power of social pressure coerced Halleck's participation in ceremonies of both marriage and war.

Halleck never understood that he was intrinsically different from Drake. But Richard Henry Stoddard, who was also homosexual, provided insight into Halleck's distress over the wedding: "Clearly this Benedick [Halleck, who is compared to Shakespeare's confirmed bachelor], if he knew himself when he wrote, would never become a married man."[63] Stoddard not only doubted Halleck's potential as a husband but also accused Halleck of lacking self-knowledge. Halleck did manage to take Drake's marriage as much ado about nothing, but only until plans for the honeymoon were crystalized.

Significantly, Halleck's objection was not to Drake's fiancée, for his letter on the marriage acknowledges that she "is good-natured, and loves [Drake] to distraction,"[64] but as with James B——r's bride, Halleck never acknowledges the name of Drake's wife, Sarah Eckford. It has been understated that "Sarah apparently caused a temporary rift" between the two men, since "until Drake's marriage the two were inseparable."[65] Robbed of his better half, Halleck modeled a new type of woman on Mrs. Drake—the bride as burglar. As with his compulsory military service, Halleck recoiled from his social obligations around this marriage. He did not wish to be Sarah Eckford's accomplice in the "crime" which was that Monday evening ceremony.

Halleck never regretted the attack on Drake's wife although her descendants were offended for generations to come. In 1881, the *New York Daily Tribune* rebuked Wilson for having "had the bad taste to publish" Halleck's letter to Maria saying that Drake married for money, prompting Francis R. Tillou, Drake's brother-in-law, to defend the marriage as having been based solely on love.[66] Charles DeKay, Drake's grandson, further defended the marriage against "the slur" of Halleck's "peevish and impulsive letter to his sister."[67] The January 29, 1817, letter was forward, but it was hardly rash. Halleck had not mentioned Drake's marriage to Maria until more than three months after the October wedding. Banished by Drake's wife, he mirrored the depressive resentment of his hero, Lord Byron, who was facing a literal exile in the same year. Rumor tied Byron's 1816 exile to charges of sodomy.

Drake's biographer, Frank Lester Pleadwell, challenged Halleck's statement that the doctor had sold himself and came close to naming the cause of Halleck's crass remarks. Pleadwell claimed that Halleck was "almost a misogynist, certainly a complete disbeliever in married happiness. Jealous of the empire which [Drake's] wife had gained over his beloved friend."[68] Halleck's "freak of fancy" reaction was steeped in language indicative of the medical views of homosexuality as physical deformity and mental psychosis in vogue in the 1930s when Pleadwell was writing. But unlike his other tirades against married men, Halleck's assertion that money was the major factor in Drake's selection of a wife may have hit the mark.

Wilson took Halleck's comments at face value and investigated Drake's financial history, which had roots tracing back to Sir Francis Drake. Wilson published his findings on the loss of the family fortune and argued that Drake had "an implicit confidence" that he hoped would be useful in escaping poverty in order to "replace his family in the position to which it was entitled"—a goal Drake held from early childhood.[69] Drake's Croaker "Ode to Impudence" must have gratified Halleck. Its narrator acknowledges living beyond his means, "With looks of brass and words of honey."[70] Drake had been a comparatively poor man who commanded his choice of beautiful women, and his new father-in-law was a wealthy merchant, rich enough that Halleck "feared the alliance of genius with wealth."[71] Henry Eckford, a marine architect, paid large bills of necessity (a deeded home in 1820) and pleasure (a European tour) for his son-in-law and provided Halleck with the ammunition for insisting that Drake profited greatly from his marriage vows. After Drake's honeymoon, he established himself in the drug business with his father-in-law's capital.

Halleck's contention that handsome young men used marriage to gain money was not unusual by nineteenth-century standards, but his exaggerated claims that male friends were all good-looking extortionists utterly denied any romantic or sexual inclination to marry. His letters and verse inverted the natural course of marriage to an unnatural state produced by sloth and even male prostitution. In Drake's case this prejudice was reinforced not only by his father-in-law's generosity but also by Sarah Eckford's homely appearance. Sarah was not considered attractive, and Halleck could not believe that she had won the heart of New York's handsomest man. Indeed, her portrait by Henry Inman is austere. "A very modest woman," Eckford appears in oval, shaded eyeglasses with tangled hair and a severely plain dress.[72] Adkins, however, did not find Drake's marriage "mercenary"[73] and shared George P. Lathrop's opinion that Halleck's condemnation sprang from his own "singular coldness, indifference, [and] rigidity" regarding women.[74] Halleck's disgust at the idea of sleeping with a woman for money was meritorious, but his general repugnance toward heterosexual intercourse merely illuminated his own sexuality. He shared the common molly belief that homosexual men only married women for financial gain.[75] With regard to Drake, circumstances merely reinforced the idea.

Drake settled into married life comfortably while Halleck grew more agitated. In 1815, he moved out of the room he had shared with Mac-Carthy into another boarding house on Hudson Street in Greenwich Village. He wasted no time gossiping to his sister about the other tenants. A sexually suspicious acquaintance identified only as Wilson, not his biographer, left the boarding house, moved "somewhere in Pearl Street, is unmarried, and always will be. Thomas Barker [Halleck's ex-business partner] boards with him."[76] It is hard to justify Halleck's comment that Wilson always will be a single man without considering that Halleck alludes to his sexuality. Although the proprietor cried upon his departure, Halleck soon left her establishment for a French boarding house, Madame Berault's. In February 1817 he complained that there were too many Americans at that residence and moved again to Monsieur Villagrand's on Chambers Street where only French was spoken. He enjoyed the pretty hostess of the household, whom he described as being "somewhere from thirty to one hundred" years old, but remained restless.[77] He began to move beyond New York.

In 1815, Halleck took a short business trip to Boston, and in June and November of 1816 he made two trips to the South for his employer. While he generally hated the inconveniences of the road, he experienced "Byronic exultation" on the choppy seas during turbulent storms.[78] Writing his mother about North Carolina, he was affronted by the "habits of debauchery and vice" of transplanted Northerners who had taken to Southern customs, including slave-owning. Even more unappealing were the hideous natives of the state regarded as nature's outcasts possessing feeble minds. Halleck may not have realized just how precarious his situation was as a visitor to the Carolinas, which were the last states to drop the death penalty for sodomy. Sodomites could be officially executed there even after Halleck's death—until 1869 in North Carolina and 1873 in South Carolina. Yet, even the Carolinas were home to same-sex activity as evidenced by a series of 1826 letters between male ex-lovers swapping tales of homosexual conquest.[79] Halleck used his looks to get along in the Carolinas, informing his untraveled mother, "a stranger always finds a more welcome reception from the women than the men, particularly if he happens to be young and good-looking, begging your sex's pardon."[80]

Halleck knew that women were fascinated with him, but he was still searching for an unmarried man of his own.

In winter 1816–1817, Halleck took his first leisure trip. As Bryant noted, Halleck always preferred to travel the country alone.[81] En route to Virginia, he explored Philadelphia, Baltimore, and Washington, D.C. All proved far inferior to New York. Halleck was confronted by the leading social issues of his day, never realizing that he would directly benefit from the war through his future association with John Jacob Astor, who had provided loans to the United States government, thereby helping to win the war and making huge profits for himself. Halleck's letter to his mother recalled this trip and the dire consequences of the recent war victory. The corpses of the British littered the roadside with hats and rags and "now and then an arm or a leg, scattered on the field."[82]

During this trip, Halleck was invited to the newly refurbished White House, but he declined the invitation to meet the ailing President Madison. At the time of Halleck's visit, Monroe was the Federalist president-elect, but he had not yet been inaugurated. While Halleck did not seem overly flattered by the extended hospitality of the president, he was excited by a glimpse of Dolly Madison out at a performance.

An excursion to Mount Vernon, though, really made the trip worthwhile. Halleck compared his tour of Mount Vernon to a Holy Land pilgrimage, yet he was critical of a youthful officer's patriotic zeal along the way. The veteran he met had been sorting through benefits with the War Office when Halleck picked him up and took him on the thirty-two mile trip to Vernon. The stranger was "fast sinking to the tomb" from consumption, "the result of long marches," and earned detached sympathy from Halleck, whose eyes had been opened to the baleful reality of military duty: "He was an enthusiast, and a victim of enthusiasm. I have not since heard of him."[83] Halleck found patriotism generally "obnoxious,"[84] but even he felt a surge of democratic pride upon seeing the Bastille's key that Lafayette had sent to General Washington. For once, Halleck lived up to the criminal identification in his writings by confessing to his mother that he had "robbed" some plaster shells from the first president's vault.[85]

Shortly after Halleck's return to New York in 1817, Drake moved to close the gap in their friendship, which had been postponed by war and marriage. Invitations to restore the friendship were poetic. Whether Drake was bisexual or not, his one poem, "To Sarah," written on their first wedding anniversary, is conspicuously passionless, whereas his "Sonnet" to Halleck is emotionally vibrant. "To Sarah" praises wifely conduct "in sickness and in sorrow," but no other physical or mental assets.[86] In contrast, Drake's sonnet to Halleck praises a friend whose heart is "weary of unfeeling men" and promises a hike to a secluded area to sit "unviewed / By scoffing eye; and let our hearts beat free / With their own mutual throb." He promises: "None there will intrude / To poison our free thoughts and mar our solitude. / Such scenes move not their feelings."[87] The lines suggest that Drake and Halleck differed from ordinary men in their desire for privacy and emotional intimacy. The sonnet's terminology, such as "mutual throb," which echoes the heartfelt exchange in Halleck's "To Menie," suggests that Drake may have in part reciprocated or subconsciously encouraged Halleck's sexual desire.

Drake's "Life and Love" expressed his disillusionment with marriage and mourned a past friendship. The "delusive sleep" of romance is shaken off: "Love is an empty name, / That leads to pain and woe, / And friendship's holy flame, / Hath ceased to glow." The narrator envies Halleck's "visioned eye" in an allusion to *Fanny:* "Ne'er may his fairy dream, / Vanish like mine."[88] Halleck's premonition that marriage would frustrate Drake's muse had come to fruition. Drake's Uranian lines echo Halleck's early poems and cherish "friendship's holy flame" above heterosexual romance that is "delusive" and "empty." The roving Halleck became more settled with Drake's renewed attention, and he enclosed two poems by Drake in the January 1817 letter to Maria reporting Drake's marriage. If Maria were reading between the lines, she would have known that her brother's competition for Drake's affection was just beginning.

Halleck was highly subjective in his criticism of Drake's calamus-drinking "Culprit Fay" ("certainly the best thing of the kind in the English language") and "Lines to a Lady," which treated "a hackneyed subject"—heterosexual love.[89] "Lines to a Lady" was not for Drake's wife but for another woman with whom the married doctor had spent a romantic evening. Besides these two poems, Halleck encouraged Drake to write others by reversing the metaphor for policing art: "Come, then, dear Joseph, come away; / 'Tis criminal to lose a day / With talents bright as thine."[90] But it was Drake who more constantly pressed Halleck to write.

Between 1817 and 1818, Drake advised Halleck to abandon business for a career as a poet and wrote an ode, "To Fitz-Greene Halleck, Esq."[91] The epistle cries shame on America, in which "no native bard the patriot harp hath ta'en," and bids Halleck, "Arouse, my friend,—let vivid fancy soar." But Halleck wrote only one poem in 1817. This untitled poem was not published until February 1868 when *Putnam's* gave it the title "A Farewell to Connecticut."

"A Farewell to Connecticut" was written for a singer, Eliza McCall, for whom Drake had already composed two poems. Adkins comments, "Though couched in personal phraseology, the poem has probably little autobiographical significance."[92] Indeed, Halleck's poem expresses more longing for the comforts of his sister and mother than flattering McCall.

Unsettled and depressed since Drake's marriage, Halleck increased letters home at this time, especially to his mother, who died in 1819. Even more critically, Halleck's poem shared its alleged subject (McCall) with Drake's poems, foreshadowing the only terms on which Halleck would take up Drake's challenge. Artistic collaboration was the target.

The two friends would first be drawn together by a tragedy laden with cardinal secrecy. On December 12, 1817, Drake informed "My Dear Fitz" that their close friend, Walter Franklin, had committed suicide.[93] Hardly "capable of writing," Drake wanted to give Halleck the news himself and added that Franklin's reasons for shooting himself were "obscure": "No writing, no paper, tending to throw any light on it, has been found." Franklin had spent his last full day alive entirely with Drake, who noticed "no agitation in his manner, no depression of spirits, to lead to any suspicion of the state of his mind." "From ten in the morning until late at night," Drake had found Franklin's demeanor "more placidly cheerful than ever" and observed

a gentleness in [Franklin's] mirth which was unusual with him, but I attributed it to our reconciliation. It was on Monday that he called on me first, and from that time he was with me almost constantly until the fatal morning. Many circumstances have occurred to prove that the deed was long premeditated. A number of expressions which he made use of in conversation with me, at the time obscure, are now elucidated; but they were used in a pleasant conversation, and uttered in too gay a tone to make any impression on me at the time.

Drake was stunned by Franklin's plan to lie on his sister's bed, place a mirror between his knees, and aim a gun at his forehead. Drake depicts the dead man as in a state of near ecstacy on the day preceding his death, having made up with him after some unspecified falling out. The above letter was signed "Faithfully yours, J. R. Drake" and implied that Halleck was already familiar with the conflict that had existed between Drake and Franklin.

In sharp contrast, Halleck had anticipated Franklin's suicide. What Drake had only realized in retrospect, Halleck had foreseen, as he conveyed in a letter to his sister three days after Drake had written him. Having just returned to New York, Halleck wrote, "One of my most intimate friends shot himself." He tells Maria that he had met Franklin, a nineteen-year-old clerk for the United States Bank, through Drake two years earlier and that "we have since been bosom friends." He describes the boy as an "extraordinary character in every respect," whose intellect was "strong, and powerful, and energetic far beyond his years; an enthusiast in poetry, in music, in every thing."[94]

Franklin had had much in common with Halleck who was sensitive to Franklin's continual gloom which, even in his most cheerful hours, and in the midst of the maddest mirth, was always perceivable. He was the handsomest being I ever saw. He was six feet high, perfectly proportioned, and had as fine a face as nature ever formed.

Rescinding the most handsome award from Drake, Halleck describes his dead friend as physically irresistible. The homoerotic eulogy to Franklin is followed by clues that Franklin was self-destructive and Halleck knew "he intended to shoot himself. . . . we had often conversed on suicide, and I joined him in the opinion that the world contained nothing worth living for." Halleck and Franklin's private discussions were apparently kept from Drake.

Halleck's graphic picture of the suicide included additional details. He adds that the pistol's

ball passed through [Franklin's] temple and lodged in the wall. His death must have been instantaneous, and without a pang, for his countenance was perfectly calm and unruffled, not a muscle distorted, nor even a curl of the lip to denote agony. I need not paint the anguish of a father's, mother's, brother's, and sister's feelings, or of a young lady to whom he was betrothed.

This reconstruction of Franklin's death scene cannot possibly have been an eye-witness account because Halleck arrived back in New York days after the corpse was discovered. Surely, the picture Halleck imagined satisfied his own need to believe that his troubled friend had found peace.

Only Halleck's letter mentions Franklin's fiancée, and his empathy suggests that he and Franklin shared a bond to which Drake was not privy. At nineteen, Franklin stood at the threshold of what would appear to be an ideal future. He was smart, making decent wages, had a loving family and friends, was exceptionally good-looking and about to marry. The anticipated wedding should have guaranteed optimism and happiness.

The discrepancy between Halleck's and Drake's insights into Franklin's personality could not have been wider. While Drake had completely misread Franklin as stable, Halleck relayed to his sister Franklin's artistry and attraction to themes "wild, and daring, and romantic." Halleck's apparently guiltless encouragement of the suicide and his inaction to prevent it suggest that he could not think of solutions to the problems that Franklin had confided in him. Franklin's conscious decision to spend his last days in a forced mood of joy with Drake might suggest that he, too, had fallen in love with the handsome doctor. The break with Drake may have been caused in the first place by Franklin's feelings for his married friend, who seemed as imperceptive about Franklin's intense turmoil as he had been of Halleck's unrequited love. If this were the case, Franklin's impending marriage would have forced his despair. As unfinished emotional business, the friendship with Drake outweighed Franklin's need to spend his final day with his future bride.

Halleck's role in Franklin's tragedy reinforces the assumption that Franklin was also homosexual. Before reconciling with Drake during Halleck's absence, Franklin had already discussed with Halleck his plan, to which Halleck had given his consent. Halleck felt that suicide was a viable solution to Franklin's overwhelming feelings of entrapment. Franklin had said his farewells to Drake and Halleck but left no suicide note or explanation for his family or fiancée. He shared his motive only with Halleck, whose last words to Maria on the suicide were those of gratitude. Thankful to God that he had been away at Sandy Hill, he was spared having to look on the immediate reaction of Franklin's family in "the first madness of that moment's agony." Pointedly, Halleck understood the mad agony of the survivors' grief but did not consider Franklin to have been mad at all. In the widening eyes of heterosexual America, homosexual "insanity" and suicide escalated in the nineteenth century as social and medical sciences reexamined sodomy as a dysfunction of the self.

Psychomedical theories on homosexuality are as ancient as the Greek Hippocratic corpus, although psychiatry did not lay the bedrock for modern homosexual pathology until the first half of the nineteenth century, when instinctive and affective monomania explained homosexuality, around 1816.[95] In 1726, the homosexual was said to have an irregular anus, a medical theory that persisted through 1857 when a canine penis was added to the physiological make-up of homosexuals. Following Heinrich Hossli's two-volume apologia of homosexuality in 1830, Karl Heinrich Ulrichs's 1862 work applied scientific principles to sexual deviation. Genetic theories in 1857 used Darwinian terms to label homosexuals degenerate. Later the central nervous system of homosexuals was considered to be abnormal, effectively replacing old religious objections with new scientific ones.[96] Homosexual advocates' innate sexual theories were deliberately omitted in Western research and Jefferson's proposal to castrate sodomites was acceptable medical treatment for incarcerated homosexuals in 1893.[97] George V allegedly remarked, "I thought fellas like that [homosexuals] shot themselves."[98] As with Franklin, sometimes they did.

Nineteenth-century homosexuals in Europe no longer needed society to condemn them; they could simply self-destruct. Some sought America in order to avert the suicidal alternative elsewhere.[99] But Halleck knew that the Constitution of the United States did not extend its protection to homosexuals any more than it did to blacks or to women. He became increasingly antinational and depressed from the time of Franklin's suicide through much of 1818. Late that spring, Drake took his wife on a delayed honeymoon to Europe, and Halleck temporarily envied Franklin. Halleck had not been asked to go along on the trip even though the mysterious Dr. William Langstaff had been invited. Wilson reprints part of a letter Halleck wrote on January 24, 1818, describing Langstaff as "a most eccentric character . . . something like Lord Byron's 'Lara,' for nobody knows where he came from, or who he is." Halleck adds that Langstaff was about his age and had a wife "a little given to drinking."[100] Halleck gossiped to Wilson that Drake's father-in-law had paid the honeymoon bill, including Langstaff's expenses. In fact, Henry Eckford may have pressed the tour upon Drake, who seemed homesick for Halleck. On May 1, 1818, the second day after his arrival, Drake wrote "To Fitz-Greene Halleck in Dumphries," mimicking Scottish dialects. "To Fitz-Greene Halleck from Irvine" was composed on May 10 at 10:00 P.M. These two poems were intended for, but omitted from, Drake's collected poems, according to Pleadwell because of their personal nature. Both of them long epistles, "To Fitz-Greene Halleck from Irvine" provides a curious postmodern reading.

Opening with the line "My Muse is almost fagged with writing," the poem claims that Drake has been writing letters all day, saving Halleck's for "the fag-end of the feast."[101] Reminding Halleck, "I wrote you late a queer hotch-potch" recently, Drake tells him of "Braw bare-legged girls, auld smoky queans." Although the term "queen" was a euphemism for prostitute, it also had its gay meaning since before the reign of "Queen James," as his subjects referred to him.[102] Drake's use of "fag," "fag-end," "queer," and "quean" are coincidentally appropriate for his addressee, and his poem further argues that "Rob" Burns would have lived longer if he had learned "to let strong drink and priests alone." Henry VIII's civic law was largely a political vehicle for eliminating Catholic monasteries, thereby confiscating their gold and England's greatest source of wealth. The linking of sodomy with the priesthood, however, persisted in Puritan views of papal Rome as sexually, especially homosexually, lenient.[103] In fact, Bradford mentioned that concubines in New England lived "after the Italian manner," and Edward Coke's *Laws of England* (1646) reestablished capital punishment for sodomy, claiming "the Lumbards had brought [sodomy] into the Realm."[104] Even contemporary films such as *Priest* (1995) continue to align the religious call and homosexuality. Drake ends his lines to Halleck by looking skyward. Star-gazing over whitecaps, the poem closes, "Ah! Fitz, my lad, I'm thinking, aye, / How blithe and happy'll be the day / When we shall meet again together."

Meanwhile, Halleck was writing "Twilight," inspired by a summer evening on the Long Island Sound as he was crossing for Guilford. The earliest poem included in Halleck's collected edition of 1827, "Twilight" was printed and reprinted anonymously (under F.G.H.) in the *New York Evening Post* (October 13, 1818, and May 8, 1819, respectively.) Watching a sunset reflected off the waves, Halleck returned Drake's love even though an ocean separated them. Twilight did not refer to the time of day, but to "an evening twilight of the heart / When its wild passion-waves are lulled to rest." The narrator watches the sunset as a silent metaphor for "the rainbow of the heart" "with a nameless feeling of regret." The nameless feeling echoes a love that dared not speak its name, a phrase popularized during Wilde's trial later in the century. Dwelling upon "our destined tomb" and the heart's "last deep beating," the lonesome speaker catches a single glimmer of hope: "The meteor-bearer of our parting breath, / A moonbeam in the midnight cloud of death." The vague and highly romantic lines conjure the parting image of Drake leaving for his honeymoon. Since that time, Halleck's poetic juices had dried up. "Twilight" was his only poem of 1818.

The poem corresponded with the predominant mood descending upon Halleck. By the fall of 1818, his darkening thoughts gave Maria good cause to worry. Like the wayward brother of *Frankenstein* (1818), Halleck was pursued across the waters by a monster of his own making. In late November, he turned to his sister, to whom he had not written since that summer twilight visit. His life had dragged on slowly since then with "my only companions, books," and he confessed that he had been "excessively ill, to say the truth, for a long time past." Unable to enjoy even an occasional cigar, he had bent the ear of his patient doctor who, "would you believe it, told me I had the hypo, so prescribed me nothing at all."[105] He had been comforted by rationalizing that Drake's incentive to marry had been financial and by the poems that Drake had sent him. But the reality of the Drakes' honeymoon jarred Halleck from the emotional shock of the wedding and Franklin's suicide. A honeymoon was meant to seal the legal agreement with sexual consummation.

Maria was perhaps less surprised at the diagnosis than Halleck who "really thought myself the last man in the world for such a disorder." He relates the condition poignantly:

a total loss of appetite, or rather—for I know not what to call it—a total indifference whether I ate or drank any thing or not; a sort of ague all day and a violent fever all night, have continued to worry me and wear me out. I felt no pain or feebleness. I was not miserable, but my mind felt a kind of indifference toward every thing like emotion, whether of pain or pleasure; in short, I was a complete stoic, and could have received the most unexpected delight without a smile, and heard of some unlooked-for stroke of ruin without a pang. . . . I then fancied all was over with me.

Halleck provides a textbook account of an eating disorder, insomnia, and the mental numbness symptomatic of a clinical depression, but his prognosis is good. Apparently unaware of the connection between Drake's absence and his hypochondria, he nevertheless ties the events up in one neat

stroke: "I really am better this week, and intend to recover. The Drakes
. . . have returned."

Halleck had evaded Walter Franklin's fate, and Maria could breathe a
sigh of relief. Her brother had survived the emotional paralysis brought
on by Drake's honeymoon, as he had managed to go through the motions
of acting as Drake's best man, in every sense of the word. Halleck's private
desperation of 1818 intensified his craft and gave rise to a new oxymoron
of silent protest. All was not over with him. The letter announcing the
Drakes' return also mentioned that MacCarthy had returned from the
West Indies a month previous, even though Halleck had thought his
friend would die there. Yet the good news about MacCarthy did not im-
prove Halleck's despondency; it was Drake who made him want to live
again.

The honeymoon had been a lost battle for Halleck, but the combat
he waged against Drake's bride pressed on. Halleck would contest Sarah
Eckford Drake's primary roles as bride and widow. It would not be a long
war, though. In 1819, Mary Eliot Hallock died, and neither Halleck nor
Maria could have known that Drake himself would follow their own
mother into the grave only one year later. Drake's wedding and funeral
were catastrophic to Halleck, who thus lost his desired soul mate twice.
He could not forget the death and would never forgive the marriage. Edmund Clarence Stedman, one member of another homosexual triangle,
dedicated *The Blameless Prince* to Richard Henry Stoddard and wrote a
sonnet, accompanying a gift of Shakespearean sonnets, to Bayard Taylor.
Stedman also assessed Halleck's post-Drake writings as drivel, writing
that Drake "stimulated the muse of Halleck, whose choicest poems were
composed before he had outlived the sense of that recent companionship."[106] While Stedman's words probably alluded to Drake's death, they
also could have been applied to his marriage.

Throughout the brief period between Drake's marriage and his death,
Maria Halleck continued to read her brother's letters. Her maternal role
as Halleck's confidant meant that she had to bear the full weight of his
disclosures. He had conquered self-loathing and retreated from relations
with foreign men, but now she feared that he had surrendered his heart
without any terms. Halleck had finally fallen in love. He fell hard.

3

The Widow Halleck

The answer is a silent one,
More eloquent than words.

Fitz-Greene Halleck, *Fanny*

ALLECK'S *annus mirabilis* of 1819 was the direct result of Drake's
renewed attention. Beginning in December 1818, Drake took extraordinary measures to close the gap with Halleck. In January
1819, he made the consolatory gesture of christening his only child, a
daughter, Halleck. Named for her father's best friend, Janet Halleck Drake
was nicknamed Joe after her father, and Drake referred to Janet as his
son. Joe Halleck represented both poets in Inman's painting of her as a
little girl in foppish male clothing. Halleck cherished little Joe as his own
long after her father was gone. Halleck's June 1821 letter to Sarah Drake
requested, "Kiss little Joe, and all that's little Joe's."[1] Orphaned at age
nine, Janet married at the age of fourteen. Halleck took a paternal interest
in her marriage and maintained a very affectionate correspondence with
her. She, in turn, honored him as godfather of her first child, Katherine
DeKay.

Janet's christening had marked the onset of Drake and Halleck's literary collaboration. At first, Drake and Halleck cowrote a series of sermons, now lost. These theological lectures were comic rebuttals to Dr.
Samuel Hanson Cox (1793–1880), a noted Presbyterian minister and educator. Halleck and Drake's sermons were read privately to James DeKay
and Dr. William Langstaff but were also intended for publication.[2] But it
was Drake and Halleck's poetry that made them notorious. Their Croaker
poems, which took the form of Pindaric odes, appeared almost daily,
primarily in the *New York Evening Post*. Although they had individual
titles, the poems were collectively named after Drake and Halleck's com-

mon pseudonym. Croaker referred to Drake and Croaker Jr. designated the more accommodating Halleck who was also called Prince Croaker. Croaker and Co. was used for poems that were cowritten. Several dozen of these social commentaries appeared from March through June 1819.

The Croaker poems captivated New Yorkers as a rare example of joint authorship. Charles Lewis Biggs writes that New York's literary couple of poets were the "rarest of all rare beings in the America of that day," while Robert K. Martin observes, "One is hard put to think of another example [of coauthors] since Beaumont and Fletcher."[3] The Croakers were close relatives of Oliver Goldsmith's mismatched family by the same name in *The Good-Natured Man*. Goldsmith's Mr. Croaker is a depressive alarmist, whereas the play's Mrs. Croaker is a boisterous optimist who believes that love reigns supreme. The choice of Drake and Halleck's joint pseudonym not only referred to a man and a woman but also reflected the tension between Drake's practical heterosexual marriage and Halleck's unyielding same-sex romanticism. The husband in Goldsmith's play also seeks a wealthy match for his son in Miss Richland. Halleck probably relished the insulting allusion to Drake's own wealthy bride.

Goldsmith's Mr. Croaker makes comments on gender, wedlock, and suicide that are intriguing in the context of the Drake-Halleck relationship. The father chastises his shy son as gender deficient ("one would think you had changed sexes") and praises silence as "his mother tongue" which "gives consent." On marriage, Mr. Croaker preaches that "one may find comfort in the money, whatever one does in the wife," and like Halleck he confesses that his own depression had encouraged a friend's suicide. Honeywood, Goldsmith's main character, and Halleck also share the flaw of seeking social approval. Thus Croaker was not only an appropriate pen name for Drake and Halleck on a personal level but also made sense for their public lines, which imitated Goldsmith's parody of high literature and social hypocrisy. "Spicy, personal and fearless," the Croaker poems were signed by D. or H. based upon which poet had written the poem—or most of the lines in the case of cowritten verse.[4]

The first Croaker, Drake's "To Ennui" (*New York Evening Post* March 10, 1819) was for Halleck, who answered with lines published in the *National Advocate* on March 12. Thus began a poetic dialogue that expanded almost daily and "had New York by the ears."[5] The poetic columnists had stumbled upon a new genre, as would Lydia Maria Child with her *Letters from New York*. "To Ennui" alluded to Halleck's 1818 depression with Drake's typical insensitivity. Crass in its style ("Let Mister Hawkins blow his nose / And Spooner publish it"), the poem revealed "Fitz is almost hypped to death" and sought medical advice for the narrator driven mad by literary drivel and a monstrous condition:

> The fiend—the fiend is on me still,
> Come, doctor, here's your pay—
> What potion, lotion, plaster, pill,
> Will drive the beast away?[6]

Although Halleck's identity was encoded originally as "F * * *," it was revealed as "Fitz" for the first complete collection of Croakers published by the Bradford Club in 1860. Drake's propensity for medical topics is evident in four other Croakers: "The King of the Doctors" (Dr. David Hosack), an ode "To Quackery," and two attacking the surgeon general of New York State.

Drake concealed Halleck's name even more fully in "To * * * *, Esquire," which invites a friend to "sparkle again" and "banish the blues" as "our wine shall be caught from the lips of the Muse." In a literary feast prepared for "my old chum," Drake's emphasis plays on Halleck's name ("Fine *greens,* from the hot-bed"); Byron prepares "black wormwood bitters"; and David Macbeth Moir brings "a Sip-witching bumper of *parfait amour.*" In a criminal metaphor, Drake is threatened with being "sentenced" to read bad literature and he accuses Halleck of poetical treason.[7] Drake's "To a Friend" also charged Halleck with choosing business over poetry.

Drake's "To Croaker, Junior" described the Croakers as a phallic horse ride of pens. A Freudian deconstruction of "To Croaker, Junior" would suggest that Drake's metaphor for collaboration was mutual masturbation. Drake bids Halleck, "Unbuckle your harness, in peace let us dwell; / Our goose-quills will canter together." These lines are followed by an analogy to Gemini, the poets like Castor and Pollux cast down to earth. In another Croaker, "To an Elderly Coquette," Drake's persona abandons fresh and fading beauties for poetry: "I kneel to the Muse, / And, instead of love-ditties, write Croakers."[8] Drake increasingly avoided personal topics in favor of national political issues and, like Halleck, he grew antinational, especially in "The Modern Hydra."

When Drake and Halleck finally dropped by William Coleman's Hudson Street home to reveal the true identities of the Damon and Pythias of American poets as they were called, Coleman exclaimed, "My God! I had no idea that we had such talents in America!"[9] Coleman, editor of the *New York Evening Post,* rejected Drake's second Croaker, "The Declaration of Independence," so Drake altered the title to "The National Painting" and submitted the poem to Mordecai Noah, editor of the *National Advocate,* who printed it on March 15, 1819. The lines attack John Trumbull's art for the Capitol's rotunda as Halleck would also do in *Fanny.* Drake is the harsher critic, though, alluding to Trumbull as "the Titian of a table-cloth!" whose work "a horse may mire upon." Conversely, Halleck's Croaker "The Great Moral Picture" attacked political criticisms of public art. Coleman had refused Drake's "Declaration of Independence" because it was too personal an attack on a national figure, yet Coleman printed Drake's next two submissions, rash criticisms of Andrew Jackson. Drake's "The Freedom of the City" portrayed masses "mincing, smiling, bowing" compliments at Jackson like "a volley in his face." Jackson is upbraided: "Dear General, though you swallow all, / I must confess it sickens me."[10] It is no wonder that the Croakers divided New Yorkers—one half "mad with anger and the other half mad with delight."[11]

Halleck's first Croaker, "Bony's Fight," followed Drake's lead and supported the addition of mushroom soldiers, untrained volunteers who sprang up overnight, to the New York State Militia. It joked that the British could now take America since the Iron Grays had disbanded. Halleck's third Croaker fueled political gossip in a fictitious letter from Alexander Hamilton to New York governor DeWitt Clinton. Unlike Drake, however, Halleck preferred more social and local subjects.

Halleck's second submission was "To Mr. Simpson," manager of the Park Theater. "To Mr. Simpson" poked fun at editors Coleman and Noah. The Halleck Croaker "To John Lang, Esq.," attacked the editor of the *New York Gazette* as well. Coleman and Noah had recently neglected to cover the theater, prompting Halleck to turn critic "out of pure love" for Simpson. Another Halleck Croaker, "To E. Simpson, Esq.," suggested acting roles for politicians. His coauthored Croaker "To Mrs. Barnes" criticized the actress, and "An Address for the Opening of the New Theatre, to Be Spoken by Mr. Olliff" (1821) was risqué in boasting that the new building was six inches higher than its "brother," which had burned down.[12] The poem also flattered his future employer, John Jacob Astor.

Halleck's 1831 "Address" for the opening of another theater also sought public support. In yet another poem critiquing stage personalities, Halleck writes tellingly: "Your ladies are safe . . . I'll let them alone, . . . But as for your men . . . Of praise that they merit they'll each have his share." Women were nevertheless in danger of Halleck's pen, and actress Catherine Leesugg is derided as "not pretty, / She's a little too large" and graceless.[13] Far removed from his Puritan ancestors who had closed down the theaters, Halleck's poetry defended the theater from long-standing opposition.

According to Wilson, Halleck was "intimately acquainted with nearly all the great actors" and once stated, "I am no such bigot for the stage as to say that it is necessarily a school of morals . . . [however,] drama rather follows than leads public morals."[14] He notes taking his seat in box number 3 in two poems, and his Croaker "Lamentings" mourned numerous famed actors. But Halleck did not appear self-conscious of his theatrical leanings and boldly praised the playhouse. With Drake at his side, Halleck offered what the *National Magazine* referred to as his "effusions" [15] with steely confidence. He was on top on the world.

By the end of March 1819, the Croakers' popularity had skyrocketed. The hyperbole used to compare the Croakers to "manna upon the desert of American letters" did not detract from the success that gave Drake and Halleck "the field to themselves." [16] Halleck gushed about the unexpected and dramatic results of his reconciliation with Drake in a letter to his sister written on April Fool's Day in 1819. He rhetorically asked, "Can you believe it, Maria, Joe and I have become authors?" and expressed the thrill of seeing and hearing themselves "praised, puffed, eulogized, execrated and threatened." [17] The Croakers enjoyed the highest form of flattery, imitation.

Hundreds of bogus poems arrived daily to newspapers; Coleman showed Halleck fifteen submissions that arrived on one morning. [18] Adkins notes four parodies published between March 19 and April 1, 1819, and cites a barrage of daily *faux Croaker* submissions. Halleck assured his sister that "the whole town has talked of nothing else" and claimed that the Croakers held the attention of virtually every New York paper. He complained of having to submit daily poems without Drake who had been in Albany for ten days. In his effort "to carry on the war alone," Halleck bragged to Maria that he had "set the whole town in a blaze" and was determined to let things cool off. [19] Yet he realized the limits of the series: "The subjects are, many of them, purely local, and will, of course, be unintelligible to you." [20] As early as 1852, the *National Magazine* realized that the canonization of Halleck's epistolary and comic poems would prove problematic. Topics "obsolete and forgotten" were "the warp and woof of the poems" and would become irrelevant to future readers. [21]

Maria, however, would have had no trouble discerning her brother's misogynist themes. Halleck's Croakers inverted a rigid masculine code to insult male enemies. His "To Simon" bids a popular male food caterer to wear his corsets and predicts, "When you die, a long procession / Of dandies shall surround your tomb." [22] Other lines consistently belittled women. Aptly titled, "Cutting" opens by bemoaning an imperfect world in which "all women are not wise or pretty" and "all that are willing are not won." The narrator is despised by the ugly and dull females he cannot bring himself to flatter; "they hate the slighting beau so!" Fending off the "fat," the "stupid," and the "bores," he rejects a half-dozen women who declare him an immovable and "immoral man." He inspires the haughty Miss McLush to hate him by confiding, "I preferred her crony," and advises the male reader that if he will "trot out people's awkward daughters— / You may scandal 'scape—perhaps!" "Cutting" concludes with an admission of feigning interest in women in order to avoid social condemnation:

> Woman never yet refused
> Virtues to a seeming wooer—
> Woman never yet abused
> Him who had been civil to her.[23]

The seeming suitor knows that the pretense of heterosexual interest sufficiently meets the social requirement. In another poem, "Ode to Fortune," Halleck and Drake together personify fortune as a woman who is resented for her interference.

In fact, Halleck and Drake's "intimacy suffered as little abatement as possible when matrimony steps between bachelor friends."[24] Halleck believed that he was winning Drake back from Sarah Eckford and basked in the victory. He divulged Drake's response to receiving Croaker proof sheets indiscriminately: Drake "laid his cheek down upon the lines he had written, and, looking at me [Halleck] with beaming eyes, said, 'O, Halleck, isn't this happiness!'"[25] Whether this account is accurate or not, the anecdote does convey Halleck's conviction that Drake was equally enraptured by the collaboration. But in spite of a close literary attachment, Halleck never adequately read Drake, who was the first to weary of Croakers.

Drake's "The American Flag" was written in spring 1819 and was probably inspired by the new flag Congress had adopted in 1818. "The American Flag" was the exception to Drake's generally unpatriotic mood and ironically became his most celebrated short poem. It was also his last Croaker, and he requested Halleck to write its final stanza, which had presented some difficulty. He did not have to ask twice. Because of Halleck's heavy hand in its composition, the poem was cosigned Croaker and Co. Halleck not only completed that poem but also wrote all of the remaining Croakers. Drake had lost interest as his health seriously declined.

Even after Drake had left New York to treat his consumption, Halleck published a dozen more Croakers before throwing in the towel. The September 1819 collection, *Croakers*, sold rapidly and became an exceedingly valuable book as Halleck suppressed a second printing. The result was an inflated price for available copies that reportedly sold for as much as twenty times the original price.[26] Following Drake's death, Halleck seemed unable to tolerate any edition except the original product. In addition to suppressing future editions, Halleck expressed his displeasure when the first complete Croaker collection appeared in 1860. Its engravings portrayed him at age fifty while Drake appeared as he had at age twenty-four. Halleck was also dismayed by inaccurate explanatory notes.

S. F. B. Morse's 1827 oil on canvas combined sad eyes with a mischievous smile in order to capture Fitz-Greene Halleck's infamous dual nature. The Morse portrait was completed about the time that Halleck produced his controversial "Field of the Grounded Arms" and is currently displayed in the New York Public Library's Portrait Gallery. (Collection of the New York Public Library: Astor, Lenox, and Tilden Foundations.)

He was unable to finish reading the 1860 edition and refused to auto-graph it.[27]

The poets followed their joint project with their longest individual poems. Drake's short career in poetry climaxed with "The Culprit Fay," a lengthy fairy tale written during August while he was still in the South. By September, he was too sick for such an undertaking. He was not alone; New York City was under a yellow fever quarantine that month. Halleck filled his lonely summer hours in New York as Drake had done during their time apart, by writing his longest poem.

Unlike Drake's "The Culprit Fay," Halleck's mock-epic *Fanny* was an enormous success. Still, it failed to relieve the crisis brought about by his physical separation from Drake. In a letter written on New Year's Day 1820, Halleck told Maria that *Fanny* was written "to render my solitary hours less irksome."[28] Although begun in summer, *Fanny* was not pub-lished until late December 1819. It was an immediate bestseller made more valuable by delays in reprinting. Halleck refused to have *Fanny* re-published until its enlarged edition of 1821; consequently, scarce fifty-cent copies "brought twenty times the original price" or ten dollars by 1821.[29] The irreverent poem excelled in "the sparkle of wickedness and fun so impossible in New England poetry," continuing Halleck's rebellion from early American austerity.[30] Its humor demonstrated his growing ten-dency to contradict private tragedy by donning a happy face.

Halleck's social satire was, in this case, heavily indebted to the con-temporary work of his literary idol, Lord Byron. Halleck chose a modified *ottava rima* and iambics for the nearly fifteen hundred lines of his hybrid *Don Juan/Beppo*. Halleck's stanzas are six lines rather than eight. *Fanny* led William H. Prescott, editor of Boston's *Club-Room,* to compare Hal-leck with Byron, as would Bryant as well. In 1820, a personal friend of Byron also flattered Halleck with a favorable comparison.[31] The *Literary Gazette* compared *Fanny* to *Don Juan* (April 7, 1821), as did *Godey's* (July 1846) and *Fraser's* (July 1850). The *National Magazine* (December 1852) drew parallels to both *Don Juan* and *Beppo.* Some found *Fanny* most like *Beppo,* and others wondered whether *Fanny* or *Beppo* came first.[32] (Because its cantos were produced serially, *Don Juan* was not considered a completed work until 1823.) James Russell Lowell joked, "*Fanny's* a pseudo Don Juan," and Ezra Pound upheld the comparison of Halleck as the American poet most like Byron in the twentieth century.[33] As in *Don Juan,* the real hero of *Fanny* is the narrative voice.

Lengthy digressions that abuse famous politicians and artists con-stantly interrupt the plot. The speaker points out his own breech in story-telling with phrases like "but to return" and "but to return once more," and with rhetorical questions such as "but whither am I wandering?" and "but where is Fanny?" Halleck and Drake bear the brunt of the narrator's joke: "'This may be poetry, for aught I know,' / said an old, worthy friend of mine, while leaning / Over my shoulders as I wrote; 'although / I can't exactly comprehend its meaning.'" He baits the reader:

> If in my story of woes, or plan
>   Or moral can be traced, 'twas not intended.
> And if I've wronged [Fanny], I can only tell her
>   I'm sorry for it—so is my bookseller.

Readers were unsuccessful in their attempt to identify a real woman cloaked behind the name Fanny because Halleck's heroine caricatured a man, Drake. The snares of feminine false beauty and masculine materialism replace virtue and chivalry in *Fanny*'s irreverent battle of the sexes. While Adkins complains that "the subject of the digression—the fickleness of woman—was foreign to Halleck's manner of thought,"[34] Halleck manages a fine job in his parody of female artifice and male avarice.

Fanny is ultimately cast aside by "a true dandy of the modern schools," where it is "a violation of the latest rules, / To treat the sex with too much courtesy." Halleck's assault on contemporary heterosexual courtship was motivated by his view of Drake's unprincipled pursuit of money and perhaps extramarital affairs. As in their relationship, the poem's "vision" and "vulgar practicality" are never reconciled.[35] The chase for Fanny (British slang for vagina) results in disillusionment and exacts literary revenge on Drake and his wife. The novel *Fanny Hill* (1750), considered pornographic and the subject of a trial dealing with the Massachusetts obscenity law in 1821, takes its title from a pun on female anatomy. Halleck's completed *Fanny* also appeared in 1821.

Fanny seems to represent both Drake, who was motivated to marry in order to rise socially, and Drake's wife, whose biography is similar to Fanny's own circumstances. *Fanny* recounts the rise of a *nouveau-riche* merchant and his daughter, Fanny, people not unlike Henry Eckford and Sarah. Fanny, who exudes youth and wealth, is the physical and social product of her ignorant father, who rises so high in "the art of making money" that the public subsequently discovers his genius because he is rich. But all that he has learned is that social clout can be bought. He is the force behind a half-dozen insurance companies, as Henry Eckford himself had been. Ambition, personified as a woman, fails to seduce Fanny's father into politics, hiding her motive under cosmetics: "She was no beauty; yet, when 'made up' ready / For visitors, 'twas quite another lady." After berating politicians who live by the Satanic motto of *Paradise Lost* ("Better to reign in hell than serve in heaven"), the narrator returns to Fanny who expects that her father will "buy out" New York's dandies who "ranged within, / Gay as the Brussels carpeting they tread on, / And sapient as the oysters they are fed." Halleck's use of "dandy"—an effemi-

nate and elitist homosexual figure in British and American poetics—
is consistently derogatory, as in the case of Drake's "Battery War." [36] The
parody of Sarah Eckford ends when Fanny spurns middle-class suitors in
her clamor for status; actually Drake had been well below Sarah Eckford's
own class level. Fanny's only redeeming feature is literary. The narrator
even tells the reader that she has read the Croakers! This detail reinforces
the idea that the poem alludes to real people, its narrator being Halleck.

At the end of the first edition, Fanny is adored by those men who had
"wearied of your duns and single life, / And wanted a few thousands and
a wife." *Fanny*'s second edition begins the enlargement with stanza 152
and was produced under a contract to add fifty more stanzas, though the
Literary Gazette would be quick to find the second edition inferior on
April 17, 1821.

As it turns out, Fanny's suitor misrepresents his assets. The secret debt
of Fanny's lover rivals that of his potential father-in-law, who is headed
for bankruptcy and has taken his daughter's advice to throw a party in
order to convince creditors that he is not out of resources. The party fails
when a chandelier falls, symbolizing Fanny's own fall from shimmering
heights. The bad memory clings like "a wife" to both Fanny and her father on the rainy day after the party. Her evicted father sings a solemn
song unfittingly sober for a mock epic. Its fifth verse served as a reminder
of Drake's untimely autumn death:

> To-day the forest-leaves are green,
>   They'll wither on the morrow,
> And the maiden's laugh will be changed ere long
>   To the widow's wail of sorrow.
> Come with the winter snows, and ask,
>   Where are the forest birds?
> The answer is a silent one,
>   More eloquent than words.

Besides insulting Drake's wife and father-in-law, *Fanny*'s plot reiterated
Halleck's familiar scenario of heterosexual pressure and escape that he
would surmount time and again.

Fanny is impressive for its same-sex tactics that excuse Halleck's bachelor status. His speaker covers up by reproaching himself: "I have too
long loved pretty women with a poet's feeling." One critic made no distinction between the narrative voice and the author of that line, retorting
that Halleck "gives no evidence of any feeling for women at all." [37] Halleck's narrator also explains his preference for smoking to marriage: "But
if you are a bachelor, like me, / And spurn all chains, even tho' made of
roses, / I'd recommend segars." James Lawson, who would be Halleck's
first patently homophobic reviewer, deemed the line absurd. Superimpos-

ing italics on the words "*a bachelor, like me,*" Lawson felt Halleck's old age confirmed his "young thoughts" and noted that Halleck "seldom unbosoms his feelings."[38] Yet, *Fanny* provided some remarkably naked personal asides, such as the following on women:

> But Fortune, like some others of her sex,
>   Delights in tantalizing and tormenting;
> One day we feed upon their smiles—the next
>   Is spent in swearing, sorrowing, and repenting.
> (If in the last four lines the author lies,
> He's always ready to apologize.)

The final couplet mocks the Romantic ideal of unrequited yearning and confesses a lack of heterosexual identification. Halleck's American Byronism was decidedly anticlimactic.

Fanny made Halleck the only American poet besides Irving whom Irving's publisher would print. Halleck, himself, mentioned this to Maria in a January 1, 1820, letter. Like *Croakers*, *Fanny* was also widely plagiarized. "Fanny, Continued," by Isaac Starr Clason, who also wrote two cantos continuing *Don Juan*, appeared in November 1820. Clason, who committed suicide in London during 1834, also wrote "A Bumper to Fanny" beckoning Halleck to "awake!" and "appear!" and challenging: "You've found the silver nib of Byron's pen; / Prove that its iron stem can plough again."[39] The *Literary Gazette* (April 28, 1821) reviewed William Bicker Walter's *Sukey* (1821), a seventy-two page imitation of *Fanny*. The *Charleston Courier* and the *National Advocate* published *Kitty*, yet another imitation of Halleck's *Fanny*. Despite all of the flattery of imitation, Halleck considered the poem a bit of hack writing and wished to remain anonymous as its author. Still, he had been unable to resist the five hundred dollars offered for the second canto.

The artistic sell-out was no less hypocritical than Drake's profitable marriage and complemented Halleck's other transgressions of 1819—he had been flirting with other men. When a friend, Charles Clinch, had placed a five-dollar reward in the papers for the return of his lost dog named Fitz, Halleck scribbled a note of regret that he could not locate the canine but offered himself: "I, however, know another puppy answering to that name, who will come to you for half the money!" Writing Maria from his Bloomingdale retreat during the yellow fever epidemic in mid-October 1819, he told her how tickled he had been by a greeting from James DeKay:

He seemed beside himself at the sight of me, and embraced me *à la Française*, by kissing each cheek, in the middle of the street, to the great admiration and amusement of the populace. He will establish himself in New York, and I anticipate much pleasure in his society.[40]

Halleck did not feel that these other friendships diminished his devotion to the absent Drake, but his humor declined along with Drake's rapidly deteriorating health.

A French physician in New York unsuccessfully tried to relieve dizziness cause by Halleck's bad ear, using a painful moxa remedy, an organic Eastern substance used as a counterirritant that burned the skin. While the physician attempted to help Halleck's hearing, Maria tried to ease his heart. By early February 1820, Halleck was leaning heavily on his sister. At this time, Drake was alone in New Orleans and wrote alternately to his wife and Halleck. Halleck, who was dieting at the time, wrote Maria, "I have been miserably low-spirited about myself."[41] Drake and Halleck reflected each other's mental states as had been the case when they were separated by Drake's honeymoon.

Drake was doubting his own worth as a poet and wanted his works destroyed. DeKay, who had gathered Drake's poetry into a coherent pile in order to cheer his ailing friend, was repaid with a reprimand. Drake wanted the stack of poems burned and told DeKay "They are valueless."[42] The *Foreign Quarterly Review* felt that Drake exercised "good judgment" because so little of his work was "worth remembering."[43] Drake also requested on his deathbed that his poems be incinerated, but his wife refused.[44] It would have been futile to ask Halleck. Drake was not a modest man and may have wanted his poetry suppressed because of its content. Some of his lines related possible infidelities. For instance, the remorseful narrator of "To ———" personifies love as "a changeable boy" who has broken his vows by kissing another's lips. "Lines to a Lady" may have been coauthored with a married woman and was not for Sarah Drake. In addition to his roving eye, Drake also maintained an unusual affection for one sister, and "To My Sister Carry" was tribute to Caroline Drake.[45] This incestuous infatuation appeared to be connected to a fetish for lesbianism.

Caroline Drake also figures in Drake's unfinished "Leon," which was compared to Byron's "The Corsair" and explored a love triangle between a husband, wife, and sister. The wife's "strange passions" and "maddening passion" create "impetuous heat"; she is flushed by a "hectic pleasure" and "scorned herself, that she could be / A moment lulled by that sweet sophistry." She can bear her husband's treachery but not that of her sister: "I feel she loves me yet, / And if my boding bosoms could forget / Its wild imaginings, with what sweet pain / I'd clasp my Florence to my breast again."[46] The personal and prohibited nature of Drake's lines led to their censorship by both Drake and Halleck. Fifteen years after Drake's death, Halleck still could not bring himself to touch Drake's works.

As late as 1881, the *New York Daily Tribune* assumed that Halleck had edited Drake's poems, which were first published in 1835. But Halleck had repeatedly refused to edit them or to write Drake's memoir. Like Halleck's publisher, Dearborn, the *Morning Courier and New York Enquirer* (December 23, 1830) also assumed that Halleck would perform the task and the *New York Mirror* (July 11, 1835) turned his criminal metaphor back on him: "Mr. Halleck, Mr. Halleck! you have much to answer for. . . . The crime of omission lies heavy at your door." The *Mirror* also charged Halleck with the crime of not writing Drake's biography a few months later, after Janet Halleck Drake (Mrs. Commodore DeKay) completed the first edition of her father's poems. Since she was only an infant when Drake died, she had asked Halleck to prepare the memoir section, but he could not do it. Janet sympathized and dedicated the edition to Halleck, her godfather. A century later, Drake's biographer offered his explanation that Halleck "was too close to Drake" to be able to write the biography, adding: "His feeling for [Drake] was so intense that he may have regarded the task as being quite beyond his powers."[47] Even before Drake's death became imminent, Halleck had only wanted to be alone with him and viewed both Drake's family and the public as intrusive forces.

Drake had returned from Louisiana in spring 1820, about the same time that business took Halleck to Canada. Upon his return in June, Halleck realized just how dire Drake's condition had become. Halleck stayed close by for the rest of that summer and watched over Drake's bedside with "more than a brother's love."[48] Assuming a wife's position, Halleck "smoothed [Drake's] pillow" and appears to have tended to Drake by himself at the end.[49] Halleck stayed up through the entire night. Exhausted and helplessly alone, he ended his vigil just minutes before dawn when Drake gasped his last breath of air. Halleck's bedside remonstrations against death were not enough to save Drake, who died on September 21, 1820, at the age of twenty-five. In that moment of agony, Halleck's own faith in life ended. He was only thirty.

A procession of thirty carriages escorted Drake's casket during the funeral procession that had been announced in the *New York Evening Post* the night before. The *Post* did not mention Drake's wife or his father but had welcomed acquaintances of his father-in-law, Henry Eckford, to attend the service. Charles P. Clinch overheard Halleck's understatement to DeKay made at the graveyard: "There will be less sunshine for me hereafter, now that Joe is gone."[50] The paraphrase of Sir Walter Scott at Johnnie Ballantyne's grave was prophetic. A gloomy cloud enveloped Halleck for the next fifty years of his life.

The implosion of grief he experienced was not dissipated among friends. Even Maria could not provide solace. Halleck kept to himself except for one letter to his sister, in which "the survivor lamented in a most touching and affecting manner the loss of his heart's companion."

Like his paragraphs extolling Drake's physical beauty, this letter has not been preserved. Wilson did "deeply regret" that perhaps the single most revealing of all Halleck's prose had been somehow mislaid.[51] But Halleck's poetic tribute to Drake survived. It was composed on the same day that Drake died. "On the Death of Joseph R. Drake" foreshadows homosexual protest literature and illustrates Halleck's division of grief over Drake and anger at a society that failed to recognize their love. It was brilliantly pathetic.

"On the Death of Joseph R. Drake" is prefaced by William Wordsworth's searing words: "The good die first, / And they, whose hearts are dry as summer dust, / Burn to the socket."[52] Poe observed that Halleck's elegy for Drake was a rewriting of Wordsworth's "She Dwelt Among the Untrodden Ways."[53] Richard Stoddard provided a second sexually curious literary cross-reference by claiming that Halleck's elegy imitated Wordsworth's "Lucy."[54] Halleck inverted gender in basing his lines on Wordsworth's poems to women and may have intended a clever sexual pun on living among "untrodden ways." The poem begins with Halleck's most famous quatrain:

> Green be the turf above thee,
>   Friend of my better days!
> None knew thee but to love thee
>   Nor named thee but to praise.

Drake's gravestone was inscribed with these lines. When the Bronx graveyard became Joseph Rodman Drake Park in 1915, a bronze tablet bearing more lines was added to the original epitaph in marble. The addition conveyed Halleck's utter anguish:

> Tears fell when thou wert dying,
>   From eyes unused to weep,
> And long, where thou art lying,
>   Will tears the cold turf steep.

The poem ends by expressing Halleck's sense of displacement at the funeral, where he could not assume the role of widower:

> And I who woke each morrow
>   To clasp thy hand in mine,
> Who shared thy joy and sorrow,
>   Whose weal and woe were thine:
>
> It should be mine to braid it [the wreath]
>   Around thy faded brow,
> But I've in vain essayed it,
>   And feel I cannot now.

While memory bids me weep thee,
　　Nor thoughts nor words are free,
The grief is fixed too deeply
　　That mourns a man like thee.[55]

The first of these last three stanzas implies a physical consummation with Drake and refutes the limits that society imposes on male friendship. To no avail, the narrator has "essayed" his claim to the widow's rights, which "should be mine." This vain effort yields confusion as the speaker consciously controls his restricted tears. Not free to share his thoughts or feelings in public, his pain becomes as fixed as a statue.

The narrator, who once felt Drake's "weal and woe," feels nothing now. The emotional numbness that Halleck felt during Drake's honeymoon recurs even as he claims a love for Drake superior to that of Drake's wife, who is alone entitled to the privilege of dressing her husband's corpse. Like modern survivors of gay partners with AIDS, Halleck's own needs are subordinate to the legal and social prerogative of the American nuclear family. Halleck shared his "On the Death of Joseph R. Drake" with DeKay but never wanted his "lyric rosebud dropped on the grave of Drake" to be published. Halleck did not even title the poem; he merely wrote "Lines" at the top of the manuscript. Adkins agrees with Wilson that Halleck wished the poem to remain private; however, DeKay gave a copy to the *Quarterly Repository*, which then published it in January 1821. It was republished in the *New York American* (February 9, 1821), the *New York Evening Post* (February 21, 1821), and the *Literary Gazette* (February 24, 1821). Halleck's poetic triumph over Sarah was enduring; the lines from his elegy still adorn Drake's black marble monument.

Poe preferred the poem above all others by Halleck, as did others.[56] One critic deemed four lines of the elegy "worth all of [Halleck's] Byronizing," while another commented on its display of "the tender regret that is usually the slow result of time."[57] Most scholars agree that "On the Death of Joseph R. Drake" is Halleck's best-known poem. Halleck's ode to Drake was highly regarded for its controlled emotion; however, for some its "repressed sobs" reflected social conformity rather than conscious artistry.[58] William Leggett's "fluttering heart" lent its "curiously romantic" sympathy to Halleck, whose epitaph he read during an 1829 moonlight visit to Drake's grave.[59] Leggett's insightful commentary and emotional response were rarely attained by the popular readership. George Parsons Lathrop, Nathaniel Hawthorne's son-in-law and Halleck's personal friend, discussed Halleck's "self-divided genius" in terms of "On the Death of Joseph R. Drake" and several other poems: "From one point of view, how versatile and susceptible was this man! from another, how chilly and limited!" Lathrop suggested that "a sudden, prosaic self-consciousness" was "arresting" Halleck's vulnerable spirit in a country characterized by "the

Joseph Rodman Drake, who was praised for inheriting his good looks, trim physique, and height (six feet, two inches) from his father, as etched by Thomas Kelly (ca. 1820). (Portrait File, Miriam and Ira D. Wallach Division of Art, Prints, and Photographs, The New York Public Library: Astor, Lenox, and Tilden Foundations.) This portrait was based on a Nathaniel Rogers miniature that featured recesses holding locks of hair from Drake and his daughter. Drake was also painted by Eliab Metcalf during a restorative visit to New Orleans in 1820.

absence of a highly developed society which could stimulate instead of limiting and repressing him. He was indubitably hurt by his surroundings."[60] The pain never lifted.

Halleck's first poetic tribute did not adequately represent his loss in a heterosexist environment. He tried again. "Album Verses," composed two weeks after Drake's funeral (October 6, 1820) was a second private poem, this one not published until 1869. Wilson suggests that the poem was for DeKay's sister, but its proximity to Drake's funeral suggests that its immortalized Beauty is in fact Drake. Like Drake's flute playing, wind breathes life into a singer's lungs. The opening phrase, "Within a rock whose shadows linger," personified Halleck's stony heart haunted by Drake's ghost. The rock is animated by an Indian muse so that life is no longer "mute and lonely." The analogy to Drake's effect on Halleck's poetic powers is blatant:

> So I—that fabled rock resembling,
> With heart as cold, and head as hard—
> Appear, although with fear and trembling,
> At Beauty's call, as Beauty's bard.

This turn in the poem showed how Halleck's chilly side was contradicted by the emotional susceptibility Lathrop observed. The narrator finds intellect useless against his muse and praises friendship above all other experience. The poet-narrator can brave oblivion, having been called by the spirit of love, and asks, "And who would live beyond that hour?"[61]

Halleck lived on still feeling that his grief was untold and composed a third poem to Drake. "To * * *" was "quite private and personal" and not intended for publication.[62] Closely related to the elegy to Drake, the three-stanza poem was not shared with DeKay. Varying from the original elegy by using third-person narration and focusing on the physical body, "To * * *" retained Halleck's phraseology and theme of silenced grief:

> There's one who long will dream of thee
> Now thou'rt at rest in death's dark sleep;
> There's one will love thy memory
> Till his own grave the night dews steep;
> And though no outward tear he weep,
> And none his silent sorrow know,
> Long will his heart her vigils keep
> Beside the spot where thou liest low.

In the stanza above, the mourner is portrayed as the sole bearer of grief. None knows the one who really loved the dead man; the lover weeps "no outward tear" and guards "his silent sorrow."

Crying on the inside, Halleck consoles himself. His heart, married to Drake, is personified as "her," infusing same-sex romance into the heterosexual tradition. "He" knows the depth of "his" loss and does not negotiate gender as in Halleck's other autobiographical verse. The next stanza displaced his depressive years onto Drake who is released from a sad life of "bitter tears," spent like a storm. It blurs a homoerotic and platonic compliment:

> And loveliest of the buried dead,
>   Sweet may thy dreamless slumbers be,
> A grave of summer's flowers thy bed—
>   You sleep in beauty's purity.

The loveliest of all who ever lived, Drake is returned to the purity of his bachelorhood in death. The final stanza alludes to Drake's marriage as a betrayal and reverberates with outrage at having been cheated of the rights of widowhood:

> As withered on thy cheek the rose
>   He banned the hour when love betrayed thee,
> 'Twas his in death thine eyes to close
>   And watch till on the bier they laid thee.
> No gloomy cypress boughs shall shade thee,
>   No marble thy sad story tell,
> The cruel world shall ne'er upbraid thee
>   With having loved and loved too well.

Halleck is prevented from tending to Drake's corpse in much the same way as he was betrayed by Drake's marriage. The marriage, in turn, betrayed Drake. The narrator tries to protect their love from the cruel world that would upbraid it. Paraphrasing famous lines on heterosexual romance, Halleck employs the words of Othello (who loved Desdemona too well) to express the depth of his own emotional attachment to Drake. Both Halleck's narrator and Shakespeare's hero learn not to doubt their love despite all worldly temptations to do so. Halleck's first elegy ("On the Death of Joseph R. Drake") did not tell the whole story as his writing of "To * * *" suggests. But this second poem also fell short.

Scribbling an additional asterisk to differentiate the poems, Halleck also wrote "To * * * *," which completely avoids the gender of his subject. He warns a youth whose bosom is "Pleasure's shrine" to have more permanent values than physical beauty. Halleck provides "a song of sorrow / The death-dirge of the gay" and warns "these charms may melt away." Recollecting his quotation at Drake's funeral, Halleck predicts that the "sun's bright beam [will] be shaded," but his aged, lonely narrator is no longer afraid of death. He eternally guards "the wild-flower wreath of feeling, / The sunbeam of the heart."[63] The image of an uncultured wild-flower wreath reclaims the official, artificial wreath that Sarah Eckford was permitted to weave into Drake's locks.

Twenty-two years after Drake's death, Halleck conveyed his experience yet again in "A Poetical Epistle," which thanked a married friend for her support during the crisis. The poem was sent to Mrs. John Rush in a letter dated March 8, 1842. Rush, "her who taught / My song, when life was in its June," is lauded alongside Drake. Echoing his own words that "there will be less sunshine for me hereafter," Halleck reflects, "Gone are the days of sunny weather / (I quote remembered words), when we / 'Reveled in poetry' together." Forced to remember the good old days with Drake in the ongoing popularity of *Croakers,* Halleck's narrator also recalls "a sick-room's bed of pain." "They are far away, those sunny days," although global praise continues to greet Halleck's "astonished rhyme" which has turned on the public: "Til half in doubt, half pleased, it curled / Its queerest lip upon the world." According to "A Poetical Epistle," the public applied an effeminate cliché to Halleck by saying that "we'd 'a bee in both our bonnets' / And he [Drake] sat listening, he the most / Honored and loved, and early lost."[64] Diverging from his intention of complimenting Rush, as he had done in the poem for DeKay's sister, Halleck alludes to Drake as a plant: "The green blade with the golden grain; / Alas! to bloom and beard in vain." Although written many years later, "A Poetical Epistle" was not Halleck's last attempt to honor Drake with the "queerest lip." Even then Halleck had not yet found the right language to translate his love.

Unlike the initial elegy "On the Death of Joseph R. Drake," "Translation from the German"[65] and "Translation: From the German of Goethe" had generic, seemingly unrelated titles, as had "Album Verses," "To * * *," "To * * * *," and "A Poetical Epistle." The narrator of "Translation: From the German of Goethe" longs for death not only as a release of the spirit from the body but also as a liberation of the individual from society. In a very loose translation of Goethe's "*Zueignung* of *Faust,* Part I," the speaker floats down a stream of water and of consciousness to his youth of "happier days, First-love and friendship." Ultimately, time has taken friends and left the narrator with "a longing long unfelt a deep-drawn sighing / For the far Spirit-World o'erpowers me now," leaving "the now a dream, the past reality." The heart is no longer stone, but flesh: "My changed heart throbs warm, no more denying / Tears to my eyes or sadness to my brow."[66] All of Halleck's tributes to Drake carried his message against social intolerance, but this poem utilized Goethe's verse to claim the right to externalize his pain. Halleck's other "Translation from the German" was also an emotional—rather than academic—exercise.

The text of "Translation from the German" is too similar to Halleck's previous elegies to have had a foreign prototype, and not surprisingly, no original has ever been identified. Halleck attempted to disguise his obsession with finding the words to communicate his eternal loss and emotional fidelity to Drake in the second translation. The poem vows:

> There's one who long will think of thee,
>   Though thou art cold in death's last sleep;
> There's one will love thy memory
>   Till his own grave the night-dews steep.

The opening repeats that of "To * * *"; its first two lines are only slightly altered and the second two lines are copied verbatim. In identical phrases, the narrator of "Translation from the German" also keeps a vigil at the spot where his friend lies, though "no outward tears he weep, / And none his silent sorrows know." Also in paraphrases from "To * * *," the poem frees Drake from his earthly marriage.

The second stanza of "Translation from the German" makes Drake's "grave the summer's bridal bed," negating his legal marriage and remarrying him to Death. Once again crowning Drake "loveliest of the buried dead," Halleck's homoerotic second stanza more boldly undermines Sarah Eckford's marriage than had his earlier "To * * *." The use of "bridal bed" could not have eased Drake's widow, who now occupied an empty bed. This stanza also borrowed from Halleck's "On the Death of Joseph R. Drake," including the words, "the turf is green above thy head." A final stanza further reiterated "To * * *."

The last stanza of "Translation from the German" only altered minor punctuation and replaced the earlier third-person narration with a first-person speaker:

> As withered on thy cheek the rose
>   I cursed the hour when love betrayed thee,
> 'Twas mine in death thine eyes to close
>   And watch till on the bier they laid thee.
> No gloomy cypress-boughs shall shade thee,
>   No marble thy sad story tell;
> The cruel world shall ne'er upbraid thee
>   With having loved—and loved too well.

The self-plagiarized octave wore the guise of a translation to protect Halleck from bearing the full consequences of his augmented protest. Still referring to Drake's marriage as treason, the narrator confesses to having cursed the wedding, though this condemnation did not suffice. It seems that the words Halleck groped for did not exist; his half-dozen elegies were followed by numerous other poems steeped in the nightmare of placing Drake's boyish body into the cold, silent ground.

Although Halleck's works were becoming redundant, more poems based upon Drake's death would follow throughout 1821. "Music, to a Boy of Four Years Old, on Hearing Him Play the Harp" envied innocence and called "up visions of past days," rousing memories "like lost friends wakened from their sleep." "Psalm CXXXVII" meshed a musical theme with social protest. The hero, an adult harpist, chooses to be mute rather than "make glad a stranger land" and hangs his instrument upon a branch. This "fettered" hostage wears a "chain" in Halleck's usual criminal motif of sexual confinement.[67] "Psalm CXXXVII" conveyed Halleck's entrapment (at Drake's wedding) and anger (at having to mourn in silence).

The situation was stated more overtly in "Love," which bore a Shakespearean subtitle: "Shall I never see a bachelor of threescore again?" At half that age, Halleck chose Benedict's line from *Much Ado About Nothing*—an apt title to describe his distaste for marriage. A tree whose buds are scattered by a bee's touch symbolizes Love's vulnerability. As in Blake's poem of experience, "A Poison Tree," the plant is fed by "the bitter tear." An omniscient narrator pontificates that it is better never to have loved at all than to have loved and lost. He advocates that the reader "crush, even in their hour of birth, / The infant buds of Love." The speaker's tears "nurse a heart-flame" as he discovers that to lose a love is to know the flame that wraps "round the martyr's head" and a light that casts darkness.[68] The oxymoron is effective and the analogy to heretical saints burned at the stake is reminiscent of Plaine's execution for homosexuality. Without an outlet, love combusts.

In a swing back to humor, "Rhyme of the Ancient Coaster" imitated Byron's criticism of Samuel Coleridge and advanced another assault on marriage. The poem's groom accepts drowning in a storm, but his bride halts the tempest. The narrator wonders: "Why sing of matrimony now, / In this brief hour of joy?" and returns to his favorite poets and cigars.[69] This shift toward the comic was followed by another return to the tragic. "The Discarded" took to heart what others had considered a practical joke.

Also composed in 1821, "The Discarded" was written out of sympathy for McDonald Clarke, a New York contemporary who was known as the "mad poet." Adkins described Clarke as "a strange, eccentric" man who took daily walks on Broadway wearing a "wild, erratic disposition" and having "many eccentricities of dress and manner."[70] Halleck shared Clarke's pain of romantic rejection as well as his fascination with graveyards, though Clarke actually slept on tombs. Lydia Maria Child claimed that Clarke's "whole life was in fact a restless seeking for his other half" and that he was often befriended by Halleck. Convinced that a wealthy woman loved him and presented with a forged invitation to visit her, Clarke borrowed suitable clothes and showed up at her mansion only to be thrown out.[71]

"The Discarded" is filled with grotesque imagery that Adkins found "foreign to Halleck's usual mode."[72] Yet, the twenty-one quatrains explored Halleck's most recurrent theme of love gone awry. Discarded by a lover and society, the narrator applies the tree metaphor from "Love," written earlier in the year. He is "a withered bough, / Blossomless, leafless, and alone." Sexual imagery dominates the conscious deathwish:

> When the quick throbbing of my brain
>   That now is maddening me is o'er,
> And the hot fire in each swoln vein
>   Is quench'd at last to burn no more.

A catalog of death's physical horrors ("shrieking," "rattling," "pangs," "lead-weights" on eyes, "white shroud" on breast, "death-foam" on lips, "death-dews" on one's hair, and "clench'd fingers in the grip / Of agony") does not enhance the tale of Clarke's cruel disappointment. They recount Drake's consumptive death scene. Halleck diverges from Clarke's tragic love story to tell his own.

The solitary narrator wonders who will "print on my lip the unanswered kiss." The verb "print" appropriately puns on the poetic vocation of Halleck, Drake, and Clarke. The speaker fears that strangers will attend his funeral and that the dirt hitting his casket will go unheard. A flash of the past's "bright rainbows in the twilight sky" evaporates:

> Their colours faded far away,
> Those clouds—I feel their dampness still;
>   But the bright rainbows—where are they?

The rainbow, a popular Romantic symbol, also served as an autobiographical reference to the occasion of Halleck and Drake's introduction.

The narrator of "The Discarded" is deprived of sunshine, color, and a friend to love, and so he takes up drinking: "And she I loved? I must not think / Of her—'for that way madness lies!' / Boy, start that champaigne cork—I'll drink, / And dream no more of Mary's eyes."[73] Abandoned by Drake's marriage and his death and dismissed from the widower's role, Halleck befriended a madman. His empathy for Clarke suggested his own mental state the year after Drake's death when Halleck began his slow descent into alcoholism. *Fanny* had already recommended champagne to "bathe the heart a while in bliss, / And keep the head a little time from thinking."

An "intimate" friend, Ogden Hammond, wrote Halleck a congratulatory letter in May 1821 regarding the success of *Fanny*'s expanded second edition.[74] Hammond suggested that Fanny's lover alluded to a real person and perceived Halleck's "usual good judgement throughout. My old acquaintance is craftily introduced as a finale." Requesting Halleck's copy of *Don Juan*, Hammond sent regards to their coterie and looked forward to "the gratification of once more taking [Halleck] by the hand," a phrase that may have conveyed masturbatory meaning in the nineteenth-century homosexual vernacular.

Whatever Hammond's intent, Halleck badly needed the consolation. In 1821, he was once again snared by the dubious honor of best man. Drake's favorite sister, Caroline (Cara) M. Drake, and Sarah Eckford Drake's sister were both brides that year. Drake's sister-in-law married James E. DeKay, who chose Halleck as his groomsman. Halleck was struggling to digest Drake's death as he repeated the very task that he had found so hard to stomach only five years earlier. He had now given away two of his closest male friends to daughters of Henry Eckford.

The two marriages of 1821 could not have been timed more poorly for Halleck than during this first year of grieving. His primal sense of isolation was naturally intensified. Between the February and August weddings, he wrote Maria at the end of March: "I have not written so long a letter I know not when, and you are almost the only person I do write to, for I have become dull, savage, and solitary, within the last year."[75] He cooperated with the Eckford sisters' plans for DeKay's honeymoon that paired Halleck with Sarah. Henry Eckford sent the foursome to Quebec, Canada, and may have deemed Halleck a worthy replacement for Drake. Halleck declined a second trip to Peru that Eckford subsequently offered. The relationships of his innermost social sphere were taking on incestuous dimensions. The Drakes' daughter (Janet Halleck Drake) would marry James DeKay's brother, Commodore George Colman DeKay, sealing the DeKay-Drake-Eckford link.

Halleck had also joined Caroline Drake's wedding party as an usher and wrote "A Valentine" for her. "A Valentine" was given on the eve of Caroline Drake's wedding to F. N. Tillou and was printed posthumously in the *Independent* on March 7, 1872. "Curtain Conversations," a Croaker published in 1827 under the title "Domestic Happiness," copied "A Valentine's" first stanza. A conspicuously dark poem for the occasion, Cupid's lamp is extinguished at the poem's end. The first-person narration takes on light and dark turns vicariously from the groom's perspective. From Cupid's purple wings hovering over the newlyweds, the poem ends with only a firefly's "unseen" "purple hue" lighting their way. The pledge of happiness made under dying celestial lights is contradicted by the dim future that is foreshadowed.[76] Romantic skepticism gave way to sarcasm in a later, published version of the poem. Mrs. Dash shoos Cupid away with her financial demands in the ironically retitled "Domestic Happiness." "Too proud to weep, / And too polite to swear," Dash brews her silent scorn into a storm in her husband's disturbed nightmares of "brokers, banks, and ruin." Although "he thought her pretty once," she is indeed "quite altered."[77] Once again, Love takes his lamp and his leave.

Halleck projected disillusionment onto his marrying heterosexual friends out of the conviction that he would never find a permanent partner of his own.

The compositions of 1821 betrayed his confusion as he tried to rebuild his emotional life and were written for private consolation rather than public consumption. "A Sketch," "Music," "Psalm," "Wyoming," and "Love" were not published until the 1827 edition of Halleck's poetry, and "Rhyme of the Ancient Coaster" and "The Discarded" were not published until a decade later when they appeared in the *New York Mirror* in 1831 (January 15 and 29, respectively). "In Her Island Home" (1821) first appeared in Halleck's 1869 collection. Even several light Croakers of 1821 were for specific personages: "An Address for the Opening of the New Theatre, to Be Spoken by Mr. Olliff"; "To Walter Browne, Esq."; and "Farewell, Farewell to Thee, Baron Von Hoffman." Yet Halleck himself was a personage of some note in New York City.

Not surprisingly, the first public request to intrude on Halleck's grief was for an elegy to be composed for the grave of actor George Frederick Cooke. Halleck obliged but would reject future requests. The heavy tears that ran down his face during the Cooke commemoration were shed for Drake. Halleck had attended Cooke's funeral in 1812; the commemoration was nine years later when the body was relocated to a new grave in need of poetic inscription. According to Wilson, "Tears fell from [Halleck's] eyes in abundance, and as the evening closed, he walked Broadway" alone.[78]

Halleck retreated to Wyoming in the summer of 1821, where he had first visited in winter 1816–1817. In a warm letter to Maria, he joked about an elderly woman who had shared his coach. Having thrown out his cigar as a courtesy, he was shocked when she pulled out her tobacco and proceeded to smoke for the next fifteen miles. Halleck recalled Sydney Smith's claim that a kiss stolen in youth would be a last thought, and Halleck predicted, "I shall on my death-bed undoubtedly recall with horror, as I do at the present moment, that fearful pipe and its smoker."[79] The trip resulted in "Wyoming," which is a Byronic critique of Thomas Campbell's "Gertrude." Its two women represent extremes: a sixteen-year-old farm hand, Gertrude, and "a woman, widowed, gray, and old."[80] Halleck placed a copy in a June letter to Sarah Drake although she would not have found the widowed heroine a flattering likeness.

In fact, Halleck's sole consolation in his grief was that Drake's marriage was over. Sarah Eckford Drake died eight years after her husband, on November 29, 1828, but did not exercise her right to be buried with him; Drake would lie buried alone. It became Halleck's "dearest wish" to be laid at the side of Drake even at the expense of exhumation.[81] He expressed his desire to be buried with Drake or to have Drake's remains moved to Guilford decades after the interment. The latter scheme was nearly carried out in 1903, when prefinanced plans were set to move the bodies of Drake, his wife, daughter, sister, and nephew to Guilford.

The relocation of Mrs. Drake and the others would, of course, have been a misunderstanding of Halleck's request. His sense of competition with Drake's wife was expressed in letters to Maria after Drake's wedding and in his private poems after Drake's burial, but his actions demonstrated a greater concern for social appearances. Halleck managed to overshoot his social obligation to Drake's widow. Just as he had distorted the public perception of his service in the War of 1812 to his advantage, he performed the motions of comforting and befriending Sarah Eckford with tremendous flair. Still, an undercurrent of resentment surfaced in his humor. In the year of Drake's death, 1820, Halleck only produced three Croakers ("The Dinner Party," "The Tea-Party," and "The Great Moral Picture"); the lines in DeKay's album; and "On the Death of Joseph R. Drake." One of three Croakers that Halleck had written overtly attacked Drake's widow.

The male trio in "The Tea-Party" (Halleck, DeKay, and Langstaff) is disrupted by two women who invite themselves over while "the tea-urn is singing / the tea-cups are gay." "Disturbing the bachelor's [sic] still quiet joys; / A pair of young witches have doomed them to death," even though they are "not as ugly" as their "distant relations," *Macbeth*'s evil sisters. The women are surprised to find that the men have avoided them by going out for whiskey at the appointed hour for tea. One witch is identified as Mrs. J. D. (Mrs. Joseph Drake), who shares "a smile on each lip, and a leer on each brow" with the other female intruder. The cat-like Mrs. J. D. finds "the cage there, but the bird is away."[82] Halleck outwits her and takes flight from the marriage trap.

Sarah Eckford Drake should have retaliated or demanded an apology from her dead husband's best friend for that poetic insolence. Both obvious and subtle jabs at her had been constant elements of Halleck's verse since Drake's funeral, but Drake's widow wanted much more than revenge on Halleck—she wanted to marry him.

4

Conquer and Divide

I have been, to my own astonishment, quite a ladies' man.
Fitz-Greene Halleck to Maria

SARAH ECKFORD DRAKE demonstrated one-sided romantic interest in Halleck after her husband's death. Joseph Drake's biographer states that Drake's widow "could have changed her name to Halleck. But Halleck was a confirmed bachelor."[1] Bachelorhood was just about the only stable feature of Halleck's life after losing Drake. His year of mourning, 1821, was filled with manic attempts to reestablish equilibrium. A series of elegies to Drake, including numerous poems indirectly retelling the tragedy, were valuable scribotherapy. But even these proved insufficient. Halleck was not really angry with Sarah, but rather at the culture that approved her love for Drake while condemning his. In the process of coping with his pain and frustration, Halleck retraced Drake's trip to Europe and took a fresh excursion of his own into politics.

Halleck had to deal with more than Drake's death and American law. His professional life also began to fall apart, so he redirected his emotional energy into verse that defended his business circle. Eighteen months after Drake died, Barker's business began to decline through a series of legal entanglements. The trials compounded Halleck's depression and augmented his contempt for America's judicial system. According to Halleck, "not a cool word" had passed between Barker and himself during their twenty years together.[2] By 1821, though, Halleck's concentration for bookkeeping was slipping away and he knew it. In early April 1822, he wrote Maria that "the complaint in my head" had satisfactorily been treated by "bleeding and hot water." His chronic earache or debilitating migraine was accompanied by psychological disease. He explained the delay in shipping his sister a trunk full of new books: "I am so low-spirited when the 'dark hour' is on me, that I can attend to nothing." The May letter that followed also carried bad news. An "intimate friend" had drowned.[3] The victim, Mr. Delpha, died when a steamer from New Haven sank. Delpha does not appear to have had particularly close ties with Halleck; however, the accident naturally aroused Halleck's tremendous sensitivity to death. Peace still eluded him a full year after Drake's death. Even Wyoming had not proved far enough away from his predicament.

From New York City to the western prairies, America did not seem to offer Halleck any space where he could grieve freely, so he left America as he had once fled his hometown and traveled the course of Drake's honeymoon trip. The literal and figurative journey paid off handsomely and provided emotional compensation for the European tour that Halleck probably would have made with Drake if Sarah Eckford had not taken his place. Halleck was also running away from the feminine snares then set for him.

Halleck bragged of having letters of introduction to Byron, Campbell, Moore, Scott, Southey, Wordsworth, and Irving (in England at the time) as well as to Lafayette and Talleyrand. Among others, J. Fenimore Cooper and Dr. David Hosack, whom Drake had lampooned, had provided the introductions. Halleck did not actually meet any of these men, though Byron and Campbell were his literary heroes. He told Maria, "It did not comport with my plans" to socialize and he had gone "to see things, not men." He "diffidently withdrew" from meeting Coleridge, and Samuel Rogers wrote to Irving that he was perplexed that Halleck did not visit him, chastising, "He must not content himself with looking on the outside of my house, as I am told he did once—but knock and ring, and ask for me as an old acquaintance."[4] But Halleck's agenda remained intensely personal and he behaved accordingly.

Just months before Halleck's trip, his "Critics of England" appeared in the *Quarterly Review* (April 1822). The poem shouts, "Growl, critics of England, growl on, ye hired hounds / Of a pitiful court! At America's name," and claims that American children are reared on "hatred for England" so that "traitor-bones" do not develop.[5] Despite the insults hurled at it, England housed many admirers of *Fanny,* but Halleck shied away from the British public just as he abstained from private visits. The recollection that Halleck was accompanied to Europe by Mr. Barker's eldest son is either completely inaccurate or else the two men parted immediately once overseas.[6]

Halleck's despondence upon leaving America was conveyed symbolically by a make-shift will he had entrusted to a friend, William Davis, "in case any accident should happen to prevent my return." Halleck also told Maria that he had left pictures and books with DeKay, "which he will send to you in the event of such a state of things. I expect to return in December, but persons must die in Europe as in America."[7] The creation of a will and a gift package for Maria could have been performed without her knowledge, for these fatal considerations only raised concern about a brother who had confided his suicidal thoughts during Drake's European tour four years earlier.

Halleck departed on July 1, 1822, and did not return for six months. His travel correspondence and notes have been lost. He did tour Ireland and Wales, where he stumbled upon his "Yankee Ravings," previously titled "Critics of England," in a newspaper. He dined with famed publisher William Blackwood in Scotland and saw Charles Lamb's desk in England, but he did not meet the man. Otherwise, he entertained himself by frequenting the theater and attending funerals. After a London funeral, he attended one in France, the "most hospitable country." Halleck declared, "The gay lilied fields of France" had ruined his opinion of America's climate.[8] His return trip was hampered by stormy seas and resulted in the complete loss of hearing in his left ear. Some had thought the ship was lost at sea. For Halleck, however, the new travel adventure, which he now held in common with Drake, proved cathartic.

Back in the United States in time for the summer of 1823, Halleck renewed old friendships and, consequently, found himself at more weddings. Early in 1824, he wrote Maria after attending a Mademoiselle Estelle's nuptials that he "seemed fated to be present at all weddings except my own." The astute and introspective comment grew more prophetic with the passage of time. By April 1824, he was bound for Philadelphia as a groomsman for Barker's brother-in-law, Samuel Hazard, and assisted "as the French say, in marrying him." Halleck would have undoubtably agreed with the French connotation of the groom as a passive object. Halleck's corresponding bridesmaid was Agnes Hamilton, whose income he estimated at about one and a half million, adding, "There's a target for a bachelor to aim at."[9] He never took a shot.

Halleck knew he would always be a groomsman and never a groom and grew more engaged in his art. He joined the Bread and Cheese Club (ca. 1824–1830), which originated in J. Fenimore Cooper's room at the back of a New York bookstore. The club approved new members with bread and voted against admittance with a bit of cheese. Cooper expressed some empathy for same-sex desire in his "To a Friend." An exceptional piece in Cooper's canon, "To a Friend"[10] praises a male's tender voice, wavy hair, and eyes "like deep pools scattering fire." "Thy charms in their diversity" so frighten and astonish the narrator that he dare not look upon the other "in their mood, / For fear of my desire, / Lest thou that secret do descry / Which evermore I must deny." This unrequited love leaves the speaker "hard, hard" for "hard is the world that does not give

/ To every love a place" as he chooses to protect his reputation and his soul. About the time that Cooper's club was forming, Halleck also met Bryant, whom New York City's mayor regarded as the inferior poet.[11] The *Literary Gazette* (July 25, 1829) called Bryant and Halleck the nation's best poets, and the two poets were ranked as "quite equal" as late as 1957.[12]

As a poet, Halleck was more confident than ever, for Europe had polished his writing. His new poems were intended for publication and shifted to public issues. While dating Halleck's poems remains problematic, at least three minor poems were written about this time. Halleck's close friend, Charles P. Clinch, had requested several song lyrics for his drama, *The Spy*, based on Cooper's novel. The lyrics were for the part of Frances and were sung at the Park Theater between March and November 1822 and at the Chatham Theater in June 1826. Not surprisingly, Halleck also produced two poetic translations following his European tour, one French and the other Italian.

The first major poem rooted in the trip was "Alnwick Castle." "Alnwick Castle" was probably written in October 1822 but was published over a year later in the *New York Evening Post* (December 6, 1823). It was translated into French in 1858–1859, during Halleck's retirement. It was signed C., for Croaker, in staunch loyalty to Drake. In the poem, feudal lore is replaced by modern laws and an intrusive government that reduces Highlanders from mythic proportions to lowly creatures who have "consented to be taxed, and vote, / And put on pantaloons." Social progress makes strange bedfellows; the Turk is "England's friend" and "Christendom looks tamely on" as "the Moslem tramples on the Greek."[13] Apparently, an English theme gave Halleck "the freedom as a poet which he never achieved on American ground."[14]

"Burns," the second major poem inspired by the trip, recorded Halleck's pilgrimage to the Scotsman's birthplace. Halleck visited Burns's cottage on October 10, 1822. A copy of Halleck's ode to the poet would eventually hang in the main room there. The poem is dated April 1823, but it was said to have been published anonymously in England and Scotland prior to Halleck's return. In America, it first appeared as a preview of the collected poems in Bryant's *United States Review*, an outgrowth of Robert C. Sands's *Atlantic Magazine*, in early 1827. Subsequently, it appeared in the *New York American* on January 11, 1827; the *New York Evening Post* four days later; and the *New York Mirror* five days after that. The poem's dialect is reminiscent of the poems Drake had written to Halleck while in Scotland. Burns's grave is fused with Drake's own turf as the speaker identifies with a dried rose: "My sunny hour was glad and brief . . . [but doom] withered my life's leaf like thine." As in the elegy to Drake, a green wreath binds Burns's hair and he is lauded for his "language of the heart." His words penetrate "where mourners weep, where lovers woo." Among "Meccas of the mind" in the world, Burns's shrine is a monument to liberal thought, "to no code or creed confined." "Burns" espouses Halleck's own political agenda and ends with disdain for grave sculptors' "funeral columns, wreaths and urns" because real loss can only be "graven on the heart."[15] Ironically, death acts as the physician in the Drake-like elegy.

"Burns" joined two other elegies of 1823 that also incorporated Halleck's obsession with death. The second elegy was for a friend, William Allen, who had been killed while Halleck was overseas. Allen was born on the same day and year as Halleck, for which reason his death may have jolted Halleck into remembering his own mortality along with Drake's demise. "Lines on the Death of Lieut. William Howard Allen of the American Navy" was the first poem written upon Halleck's return. Allen's Hudson monument is inscribed with lines from the poem, which first appeared in the *New York Evening Post* for March 4, 1823. Allen had been a witness during Barker's lawsuit and Henry Eckford raised money for the celebrated officer's surviving family. The poem on Allen portrayed the naval officer as a martyr who had been shot fighting pirates off Cuba. Defending the homeland of Carlos Menie may have added sentimental weight to Allen's mission in Halleck's heart, but as if the heroic death were not romantic enough, Allen's mother literally died of grief within a few hours following the report of her son's death.[16] Along with Drake, Allen dropped prematurely, "like summer fruit from off the bough." Halleck and his speaker are readily confused. The survivor's "grief-worn cheek" mirrored Halleck's face, "when all we love is in the tomb."[17]

A third elegy was for the Greek warrior Marco Bozzaris, who died August 20, 1823. Anecdotal materials suggest that "Marco Bozzaris" was composed two years after its subject's death. It was published in the first edition of Bryant's *United States Review* in 1825 and was reprinted in the *American* (June 7, 1825), the *New York Observer* (a month later), and numerous periodicals ever since. The *American* did not find it necessary to name the author because "within that circle *none* dare walk but he [Halleck]."[18] Halleck's renewed fame came effortlessly on the heels of his European tour.

Halleck had responded to a request for a poem by dashing off the lines for "Marco Bozzaris" and handing them to Dan Embury, his good friend and coworker, with the words, "Will this do?"[19] The *Foreign Quarterly Review* called the poem Halleck's masterpiece.[20] "Marco Bozzaris" made Halleck the "favorite poet of America" and became a "favorite school recitation."[21] Richard H. Dana thought "Marco Bozzaris" America's best lyric poem,[22] and the lines from the poem that introduce chapter 33 of the *Last of the Mohicans* (1826) shows Cooper's high regard for it. Halleck was meticulous about good manners, yet he veered clear of Cooper and never responded to the compliment.

Cooper's novel was overall rather homophobic, though. Its first chapter warns about colonists "who should have remembered their manhood, [but became] the slaves of the basest of passions." Later in the novel, an old squaw threatens Uncas with berdache status by taunting him: "Your nation is a race of women. . . . The Huron girls shall make you petticoats, and we will find you a husband." The sexual threat is extended to entire tribes which "have forgotten their sex."[23]

Surprisingly, Maria did not learn of Halleck's most famous poem for several years. Halleck's March 1827 letter was an incredulous response to his sister's complaint of discovering "Marco Bozzaris" by chance: "I am somewhat surprised and quite amused [that you had not heard of] my *chef d'oeuvre,* the keystone of the arch of my renown." Halleck bragged that "Marco Bozzaris" was "puffed in a thousand (more or less) magazines and newspapers" in America, England, Scotland, and Ireland and had been translated in France and Greece. It was "spouted on the stage . . . in schools and colleges" and served preachers in the pulpit. At length, he regained his natural modesty: "Keep this letter to yourself; it contains more about myself and my verses than I have ever said or written before, and much more than they are worth." For all of the hyperbole, Halleck could not understand how Maria, "almost the only person living (for I have become accustomed to it) to whom the music of my fame can be delightful," could fail to know of the poem.[24] Halleck's parenthetical comment reminded his sibling—and himself—that he was adjusting to Drake's death.

"Marco Bozzaris" commemorates a Turkish-Greek battle in which Death, personified as male, comes to the Greek soldier as "to the bridal-chamber." As in the elegies to Drake, this visit suspends a heterosexual marriage and Bozzaris's real wife is not mentioned. Digressing to Drake's death scene as he had done in "The Discarded," Halleck bemoans Death's reign, not only in war but also "when the heart beats high and warm" in dance and drink. A frightening catalog demonstrates his expertise at death watching: "the tear, / The groan, the knell, the pall, the bier; / And all we know, or dream, or fear / Of agony, are thine." Death comes to Bozzaris as the "sky and stars to prisoned men," keeping Halleck's criminal metaphor intact.[25] The Greece of his imagination liberates men from the social obligations of marriage and war.

While there was a general surge of empathy for Greece throughout the new American republic, the topic of Greek emancipation more securely linked Halleck to Byron. In fact, Byron's military presence in Greece had inspired "Marco Bozzaris." George D. Canale noted, "Byron was torn from a career of dissipation by admiration of the 'new Leonidas,' and

Halleck made his [Bozzaris's] fame universal."[26] Hershel Parker observed that "Marco Bozzaris" was Byronic in both sentiment and subject matter, and Van Wyck Brooks claimed that "if Byron had never existed, [Halleck's "Marco Bozzaris"] could have represented Byronism."[27] Halleck took up Byron's agenda in order to collaborate as he had done with Drake. This literary act not only displayed Halleck's loyalty to the exiled Romantic but also proclaimed their common sexual allegiance. Halleck had already written "Magdalen" (1823), which included a note explaining that the verses were written "for a love-stricken young officer on his way to Greece. The reader will have the kindness to presume that he died there." Byron, always presumed love-struck, was also on his way to Greece in 1823. By early summer 1824, news of his death at Missolonghi (April 19) reached Halleck, who was "profoundly affected."[28]

In almost the only eyewitness account of his ever having wept, Halleck's old friend, Mrs. John Rush, saw that he was "quite overcome, and could not restrain his tears." As "a great admirer of the poet [Byron], if not of the man," Halleck "walked up and down the drawing-room wringing his hands, saying, with brief pauses between each remark: 'What a terrible loss to literature!'—and 'Byron dead, and I did not see him!'" For a moment, Halleck regretted his European solitude. Rush's account conveyed alarm. Her stoic friend was crying over a stranger. He paced, wrung his hands, stammered, and wailed that "poor Byron" could "be taken away at thirty-six!"[29] Halleck's poetry rarely aspired to the dramatic pitch of his real-life reaction to the loss of Byron.

Halleck's distress was exaggerated by a profound connection with the British poet turned sexual outlaw. Both men were survivors of younger men whom they could not satisfactorily eulogize despite multiple attempts. Byron's love for John Edlestone, who was born in the same year as Halleck but died at age twenty-one, was expressed and reexpressed in a poetic series that conveyed Byron's same-sex desire as well as his tragic loss. Halleck's love for Drake was not returned in kind, and similarly, in the last year of his life, Byron was rumored to have suffered unrequited love for his Greek page, Lukas Chalandrutsanos. Byron's attempt to personally nurse Chalandrutsanos for fear of the boy's death shortly before dying himself stands out as one of the few selfless acts of Byron's existence. Chalandrutsanos survived his benefactor, and a Greek commemorative statue depicts Byron "expiring in the arms of his Greek page."[30]

Halleck, shunned by Guilford and denied the rights of a widow, related to Byron's exile as well as his role as nurse. Both scoffed at matrimonial oaths: Byron by breaking them and Halleck by refusing to take them. Byron's marriage lasted less than one year before Byron's wife was granted divorce; she had hoped to "marry a poet and reform a rake" who turned out to be "a Caligula."[31] Halleck said that he had "lost on Byron's death a brother,"[32] and Drake, a love object also referred to by Halleck as a brother, was inseparably meshed with Byron, an icon of sexual and literary liberation.[33]

With the passing of Drake and Byron, Halleck began more ardently to condemn American values. Although Halleck's personal life was rather bland by comparison, his art was heavily spiced with Byronic influence. Halleck's "Mr. Clinton's Speech, January, 1825," is a burlesque on political gibberish that is criticized as viciously as were the bogus assurances satirized in the poem. The suave speaker, "a Sancho," fosters an illusion that "all is quiet as a Sunday," a line repeated from an earlier poem.[34] Halleck attacked his homeland's hypocrisy as vehemently as Byron had exposed Britain's moral pretense. In *Byron and Byronism in America*, William Ellery Leonard argues that Byron heavily influenced Halleck's poems, including *Fanny*, "Wyoming," "Marco Bozzaris," "Alnwick Castle," "Connecticut," and "Lines to the Recorder," which steals a joke from "The Vision of Judgement."

Halleck's "Connecticut" was itself a powerful American version of Byron's "The Vision of Judgement" (1822), which spawned further comparisons of the two poets. The poem's first half appeared in the *New York Review, Athenaeum Magazine*, the *New York Evening Post*, and the *New York Mirror*. The poem was also parodied in "Extract from an Unpublished Poem" published in *Richardsiana* in 1841. The first half of "Connecticut" appeared in 1826 when sodomitical convicts were being interviewed for the record.[35] Halleck, no longer a prisoner to his grief, launched a poetical campaign resisting American law and legislation.

Halleck's negative view of American justice as generally corrupt and historically cruel toward social outsiders was worsened by the persecution of his employer, who was accused of insurance fraud in the New York Conspiracy Trials of 1826. This notorious string of trials pitted the district attorney, Hugh Maxwell, against Jacob Barker, Henry Eckford, and other personal and professional associates of Halleck. The first trial was in September/October 1826 and resulted in a hung jury. The second trial was in November 1826; Barker was found guilty. A third trial in 1827 reached the same verdict. Consequently, Halleck's livelihood and loyalty became very public matters. His "Billingsgate McSwell" hotly defended his camp.

"Billingsgate McSwell" was circulated privately and not published until after Halleck's death. Hugh Maxwell was clearly Halleck's target. The poem's prosecutor has an impressive familiarity with laws because he has broken so many of them. Allowed to "slander, stain, insult," the public servant is "now attorney, bailiff, judge, / Informer, witness, spy." In Halleck's inverted justice system, the district attorney appointed to guard against corruption is in fact its source. He admits to killing his victims in

cold blood: "From bully to attorney the / Transition is not great." Hyperbole mocks the infallibility of the holy pope (McSwell/Maxwell) who has
reformed the Inquisition line and who, "like a worm," takes a "traitor
fee" and turns every grand juryman into his "slave." The sale price on
justice muddles the criminal and the legal. Personified by a woman "fair,
fat, and forty," Scandal fails to seduce McSwell, just as Fortune failed to
win Fanny's father with any of her feminine qualities. The Conspiracy
Trials stirred Halleck's political pessimism. Pondering the profession of a
mutual acquaintance, he quipped to Evert Duyckinck: "I am not sure that
he ever was a lawyer, and do not wish to give an innocent man a bad
name."[36] The legal profession was also attacked in Halleck's correspondence in which he joked that a friend had "lamented that [a mutual
friend] should have exchanged an *honorable* profession for that of a
lawyer!"[37]

"Lines to the Recorder" continued Halleck's assault on the United
States government through 1828. The poem is dated December 20, 1828,
and was published under the pseudonym Thomas Castaly in the *New
York Evening Post* (with a preface by Bryant) and in the *New York American*. Halleck requested both printings in a rare move of immodesty that
helped shift editorial sympathy in favor of Barker.[38] Over three hundred
lines long, "Lines to the Recorder" was an epistle to Richard Riker, the
New York City recorder who was scapegoated as a party leader for making "the citizen a slave" by imitating politicians like the satirical McSwell.
Foreshadowing Halleck's later irony that would reverse sex and morality,
the poem inverts the legal system and criminal character. Its narrator
emasculates Riker whose modest blushes are "like maidens on their
bridal days" and roasts Riker in bemused shades of gender confusion:

> True, "many a flower," the poet sings,
>   "Is born to blush unseen";
> But you [Riker], although you blush, are not
>   The flower the poets mean.

Riker rules "like Sancho," a master of "illegal right and legal wrong."
The simile echoes the poem satirizing Clinton, another Sancho, and the
oxymoron jumbles law and crime, as had Halleck's previous attacks on
the American democratic system.

Hope is placed with "younger brothers in the art" before Halleck
makes fun of himself:

> And Halleck—who has made thy roof
> St. Tammany! oblivion-proof—
> Thy beer illustrious, and thee
> A belted knight of chivalry!

The lines played on Halleck's image as a bachelor given to drink. In 1826, Isaac Starr Clason, a New York actor who wrote *Horace in New York,* had cried "Halleck—Halleck, come forth!" to pour out verse against the competition that was considered "thin small beer!"[39] But now Halleck recognized his own growing reputation for drink and also made a pun about his presumed virginity at age thirty-eight: he is the belted knight, therefore chaste. As in multiple allusions to Drake in Halleck's general poetry, "Lines to the Recorder" communicates its lonely speaker's fear that few are left to shed "sorrow's holier tears, [that] will keep / The grass green where in death I sleep."

Despite his losses of Drake and Byron and his mounting legal concerns, Halleck wrote Maria that he had been stricken by what he called "occasional attacks of giddiness" by the end of May 1827. However, as Bryant noted in an 1827 review, Halleck remained "reluctant in coming before the public. . . . as if he were actually afraid of an unfavorable reception." Since Halleck presented "the phenomenon of a writer, whose works are universally admired, and scrambled for as fast as they appear," Bryant was vexed.[40] *Alnwick Castle and Other Poems* was published anonymously in February 1827 but moved Halleck to the forefront of the Knickerbocker pack at that time. His May letter home communicated that the happy success of his first collection of poems was tempered by intrusions upon his "unsocial habits and love of solitude." He tabulated for his sister averages of a dozen invitations per week to balls and parties that did not start before 10:00 P.M. as a rule:

During the past winter I have been, to my own astonishment, quite a ladies' man, a particularly fashionable person. I scarcely know how I got into the whirlpool, but I did get in in the early part of the season, and find it impossible to get out until the season is over. My name is on the visiting-list of all our ultra-fashionables. . . . It is pleasant enough while one is there, but . . . hardly enough so to compensate for the trouble of dressing. I have become . . . quite *au fait* in the small-talk of society, and can say much about nothing at all as if I had been taught by a lady-patroness. . . . I shall, if not forgotten by next year, invent some excuse for declining all future civilities in this way. The last season has been really a carnival, in consequence of a number of weddings, some twenty or thirty.[41]

Halleck's desirability should not have surprised the handsome and witty poet who claimed he did not know how he ended up at parties not worth the effort of formal attire. To his dismay, Halleck had inherited Drake's earlier title as New York's most eligible man. Yet Halleck was not a groom in the circus atmosphere of weddings that he counted by the tens. He seemed oblivious to the fact that bachelorhood was deemed a social crisis in nineteenth-century American society. At any rate, he embarked on a poem intended to launch a second series of Croaker-like social commentaries in the summer of 1827 but soon found himself unable to produce the project without Drake.

Written to start a series of "letters from town," "An Epistle to * * * *" appeared as "No. 1" in the *New York Evening Post* (August 1, 1827). No others followed. It was republished in Halleck's 1839 collected works and George Lathrop reviewed it. The campy "No. 1" opens: "I am writing not to you but at you," and the narrator jokes, "I'm in town, but of that fact the least said the better," before beginning to gossip. He wonders if his friend is busy with "puns, poems, or love," "dancing on Sundays," or "with maidens who seek wedding-rings" before shifting to political insults. Daniel Webster thrives "under something they call the American System" and John Quincy Adams, DeWitt Clinton, Andrew Jackson, and Henry Clay are criticized in turn. Despite his continued assault on American heroes, Halleck's preeminence spread, but the artistic rebound felt empty without Drake.

Samuel Kettell's three-volume *Specimens of American Poetry* (1829) was a landmark anthology that exported Halleck's poetry in its British and French editions. In general, editors did not carefully distinguish British from American writers until the second half of the twentieth century. *Selections from the British Poets (Chaucer–Present)* (1851) was typical in including poems by Bryant and Longfellow; likewise, Halleck's works were included in Quiller-Couch's *Victorian Verse* (1925).

Because of Halleck's high public profile, New Yorkers kept a keen eye out for the man behind the poetry. In February 1828, the first significant sketch of Halleck appeared in the *New York Mirror*. His portrait by Samuel F. B. Morse, which hangs today in the New York Public Library, and his honorary membership in Yale's Phi Beta Kappa were among the honors that swiftly followed. Halleck responded by shaping more public topics into verse. In 1828 Halleck wrote "Forget Me Not—Imitated from the German" for the *Atlantic Souvenir,* "Red Jacket" for the *Talisman,* and "The Field of the Grounded Arms" for Nathaniel Willis's second edition of the *Legendary* gift book. Halleck's peak of social and literary acceptance temporarily relaxed his personal guard and allowed him to experiment. "The Field of the Grounded Arms" shocked critics with its new and innovative form—a form that suggested what would later be termed free verse.

While Halleck's poem is not technically free verse, it certainly caught poetic analysts unaware in its generally radical form. The poem broke from conventional stanza meter and end rhyme and showed irrational grammatical transitions between lines. Halleck's return from Europe immediately before "The Field of the Grounded Arms" raises suspicion that he may have been exposed to experimental French and English free verse taking root there at the time. The important fact is that Halleck's contemporaries considered this work a new "species" of writing "whose constituents it would be difficult indeed to explain or trace home" even a decade after its appearance.[42] Halleck appeared consciously pleased with the new poem; it was one of few poems originally published with his real or full name.

Newspapers, however, were up in arms over "The Field of the Grounded Arms." The *Emerald and Baltimore Literary Gazette* found the form prosaic or scriptural rather than poetic but saw "a poetic gem" in each line and "an ideal which can never be equalled, while at the same time [Halleck's] production astonishes the world."[43] The *American Quarterly Review*'s esteem for the spirit of the poem was undermined by its independence from "any of the poetry, of music around or within it."[44] Poe found the poem disagreeable in the April 1836 *Southern Literary Messenger,* but James Lawson's review in the same publication deemed its "language felicitous" six years later in April 1842. Adkins's claim that William Collins or Andrew Marvell may have inspired the modified Horatian stanzas lacks any evidence and does not explain the critical diversity over "The Field of the Grounded Arms" that Adkins himself demonstrates raged for years.[45] Wilson also shows that wildly diverse opinions greeted the irregular poem. It would seem Halleck was in a field of his own.

Comparing its form to a broken vessel, William Leggett "should never have suspected it of being a poem" and complained that the "want of form" resulted in only an uncontrolled, prose-like outpouring of Halleck's ideas.[46] The intentional disregard for conventional meter affronted most American readers. But Charles P. Clinch's letter lavishly congratulated Halleck on his unique "rhapsody" as "the finest poem of the age" and added that "The Field of the Grounded Arms" was:

the most finished poetry in the world . . . [and] shall be my text-book. There is not a line of it but what is an illustration of the spirit of poesy . . . the entire piece is, in my estimation, perfect.[47]

Such an enthusiastic reception was atypical even by mid-century, when Thomas Powell's *Living Writers of America* (1850) remained "agreeably surprised" by the controversial "Field of the Grounded Arms." Bryant, however, twice concluded that the poem provided an exception to Halleck's universal popularity because of its "peculiar measure" and because of "the peculiar kind of verse in which it is written."[48]

The poem's final lines, which alluded to Halleck's sexual philosophy by comparing American heroes to "the Greeks of old," were dropped in Bryant's *New York Evening Post* (December 16, 1828), prompting Clinch's remark: "He is as bad as Leggett, who objected to its want of rhyme!"[49]

The *New York Mirror*'s reprint on December 20, 1828, included the last stanza, but the *New York American* of January 5, 1829, did not. Halleck himself dropped the final stanza in his 1836 collection.

Halleck's attempt to pump new air into the wheezing exercise that American verse had become was related to his social displacement. He was not at peace with American letters because he was not at home in America. The Croakers and *Fanny* had resisted the solemn content of earlier national poetry, but breaking conventions of form presented a larger challenge. Running parallel to a sexual revolt that would claim new uses for the male body, "The Field of the Grounded Arms" demonstrated that a poem's body could be adored in previously inconceivable ways. For Halleck, the worst feature of his new poem was that it had brought him unwanted attention.

Critical fallout brought on by the poem and the 1829 death of Israel Hallock caused Halleck to refocus on business. The tumultuous reception of "The Field of the Grounded Arms" led to a self-imposed hiatus. Readers clamored for more poetry but little came. Bryant urged Halleck to write more as soon as *Alnwick Castle and Other Poems* was out and did so again in 1836. Cooper pondered Halleck's silence in a letter from Florence in 1829 while the *New York Evening Post* broadcast a petition to Fitz-Greene Halleck, Esq., on September 11, 1829, and the *Morning Courier and New York Enquirer* asked, "What is Halleck about? . . . no echo has replied" (December 13, 1830). *Truth* (1831) tried poetry and patriotism to evoke Halleck: "Wilt thou be silent? Wake, O Halleck, wake! / Thine and thy country's honor are at stake!"[50] For seven years, the *New York Mirror* claimed that Halleck's muse was held prisoner in the "unhallowed office of a broker" (March 31, 1827), subject to a preference for "his cash accounts" (May 24, 1834). Halleck finally spit something out.

The 1830 Croaker "Epistle to Robert Hogbin" was anonymously signed "A Working Man" and lampooned a labor union in the *New York Evening Post* (November 16, 1830). The *Post* published Hogbin's rebuttal, "Reply of Robert Hogbin, workingman, to Rhyme Weaver," on November 23, 1830. It warned, "the march of mind progresses" with no care for conservative values, echoing Blake's political poetry. The "Epistle to Robert Hogbin" was Halleck's last Croaker and boasted, "We workingmen prophets" have "broken the chains of laws, churches, and marriages."[51] Indeed, by May 1829 Halleck simply refused to attend one more wedding, even that of an old friend.

On May 21, 1829, Halleck sent humorous regrets to George Foote, who was taking a spring bride, in defense of "'Us Old Batchelors,' as the envious nickname us."[52] While Halleck declined almost every social obligation, he did continue to pursue civil issues, urging Congressman

Henry Inman's 1828 oil on canvas, felt by many to be the best likeness of Fitz-Greene Halleck, commissioned by editor George Pope Morris of the *New York Mirror.* (Collection of the New-York Historical Society.) The New-York Historical Society also has Inman's pencil drawing and profile of Halleck and an oil on wood of Halleck (ca. 1825). Inman also painted portraits of Drake's wife and daughter. Albert Newsam's lithograph of Halleck (ca. 1831) was closely based on the Inman portrait and is currently housed in the Smithsonian Institution's National Portrait Gallery.

Gulian C. Verplank to strengthen the copyright law. Verplank helped pass the 1831 bill that doubled the copyright term from fourteen to twenty-eight years. The congressman quoted Halleck's "Marco Bozzaris" and "Burns" on April 28, 1831, during a speech at the dinner honoring Verplank's effort to protect authors. Verplank's prose provided what Halleck later termed "American specimens of English literature" that advanced the literary reputation of the United States abroad.[53] Halleck had reached a point at which he could exercise his own influence as author, critic, or politician.

Halleck retreated while his influence was at its pinnacle. Although he was first in a series of literary portraits in the *New England Magazine* (August 1831) and was engraved by Henry Inman in 1831, Halleck wanted to become invisible. His disappearance fostered rumors. George S. Hillard's literary portrait speculated that Halleck was about to edit a New York paper, but in early August 1831, Halleck lamented the impertinence of this announcement to Maria. The power of the press made him sick: "I can neither eat, drink, nor sleep, with any pleasure." He pursued an apology for the rumor, telling Maria that he was "exceedingly annoyed by the affair, particularly at this moment, when I do not wish to appear before the public."[54] A retraction ensued.

Halleck got three other wishes in 1832. Twelve years after his death, Drake's "To Fitz-Greene Halleck" was published in the *New York Mirror* on March 4. Drake's lines begged Halleck to sing America rather than romance. Then, two months later, Halleck ascended to his professional zenith as John Jacob Astor's private secretary. Halleck also took on that year the literary project of his dreams. Ironically undertaking the labor he found most odious—editorship—he was hired by George Dearborn to produce "*emphatically* the first complete edition" of Byron's works.[55]

The seven-hundred-page *Works of Lord Byron* was, in a word, thorough. It included abstracts, notes, imitations, observations, parliamentary speeches, translations, unpublished works, the will, and one chapter of a novel. Halleck readily identified with his subject and wrote a thirteen-page introduction, "The Life of Lord Byron." Halleck blamed Byron's twisted love life on rejection by his wealthy older cousin, Mary Anne Chaworthan, whose scorn for the school-aged Byron had the "fate and consequences" of inducing permanent moral dysfunction. Halleck's conclusion that "allusions to the subject as one of painful and of powerful interest, are to be found in almost every page of [Byron's] works" aptly described the psychological presence of Drake in Halleck's own verse.[56] Besides reinforcing his scorn for rich girls, Halleck's view of Byron at fifteen perhaps also drew on his own memory of rejection by Carlos Menie.

Halleck and Byron shared other interests and qualities as well. Byron found acceptance in the Merry Monks who reflected his own youth-fulness and inclinations. The Merry Monks had a homoerotic quality in common with Halleck's own fraternity, the Ugly Club. Byron's Monks were outfitted with crosses, beads, and tonsures. Perhaps alluding to the stereotyping of monks as homosexual, one member said the performance of religious drag "often gave a variety to our appearance and to our pur-suits!" Halleck noted the personal attack on Byron's dual nature of "fun" and "gravity," yet Halleck's own "rapid transitions from gay to grave" had also drawn criticism.[57] Each poet had also faced three premature deaths. Suicide, illness, and accident took Franklin, Drake, and Delpha from Hal-leck. Byron grieved for Matthews, "a young man of extraordinary prom-ise"; Wingfield, "one of his Harrow favourites"; and "Eggleston," his "protege at Cambridge, of whom he was romantically fond."[58] Like Hal-leck's poems for Drake, Byron wrote a series of elegiac Thyrza poems to John Edlestone who died so tragically young. A sexual component sets apart Halleck's depiction of the "romance" with Edlestone. Byron com-pared the passionate love between himself and the younger man to that of Jonathan and David, and Halleck's childhood poems on the biblical pair show just how far back his philosophical connection with Byron went.

Byron's one-year marriage failed to reform him and Halleck stressed the bride's wealth as Byron's motivation to wed. Recalling his own feelings as Drake's groomsman, Halleck imagines, "The disastrous result of the marriage appears to have been anticipated by [Byron] even at the bridal altar." Halleck is defensive concerning the obscurity of reasons for Byron's separation: "Exaggerated statements of [Byron's] private conduct, and dark hints and vague insinuations of the most criminal profligacy, were circulated and believed." Minimizing Byron's sexual escapades, Halleck places Byron's sexual indiscretions in the context of the criminal but ar-gues that his affair with Countess Guiccioli prevented less noble entangle-ments: "The liaison, however reprehensible, had the good effect of wean-ing him from still more disreputable attachments."[59] Historians still argue whether those attachments were to male or female prostitutes, though they were most likely to both.

Byron's half-sister destroyed Byron's memoirs even though he had hoped that Thomas Moore would publish his "Life and Adventures," but Halleck included some of the materials that Byron's sibling, Moore, and John Murray found too distasteful to publish. Byron's recollection of greeting male friends with kisses and of painted Turkish boys ("the preti-est little animals I ever saw") are faithfully preserved. Halleck includes Byron's enthusiasm for Turkish pederasty but omits the actual word "sod-omy" from one of Byron's letters: "Was [Perry] ever in a Turkish bath—that marble paradise of sherbet and * * [sodomy]?" Byron's familiarity with homosexual allusion is evidenced by letters to Murray on nude wrestling and by his observation that historical and literary men often had emotional propensities "natural in an effeminate character."[60]

Halleck produced the most honest version of Byron to that date, but in doing so he committed the very crime of intrusion that he abhorred in the press. On the other hand, he also seized the opportunity to oppose censorship. Halleck frowns on Murray's suppression of *Don Juan's* dedication to Southey and boasts that his edition sheds light on Byron's "suppressed memoirs" of his mother and marriage. He released "repressed" poems and exposed Byron's attempts to edit himself. "English Bards and Scotch Reviewers" was "suppressed" and unsold editions were recalled and destroyed as was "Hints from Horace," which Byron wanted withheld until his death. Byron tried to "suppress" the poorly received "Waltzing" and denied other poems in an effort to perpetuate the myth of his own genius. Eventually, he tried "suppressing every line he had written," including "Childe Harold" and the hugely popular "Corsair."[61] Feeling oppressed by their societies, Halleck and Byron both exhibit a striking tension between self-expression and self-repression. Ironically, Halleck freed Byron's repressed sexual poems even as he repressed his own name as Byron's editor. The second edition of *Byron* (1836) finally revealed Halleck as its editor. Illustrating Byron's range of erotica, Halleck included the Thyrza series, "To Romance," and "The Deformed Transformed." "The Cornelian," previously printed privately in *Fugitive Pieces and Poems on Various Occasions,* was for Edlestone, as was "Pignus Amoris," which was not published until 1898. Halleck would be seduced into editorship once again in 1840, when Harper Brothers published his *Selections from the British Poets* in two volumes. As the saying about marriage goes: the first time was for love, the second for money.

While he was working on his *Works of Lord Byron,* Halleck also entered his second career. Perhaps due to his literary reputation, he was hired by Astor as "a sort of secretary and companion" after Barker's ruin.[62] Astor, the wealthiest man in the country, had made a fortune in fur trading, opium dealing, real estate, and war-time loans to the United States government. When a Parisian paper mistook Halleck's occupation as *"une riche banquier"* in 1835, he told Maria the French had confused the groom for his master.[63] Halleck was a great favorite of the millionaire who "invited the poet to reside with him and take charge of his affairs."[64] Halleck entered the service of New York's leading aristocrat on May 15, 1832. Contemporary readers still believed that poetry and poverty were connected, and literary critics considered the two men strange bedfellows, prompting the *Foreign Quarterly Review* to remark: "[Halleck,] strange to say, is superintendent of the affairs of Mr. Astor."[65] But the millionaire's confidence in the poet was absolute. A letter from Halleck to Maria in

May, when Astor left for Europe, expressed surprise at being trusted with management so suddenly.

By the late 1820s, Irving, James Paulding, and Halleck had become "New York's leading authors" who "commanded national audiences." [66] An 1830 review of Catherine Sedgwick's *Clarence* in *Colburn's New Monthly Magazine* noted Halleck's escalating fame, as did London's *Monthly Magazine* in 1831. *Athenaeum* featured Halleck early in 1835 and 1836 while *Revue des deux mondes* noted Halleck in 1835. London anthologies including works by Halleck appeared in 1830 (*The Laurel, The Lyre*), 1833 (*Readings in Poetry, Poetry of the Affections*), and 1836 (*Gems from American Poets*). The local demand for Halleck was also great.

Astor had left Halleck holding all the cards: "I accepted a proposition made me by John Jacob Astor, to take a charge in his business. . . . This will probably, if I wish it, be a permanent arrangement, and, possibly, a profitable one." The work relationship also had social benefits. At Astor's home in 1833, Halleck met Irving, who commented enviously on Halleck's "handsome salary" and living quarters. Halleck remained a live-in guest for many years, both in Astor's winter townhouse and at Hell's Gate, which Irving described in 1835 as "a kind of bachelor's hall. Halleck, the poet, lives with [Astor]." [67]

A year into the new job, Halleck wrote Maria that he had abandoned society two years previous. Even Halleck's relationship with the theater was suspended. Francis (Fanny) Anne Kemble, who was probably the most famous actress in America, had become a close friend of Halleck as had Charles Mathews, the English comedian. But of Kemble's soiree and one other party, Halleck wrote, both "were so pressed upon me that it was less painful to say 'yes' than 'no,' I have not mingled with the 'gay world' for more than two years in a single instance. I hope to be able to be more social some day or other, though I know not on what the hope is founded." [68] Henry Tuckerman, who often met Halleck at a French café, saw that his friend had "cut loose from general society," which in return had begun to exclude him as the favorite of mothers who had once hoped to land Halleck for themselves and later tried to marry him to their daughters.

Halleck's growing isolation was clear to strangers as well as friends. Richard E. Mount recalled that Halleck feared being "'called out'—for of this American propensity he had a horror." [69] Bryant's 1836 letter noted, Halleck "has forsworn society altogether," and the *Knickerbocker's* January 1836 review of *Alnwick Castle and Other Poems* asked: "What right has [Halleck] to establish the light which God has so copiously given him, under a bushel? How can he answer to his conscience for concealing it from the world?" The *Knickerbocker's* biblical metaphor continued: "He crucifies all the unwritten creations of his splendid imagination" that were sacrificed for business. Indeed, Halleck's poetry reflected an "undercurrent of loneliness" as he withdrew from public life, and "popular applause alarmed more than it could encourage him."[70] He was reprimanded for his "selfish" choice: "He has no right to stifle the stirrings of the power within his soul."[71] But solicitations for poems on local and national events were promptly refused—even one for a theatrical benefit, Halleck's favorite cause. Only a few poems and Italian translations (dated January 1834) were produced during his sixteen years with Astor.

Among the translations were poems by Piero Maroncelli that were written in an Austrian prison (ca. 1822–1830), where he and his companion, Silvio Pellico, were incarcerated. The Italian poets provided a rare parallel to Halleck and Drake. As a free man, Maroncelli complimented Halleck's translation. The crime motif in Maroncelli and Pellico's story was irresistible for Halleck, who was still bound by the grief that he had experienced fifteen years earlier. The nature of his love and the social confines arresting it had not budged.

At age forty-five, Halleck still could not bring himself to edit Drake's collected poetry. Although not especially qualified to organize Byron's works, Halleck was undeniably the only person who could accurately arrange Drake's poetry, published for the first time in 1835. Halleck's publisher, George Dearborn, could not induce him, and so Dearborn coordinated a new edition of Halleck including Drake's works. Except for three poems already published in annuals and periodicals, *Alnwick Castle and Other Poems* was essentially a reprint of the 1827 edition. Favorable reviews were redundant, including Bryant's "Writings of Fitz-Greene Halleck" in the *New York Mirror,* September 24, 1836, and Poe's article "Drake-Halleck," in the *Southern Literary Messenger* of April 1836. Willis Gaylord Clark reviewed the edition for the *Knickerbocker,* which his brother edited, and gushed over Halleck's "beautiful volume of most beautiful poetry," proposing, "Should I beget children, it shall descend to them." Clark declared that "such poetry would thrill an oyster, if the march of mind had penetrated the dominions of conchology," and confided:

Your work will be handsomely reviewed in the next number of the *American Quarterly,* and the part relating particularly to you will be from my pen, . . . I tell you this as a profound secret, to be repeated to no one,—since you are the only person to whom I shall mention the matter. I shall send you the number as soon as it is published . . . I do not mention this as likely to please you . . . whose name has been great so long in mouths of wisest censure. The elegance of your volume is striking and, for America, unique.

The excess of this praise is only tempered by Clark's harsh appraisal of "The Field of the Grounded Arms," which he liked less than any other piece: "but you will forgive me, if I think even harmony would have im-

John G. Taggart's 1854 oil on canvas of Fitz-Greene Halleck. Based on Charles Loring Elliott's 1847 portrait, this portrait shows the poet about the time of Astor's death. (Collection of the New-York Historical Society.)

proved it."[72] Even such a devotee as Clark was not blind to the gross variation that "The Field of the Grounded Arms" introduced into Halleck's collective work, as well as into American poetry itself.

Similarly, Halleck's bachelorhood was disturbing some of his closest allies. The absence of women in Halleck's life and poetry was conspicuous. The few lines to women at this juncture of his career revered motherhood or ridiculed divas. "Woman" praises the maternal instinct and its narrator takes the female perspective asking: "What is man's love? His vows are broke, / Even while his parting kiss is warm."[73] Bryant felt that "Woman" exceeded "those commonplace and empty compliments to the female sex" in more romantic poetry, and he later stressed the poem's domestic associations.[74] "A Poet's Daughter, Written for Miss * * *" was first published in the *New York Mirror* (1831) and was the result of a commission by poet Samuel Woodworth who wanted some lines written for his single daughter, Harriet.[75] Although "A Poet's Daughter" was not for Janet Halleck Drake, it recalled the old pang for her father.

Halleck writes for a young girl but drifts into familiar emotional territory:

> Youth's coffin—hush the tale it tells!
> Be silent, memory's funeral bells!
> Lone in one heart, her home, it dwells
> Untold till death,
> And where the grave-mound greenly swells
> O'er buried faith.[76]

"Silent," "lone," "untold" grief over a premature death pervades a poem that is supposed to be about a living girl. In the poem's central simile, an aged mourner stands "like the oak storm-tried." "A Poet's Daughter" repeats the metaphors in other poems about Drake's green turf by including a tested tree and rainbows. "To Mr. Halleck" was an anonymous poem written as a response to "A Poet's Daughter." It accused Halleck of loving money more than "the gay wand'rings of thy muse" and scolds: "Shame on thee, though each passing day / I love thee closer."[77] Halleck's platonic praise for a female apparently did not satisfy some of his readers.

The proverbial sexual challenge, Halleck's homosexuality tantalized both critics and women who actively tried to entice him. As a young man, he "exercised a singular and irresistible fascination" over "superior women" who "worshipped" him.[78] One such female admirer from Guilford had flowers sent to his New York residence upon his arrival in 1811. Halleck's "The Wild-Flower Wreath" thanked the young lady and was published by Wilson in the *Independent* on February 29, 1872. Even mature women took the "position of wooer" in one-sided flirtations with Halleck.[79] When Halleck was not poking fun at enamored women, they were humiliating themselves. One socialite declared: "If I were on my way to church to be married, yes, even if I were walking up the aisle, and Halleck were to offer himself, I'd leave the man I had promised to marry, and take him!"[80] Halleck was duly flattered and penned the following epigram for another young lady who sought out his autograph through Mrs. John Rush:

> There wanted but this drop to fill
> The wifeless poet's cup of fame.
> Hurrah! there lives a lady still,
> Willing to take his name.[81]

She may have been willing, but the poet slips away.

As in 1821, Halleck's only poem of 1832 was a February Valentine, "Lines to Her Who Can Understand Them." It was for Miss Lummis (later Mrs. E. F. Ellet) who had anonymously sought his autograph while visiting New York. The poem calls women "still my worshipped being, / In mind and heart," but not in body.[82] Instead, he pays "the platonic compliment,"[83] hoping Lummis will find someone to love but repeatedly asserting that it must not be Halleck. His sexual orientation had not changed, but the media had. The topic of sexuality "began to pour from the American presses in the 1830s and 1840s,"[84] and "about 1830 an intellectual paralysis seemed to fall upon Halleck."[85] The exposé in 1836 of New York's Man Monster, a black brothel dweller who regularly cross-dressed as a woman and the *Herald*'s exposure of buggery a decade later provide a glimpse into homosexual New York during this era.[86] More frequently, articles and tracts warned against any sexual activity. During the early 1830s, Sylvester Graham's popular writings and lectures urged sexual abstinence for young men and preached the dire and public consequences of masturbation, setting off a flood of similar publications. Halleck reacted sharply when his bachelorhood was questioned; it was gradually becoming a signifier of homosexual desire.

James Lawson was the first to question Halleck's sexuality. Halleck had returned a book Lawson loaned him with a reprimand on December 1, 1831. The letter turned sour regarding the toast Lawson had made at the St. Andrew dinner when he equated a very minor poet with Thomas Campbell. Halleck asked what had gotten into Lawson, suggesting perhaps bad liquor, and rebuked him: "You have a very good memory badly employed."[87] Lawson deflected his anger in an 1842 review. Having no term for Halleck's lack of desire to marry, Lawson wrote: "There is something like isolation in his heart; and strange to say, it is without morbidity."

Halleck had "indeed heard the voice of praise, certainly longer, and perhaps louder, than any other living poet of America—and yet we have never met with a critical analysis of his works," complained Lawson. But Lawson's analysis was more Freudian than poetic. Halleck's odd peace with bachelorhood, he speculated, was derived from an unhealthy mental state evident in his verse.[88] "The ambiguity of the phrase," "the incongruity of images," and the "anti-climax order" of his poetry were all irregular. He had no family, but fathered "unnatural similes" and "unnatural transition," and "his alliteration and antithesis, if effective, are unnatural."[89] Lawson's choice of adjective turned his critique from the poetry to the poet. Halleck was being outed.

William Leggett's 1828 review had foreshadowed Lawson's implication that Halleck's form was symptomatic of a personal breach with nature. Leggett felt that Halleck's art was not entitled to the title poetry without rhyme and found form—"as in human nature"—essential for a healthy creature. Arguing that blank verse might have redeemed "The Field of the Grounded Arms," Willis Clark added insult to injury in 1837 by calling the poem "a truly amphibious and hermaphrodite composition" in his review of Halleck's poems. But Lawson's piece in the *Southern Literary Messenger* represented a more personal attack on Halleck, who was dismayed when it resurfaced like an emotional sea monster more than a year later in the *New World* (November 1843).

On the heels of Lawson's review, the *Broadway Journal*'s "Attack on Alnwick Castle" assaulted Halleck with its homophobic commentary. Poe was credited with the article, but he denied anything to do with what he deemed a "very malevolent and flippant attack" on Halleck. Poe argued that he had consistently shown high regard for Halleck's work in two biographical sketches and numerous reviews. Still, Poe "endured the loss of Halleck's good will" until Halleck discovered that it had been written by James Russell Lowell "at the malicious instigation" of Halleck's former associate, Mr. Briggs.[90] "Attack on Alnwick Castle" is, in fact, included among Lowell's works in Herbert Smith's edition of his literary criticism. Editor Charles F. Briggs charged Lowell, "Please abuse [Halleck's poems] to your hearts contents."[91]

The May 1845 "Attack on Alnwick Castle" charged that Halleck had received much more praise than he merited and emphasized his shortcomings by employing rhetorical negatives, using "no" four times and "none" six times within the space of two paragraphs. Underneath the hostile attitude toward Halleck's work lurked the suggestion that he was emotionally "deficient," "even in some of the yet coarser elements of a true poet." The review continued, "He seems to lack comprehension of those whose meaning is more interior, and whose charm is due to remoter and less tangible sympathies," before more pointedly suggesting Halleck's flaw.

"Attack on Alnwick Castle" notes the absence of a female muse for Halleck and lists the female inspirations for Dante, Shakespeare, Wordsworth, and Coleridge. In this company, Halleck fails to convincingly meet the heterosexual standard: "Love has been so reverenced by true poets, and woman so worthily praised, that a poet's treatment of either of these hallowed subjects might almost be taken as a test of his power." Halleck can only express "his theory of love," an "indifferent love," and "entirely false sentiment." In telling the reader that the secret of poetry "lies in the heart," the 1845 review reveals Halleck's emotional crime, his illegitimate love for men. The public had become well aware of New York's growing homosexual population. In 1846, the *New York Herald* exposed a shop-keeper for engaging in the same-sex acts "nightly practiced on the Battery" and two men were exposed for their daily "carnal intercourse" in a boarding house.[92]

Adkins found the *Broadway Journal's* review "conspicuous for its ob-tuse estimate" of Halleck's poetry.[93] A letter to the editors of the *New York Evening Post* likewise noted an "offensive" article in the *Nation* as highly unusual and hotly defended Halleck from the "personal pique" regarded as revenge. The undated letter was written during Halleck's re-tirement as a protest of the *Nation's* review, which was "a paltry effusion of spite, malice and ignorance," resulting from a "slashing, rowdy style of criticism." The author wanted his letter to be printed "or use it to light a cigar."[94]

Less confrontational critics simply sealed gaps when dealing with Hal-leck via heterosexual apocrypha. One writer reported an affair between Halleck and a Quaker woman, and Adkins provides a second-generation account of hearsay that Halleck had fallen in love with a Bostonian, Emily Marshall, and considered marriage but decided against it because he lacked funds.[95] In Adkins's otherwise meticulously documented biogra-phy, this episode lacks any documentation whatsoever, including any cor-respondence with or about the woman mentioned. Both the *Philadelphia Press* and the *New York Times* in December 1874 recounted an incident of the leap-year boldness of Abbie Flanner, also known as Ellen A. F. Campbell, of Mount Pleasant, Jefferson County. This episode in Halleck's life was retold in *Bookman Magazine* in 1918 by Stanley M. Ward.

On New Year's Eve 1835, Flanner, a "very homely" woman infatuated with Halleck, sent him a poem.[96] Halleck replied fittingly with "To Ellen, the Mocking Bird," echoing back her own verse form. He enclosed lines to Miss Campbell on February 29, 1836, along with a copy of the second edition of *Alnwick Castle and Other Poems* in his only known letter to Flanner. A half-dozen of her surviving letters idolize Halleck and de-grade herself:

You have already done me but too much honor. I know it is impossible you can derive any pleasure from such a correspondence. Perhaps in pity you ought not— for I feel that I am "playing with fire"—but if it be true, that "what comes from the heart carries conviction to the heart," . . . [then] "send one gentle thought to her, / Whose spirit ever turns to thine, / Like Persia's idol-worshipper, / Or Mos-lem to his prophet's shrine."

Flanner regretted such forward advances after "she had commenced the acquaintance" and realized that her actions "place her in the character of a wooer."[97] The correspondence "created a new era in my existence," wrote Flanner, who found that she was "no longer the unambitious, contented cottage-maid."

By the end of March 1836, Flanner knew that Halleck could not respond to "the crowned hopes, and fears, and doubts, and daring of a woman's heart." She questioned her own worthiness and tested his indifference with a threat of retraction, having thrown lines written to him into the fire:

Every step that I have made in your acquaintance has increased my timidity. With a reckless laugh I flung my first offering on the current of accident, little thinking it would ever bring me back tears and smiles, anxious thoughts and fevered dreams. Yet I cannot repent it . . . .This is probably the last time I shall address you, but e'er I make my parting bow, permit me to return my most sincere and cordial thanks for the gentle courtesy with which you have entertained my idle folly, and more than crowned my most ambitious hopes. I never, till now, repined at the want of talents, fashion, and accomplishments, that I might, fearlessly and undisguisedly, challenge your friendship and esteem. It may not be. You will soon forget this idle correspondence and my very existence, but the name of Fitz-Greene Halleck is forever engraven by the hand of gratitude on the heart of ELLEN.

Yet despite the threat to quit, Flanner persevered, with continued lack of success. In September 1836, she revealed that Halleck was in her dreams and told him that a book she had hoped to pass on to him had not yet arrived. Her description of the postal delay paralleled her anticipation of a more romantic address from Halleck:

"By disappointment every day beguiled," day stole upon day, and week upon week, and all my applications (repeatedly made at every probable place) have proved fruitless. My last messenger has just returned, and brought, as usual, only "hope deferred."

Feeling as though she had transgressed the boundaries of her sex, Flanner's time passed by without result. In February 1837, she thanked Halleck for his "humorous" response and used his own crime metaphor to describe herself. Halleck's last letter had "delivered my 'woman's pride' from 'the bastile of a word,' for whose adamantine bars, perhaps, I have not shown a proper reverence, but such a prize as I gained was worth the daring—beyond my most sanguine hopes, but never to be repeated."

Flanner's last-ditch effort came in mid-April 1837. Halleck had not written since 1836. Flanner "resolved and reresolved" not to write, sacrificing "pride and 'etiquitte'": "Constitutionally and habitually cold, indifferent, and indolent I am, and yet how long and how devotedly I have knelt before the idol of my fancy." The words were literal. Flanner savored

the *New York Mirror*'s new etching of Halleck: "I have framed it, to preserve it from injury, but it is not my purpose to tell you where I have hung
it, nor how often I look at it, nor how impatient I am sometimes with the
placid immobility with which it looks on all the fanciful apostrophes and
sonnets addressed to it, as pathetic as Petrarch's, and quite as sincere."
She writes: "The impetuous ebb and flow of the vital current of my heart
. . . [though distance] might veil my blushes, if I should have the grace to
blush . . . I would go a pilgrimage to look on the magnificent brow and
eloquent eye." After eighteen months, the deflated admirer finally retreated. Both of Halleck's biographers felt Flanner's effort to court Halleck was an exercise in futility from its very inception.

Wilson admits Halleck did not save Flanner's poems offering "her
hand and heart."[98] Despite six pages Adkins allots in his biography to
Flanner, he concludes, "It is doubtful whether Halleck ever took seriously
this flirtation" and reveals that Miss Flanner soon became Mrs. Talbot,
adding: "At forty-five [Halleck] had doubtless already shown a similar
platonic affection for a score of women. It was perhaps this gallantry of
feeling toward all women that made him truly in love with none."[99] Flanner was twenty-six years old when she initiated the correspondance with
Halleck; she married late in life for that time and died a year after her
marriage.

Halleck emerged from Lawson's review and the Flanner affair divided
against his nation and himself. He conquered his audience and prevailed
in his profession, but such victories were won at a high price. They has-
tened his choices between money and art, privacy and influence. He hated
editors but became one. He was fragmented into a cultural persona and
an intimate stranger. Even Maria seemed not to know him anymore.

Swelling political disgust and fear of public exposure fused in Halleck.
He scoffed as his associate James G. Percival accepted "employment in
that most degrading and disgraceful of all occupations—the editorship of
a party newspaper!"[100] By the age of seventy-five, Halleck grew unusually
crass in his reference to literary critics, calling them jackasses. Two years
later, he still raged at the press's disregard for privacy.

As Mark Twain would retort that the news of his death had been
greatly exaggerated, Halleck objected to a report that he had married. In
an April 1867 letter to Wilson, Halleck took "leave to enclose herein the
certificate of my being, or having been, a married man." The clipping
claimed that "Marco Bozzaris" was the result of a bet with its author's
wife. The misinformation placed him in the reverse situation of *Joe Miller.*
Halleck quoted the book: "I was not aware, my dear sir, until recently, of
your having been horsewhipped." Miller replies that he "knew it at the
time!" Pointedly, Halleck's literary allusion draws a parallel between marriage and flogging. Halleck joked:

I have not the slightest recollection of the happening of the happy event recorded above; but, as the announcement of it comes from an infallible source, that of the pen of the editor of a party newspaper, there can be no doubt whatever of the fact; and I delight in congratulating myself upon my long-enjoyed matrimonial felicity accordingly.[101]

Publicly, he let the socially advantageous error slide.

A good friend quoted Halleck's view of public attention as "rather offensive than pleasing" and reiterated his claim that fame was a punishment he must suffer: "All who desire the ear of the public must pay a penalty more or less; there is no sweet without a bitter." The affection of attractive men was the exception to this rule. Halleck recalled for this same friend a summer visit at work. "Glowing with ardor, innocence, and honesty, his eyes beaming with enthusiastic sincerity," a young man exhibited "increased emotion" as he grew closer to meeting Halleck. Halleck was grabbed by the hand and claimed that the admirer said, "I have wished, I have longed, I have sighed to see you, and I have dreamt that I have seen you, but now I behold you with mine own eyes." The anecdote sounds more like Flanner's type of fantasy than an actual memory. Halleck's further claim that the youth traveled eleven hundred miles from a river in Ohio to be "compensated for my pains" is suspiciously reminiscent of Flanner's situation in Ohio.[102] Distinguishing the significance of these two devotees does not require finding the boundary between Halleck's reality and his euphoric recall. His own words weigh in favor of the male admirer, whereas the press alone deemed Ellen's story newsworthy.

Publishers and editors appealed to the lowest common denominator of readership. When Leggett was hired for the *New York Evening Post*'s biographical author series, he appealed to George P. Morris for the facts. Morris directed, "Damn it, write the lives and omit the facts."[103] Byron and Halleck both discovered that the same press that created their mythic statures could just as easily destroy their characters. The rising action of having their work drawn into the public light was followed by falling estimates of their worth as people. The poets were acclaimed prophets but were judged harshly as citizens outside of the moral codes of the majority. Halleck conquered public curiosity with distance and silence, often misinterpreted as living in an ivory tower. Outside of the fortress, the culture was redefining sexual heretics, and the American media was forging literary shackles. It was one thing to misunderstand Halleck's attempt at experimental verse; it was quite another to compromise his precious bachelorhood. In the end, no news became good news.

Railing against "the blessings of a free country, where any unprincipled blackguard, with money enough to buy types and paper, can blacken my reputation," Halleck vented on Henry Tuckerman, who knew that Halleck objected to a developing culture insensitive to "individual-

Lord Byron. Byron's early death, which caused a rare emotional breakdown for Fitz-Greene Halleck, recalled the premature loss of Drake. (From Ralph Trautmann's steel-plate portrait in the author's private collection.)

ity—as to rights, development, and self-respect—[that are] constantly invaded by encroachments of what are called popular principles, but which are too often social despotisms."[104] Halleck's feelings on marriage and democracy were growing increasingly unpopular.

Halleck's lamentation of Drake's marriage and funeral was replaced by a general condemnation of the culture during the 1840s as his nation regressed toward puritanical absolutism. The years preceding the Civil

War drew hard lines. One was Confederate or Yankee, slave owner or abolitionist, Democrat or Republican. But Halleck would not take a political side any more than he would choose between business and poetry. Just weeks before his death, he wrote a lifelong friend:

As a Federalist in my boyhood and a monarchist in my manhood, I prefer a government representing property, and, let me add, probity, to a government of numbers. Under a democracy, a vote is of no value unless given for a candidate of an organized party . . . I could not, and cannot, submit. It demands the abandonment of the voter's freedom of action and opinion, and sooner or later he degenerates into the mere tool of a few party leaders.[105]

After years of emotional repression, Halleck began to drop many more political bombshells. He began a reign of artistic terrorism against the most basic American ideals. Acquaintances found that Halleck's political intellect grew "fond of broaching and sustaining literary and historical heresies."[106] Halleck shared his antidemocratic sentiments with Bryant, who was also under fire for criticizing the national government. Halleck's personal letter to Bryant declared that he was an "avowed monarchist," "detesting the ungodly government of the many."[107] Furthermore, Halleck abstained from voting in national elections and "was fond of saying that he had never voted for a president," despite having been befriended by several of them.[108] Lawson's homophobic attack on Halleck commented that the poet "half jestingly, avows himself a monarchist; and professes little confidence in the intelligence and integrity of the people, or their fitness for self-government," adding: "He never inculcates a pure morality, a virtuous patriotism, or an humble adoration [of beauty in] 'the glorious works of God.'"[109] In an honest moment, Halleck professed to Tuckerman his hate of "the solecisms in manners, the vulgar assumptions, the official ignorance, and social incongruities born of, or identified with, the democratic rule."[110] Tuckerman found himself suddenly far away from his usually congenial friend when a "creed, whether political or religious," met with Halleck's antagonism, which bore "an absolute defiance, as to seemingly preclude all chance of assimilation."[111]

No American party wanted what was becoming defined as a "homosexual," and Halleck did not want any American party. Divided between the myth of European sexual tolerance and the reality of an impending civil war, Halleck was not sure which way to turn. He only knew that the American revolutionaries had not freed him. In the end, he declared himself an anarchist.

5

A Return to Ganymede

Critics like noxious weeds do but cumber the ground they
spring up on. Never let your fear of them influence you.
Fitz-Greene Halleck to Theseus Apoleon Cheney

ALLECK temporarily ignored his own advice about the fear of
critics even as they choked his flowering literary career. His silence was an enormous public disappointment. The conservative
atmosphere presaging civil war compounded the critical fallout from
"The Field of the Grounded Arms." In addition, Lawson's brutal 1842
article, its republication in the *New World* in 1843, and the *Broadway
Journal*'s attack on Halleck's collected works in 1845 all had assessed him
in sexually suspicious terms. Unbeknown to his fans, Halleck was reeling
from the materialization of his worst fears: public exposure and moral
condemnation. Following the first negative judgment of his psychological
nature, Halleck withdrew and hid in Astor's shadow for an entire decade.
Calls for more poetry did not yield a word from him during his years
working for Astor. When Halleck finally did rise to reclaim his literary
throne, many wished he had not.

Halleck's later works immediately before and after the Civil War de-
constructed democracy in a country that was trying to reconstruct its government and identity. New poems also reverberated with the old pang
for Drake. In the intermediate period between his early success and his
retirement poems, he tried to avoid poetry and the public. By 1845, even
Halleck's "victims were expected to feel honored by the source" of the
sting.[1] Fame dogged his every step.

Halleck's familiar lines received undying praise, and he went through
the motions of responding to the honors that came his way. As promised,
Willis Clark's "Alnwick Castle and Other Poems" appeared in the *Ameri-*

can Quarterly Review (March 1836) and exalted Halleck. Britain's *Foreign Quarterly Review* (1844) followed suit. Charles W. Everest augmented the self-identified New Yorker in *Poets of Connecticut* (1843) and the *Knickerbocker* continued in its esteem with "The Poetry of Fitz-Greene Halleck" (December 1845). Halleck was also drafted into the Book Club in 1836 and elected vice-president of the Authors' Club in 1837. The Book Club was an intellectual fraternity that met biweekly at New York's Washington Hotel for drinks and discourse. The Authors' Club's membership included James Fenimore Cooper, Charles F. Hoffman, James DeKay, and other literary men who elected Washington Irving their president and Halleck second-in-command.

Halleck nearly swooned with embarrassment when singled out at the annual Booksellers' Dinner. The dinner was held on March 30, 1837, for Bryant, Hoffman, Inman, Irving, Morris, Paulding, Poe, and Halleck, who was too unnerved to stand as DeKay urged him to do when distinguished by Irving. Halleck later explained that "the brains ran to his heels" when he rose in public.[2] *New York Evening Post* editor John Keese used the occasion to ask: "Why sleeps the Muse of Drake's twin-brother bard?"[3] The same question lingered in the minds of students who witnessed the honorary master of arts degree conferred on Halleck in 1837 at Columbia College's fiftieth anniversary. Accentuating Halleck's poetic silence, the other honorees (Bryant and Hoffman) were producing new works.

In March 1839, Halleck's cousin, Barnabas Hallock, published a poem in Brooklyn reiterating Keese's inquiry: "Why sleeps thy harp in silence— why no more . . . ?" Beseeching a second muse for Halleck, the lines asked whether there was "No loved or lovely name, / To wake its slumbering melody again? / Amid Columbia's valleys, no bright spell / To make its numbers swell, / And move the heart like music." Reminding Halleck of his lines on Drake's grave, the speaker pushes the inquisition: "Are there none, / No solitary one, / That to thy heart a kindred music thrills?" The call for a national epic was ineffective and contained too many questions about Halleck's romantic life to earn a response. The narrator feared that Halleck's heart was "waxing cold."[4] No doubt his cousin meant well, but the lines only deepened Halleck's private angst.

Poe's 1836 criticism in the *Southern Literary Messenger* was replaced by his more favorable September 1842 essay in *Graham's*. This essay, "Critical Notices, Drake-Halleck," remains a landmark of criticism often anthologized for general observations on literature without even identifying Halleck or Drake. Rufus Griswold, who succeeded Poe as editor of *Graham's*, wrote James T. Fields about having smoked with Halleck in the summer of 1842 when Griswold's *Poets and Poetry of America* was nearing completion. Griswold wrote Halleck that Poe was writing an article on Halleck with a sketch by Inman and promised Halleck that a poem from him would receive "the highest rates ever paid for contributions," above Bryant, Richard H. Dana, and Longfellow,[5] but Halleck did not submit any work.

Reprints and new anthologies had to satisfy Halleck's readership from the mid-1830s through the 1840s. The *New York Mirror*'s 1836 reprints of Halleck's works ("Music," February 13; "Magdalen," March 19; "From the Italian," April 16; and "William Howard Allen," April 30) led the editor to conclude that his paper had published Halleck's entire canon to date. The *New Yorker* also republished numerous poems in 1836 ("Magdalen," April 9; "From the Italian," May 7; and "Lines to the Recorder," August 13). Anthologized works appeared in 1834 (*Selections from the American Poets*), 1835 (*The Gift, The Young Man's Book of Elegant Poetry*), 1836 (*The Laurel: A Gift for All Seasons*), and 1837 (*Autumn Leaves, The Fireside Book*). The next decade witnessed the same scarcity of new verse.

Harper and Brothers, who published Halleck's two-volume *Selections from the British Poets* in 1840, published fifteen hundred copies of both *Fanny and Other Poems* and *Poems by Fitz-Greene Halleck*. Appleton printed the *Poetical Works of Fitz-Greene Halleck* in 1847. Perhaps due to the assumption that his productive years were over, Halleck was frequently anthologized during the decade: in 1840 (*Poets of America* and *Selections from the American Poets*); in 1841 (*American Melodies*); in 1842 (*Poets of America* and *Gems from American Poets*); in 1843 (*Poets of Connecticut* and *Readings in American Poetry*); in 1844 (*Gems from the American Poets*); in 1845 (*Poet's Gift* and *Chaplet of Literary Gems*); in 1847 (*Pearls of American Poetry*); in 1848 (*Gems from Poetry of Forty-Eight American Poets*); and in 1850 (*Gems of the Season*). It is no wonder that Halleck's literary sloth made him the target of satire such as in Edgar Allan Poe's *The Poets and Poetry of America; a Satire* (1847) and James Russell Lowell's "A Fable for Critics" (1848).

These unproductive years were not due to the distractions of new employment, but to the critical revision of his love for Drake and noted absence of his love for women. Critics concluded that Halleck stopped writing poetry "far back in middle life" because his muse forsook him and added that Halleck wrote for money after the loss of Drake rather than *con amore*.[6] Only a smattering of album verses and translations from around 1840 survive the twenty-year span between Astor's hiring of Halleck and his premature retirement. Halleck had always had one foot in the business world and one in poetry, but having expressed his grief for Drake in a series of private poems and having completed his tributes to Byron, he seemed content to plant both feet firmly in his job.

Although it was an era of pornographic potboilers,[7] Halleck's years under Astor produced sparse poetry that had safety as its distinctive feature. For the most part, he passed off new poems as translations, freeing himself from any responsibility of their emotional content or form. Indeed, Halleck hid behind an assumed identity of translator while writing down original thoughts and feelings; therefore, if critics had wanted to grade these works, they could only score them technically.

Halleck's five German translations were all loose interpretations, when clear sources existed at all. Julius Goebel discovered that "Translation: From the German of Goethe" was "a rather free translation" of *Faust;* Carl Schreiber traced "Honor to Women: From the German of Goethe" to one of the "Roman Elegies"; and J. T. Hatfield found "Forget-Me-Not . . . from the German" a free paraphrase of Hoffman von Fallersleben's "Vergissmeinnicht." It is more likely, however, that Halleck's similarly titled "Forget Me Not—Imitated from the German" relied on Fallersleben's poem. "Translation from the German" has no known source.

Halleck's "Translation from the French of Victor Hugo" appeared in the *Knickerbocker* (January 1841) and the *New York Mirror* (January 16, 1841), which judged Halleck's version superior to the original. This poem joined his five German translations with their easily confused titles. The muddle of titles further obscured Halleck's sources. "Translation: From the German of Goethe" was written in February 1839. Ironically, Wordsworth's contempt for Goethe was shared by Halleck who judged *Faust* the worst book he had ever read; Halleck recommended Marlowe's verse in place of it.[8]

Halleck's version of Goethe not only relates Drake's death but also serves as a preview of Whitman's mystical style. It opens with the curious incantation from the dedicatory preface to the completed *Faust:* "Again ye come, again ye throng around me, / Dim, shadowy beings of my boyhood's dream!" Wondering whether he should bless the spell that bound him to boyhood friends, the narrator will "still bend" and decides: "I yield me as ye found me / In youth your worshipper." The sexually passive speaker uses seminal imagery as a "stream of air" magically envelops past bodies and "flows by my lips, youth's joy my bosom breathes." These "lost forms and loved ones" are inhaled in Coleridge-like meditation. Memories sprung from the ground bring "long-slept sorrows" and remind the narrator of his "life's strange labyrinthine maze" of premature love and loss. Doting on Drake, Halleck writes, "They hear not these my last songs . . . my springtime friends have gone." Public praise is painful and pent-up tears are allowed to flow: "Though stranger crowds, my listeners since, are beating / Time to my music, their applauding tone / More grieves than glads me." The autobiographical speaker's "faint voice" dies like tones of a wind-harp hung on a branch. The crisis of social repression results in the bard's resignation as it had in "Psalm CXXXVII," written when Halleck was still in Guilford.

Unlike his "Forget Me Not—Imitated from the German" (1828), Halleck's 1838 "Forget-Me-Not: *Myosotis avensis* from the German" was meant for private eyes. This "Forget-Me-Not" was inscribed for Mrs. J. J. Roosevelt's album in November 1838 and was published five years later in the *Knickerbocker* for July 1843, probably without consent. Charlotte Cushman, an actress, responded to the poem with "Lines to Fitz-Greene Halleck, on reading 'Forget-Me-Not'" (the *Knickerbocker*, October 1843). Cushman was at the center of a lesbian circle in Rome and her response to Halleck's poem suggests that a contemporary community of homosexual readers was, in fact, enjoying Halleck's work.[9]

The flower in "Forget-Me-Not" expresses grief as had the mournful trees in "Love," "The Discarded," and "A Poet's Daughter." Halleck reaffirms his love for Drake through an appropriate symbol of fidelity in 1838's "Forget-Me-Not" and in the poem's 1869 version. The earlier, private version is highly romantic. Blue petals represent "Faith's unchanging hue" and lie along the stream's "gentle side" in physical embrace amid a "silent fount." An unspeakable love resides in a colorful life form that mirrors both the narrator's heart and Drake's face:

> Wild as the azure of thine eyes,
> Soft as the halo-beam above,
> In tender whispers still it sighs
> Forget me not, my life, my love!

The "sweet flower" holds a vigil as Halleck's "Translation from the German" had done. Its grave watch is focused: "There where thy last steps turned away, / Wet eyes shall watch the sacred spot." The phallic "drooping stem" and seminal "dew-drops" on the blue leaves "may well declare" the otherwise voiceless "secret grief."[10] The lines, obviously conjuring up the loss of Drake, were tempered.

The 1869 variation of "Forget-Me-Not" was intended for publication and edited out much of the earlier version's sexual energy. The flower blooms silently and smiles on the poem's object in "purity"; Drake's immortalized blue eyes are replaced by ethereal, starry eyes. The flower's dew drops whisper its own name. Emotional distance is maintained through a new closing: "young passion grieves, / For one beloved afar."[11] Altering lines and using distant European sources, Halleck's clever strategy effectively blocked any fresh criticism.

Besides the translations, Halleck made one other return to an earlier theme. "The Winds of March Are Humming" did not recount Drake's death but rather Halleck's old satires on marriage. Although Wilson dates the poem to 1844, it appeared in the 1839 edition of works as "Song by Miss * * * *." Retaining his mask of translator, Halleck based this work on Thomas Moore's "To Ladies' Eyes." The poem was requested by George P. Morris for the *Evening Mirror* (1844) and appeared as an annual favorite in the *Home Journal*. Wilson referred to the poem as a "song of the unmarried." In it Halleck achieved literary transsexualism.

Halleck adopts female first-person narration in "The Winds of March Are Humming." Reminiscent of his adolescent "Trifles 'Light as Air'" to Carlos Menie, the teen-aged girl fears that time and opportunity for marriage are passing, even though she is reassured that she is too young to wed. She complains, "I've done a bridesmaid's duty / At three or four [weddings]," corresponding to Halleck's multiple turns as groomsman. She adds, "In vain, at balls and parties, / I've thrown my net," and while only in her second winter as a socialite, the refrain repeated at the end of all four stanzas frets: "I / Have no accepted lover: / Don't ask me why, don't ask me why." [12] The unchosen belle's ambiguous chorus is poignant for Halleck whose strange love was not accepted. "The Winds of March Are Humming" belongs with later writings by Halleck that laugh at the central mystery about himself.

Halleck compensated for his lack of self-awareness with a keen understanding of other famous men. In spring 1837, Prince Louis Napoleon Bonaparte frequently sought out Halleck, who found the Frenchman dull and "as mad as a March hare, or as my poor friend McDonald Clarke." [13] Regarding Bonaparte as politically deluded, Halleck complained that the shy royal was only excitable when eyeing attractive women and could not look other men in the eye. He found the prince disagreeable in all areas except his condemnation of "that much-puffed 'liberty of the Press.'" [14] Halleck also studied Dickens, who looked Halleck up upon arriving in New York during February 1842. Despite their long and cordial friendship, Dickens published a poor review of Halleck, calling him an imitator who lacked originality even in "his gayer effusions." [15]

In between hobnobbing with celebrities, Halleck sharpened his wicked rapport with friends. One "facetious friend" was Charles Augustus Davis. Wilson regretted that Halleck's letters to Davis, with whom Halleck maintained correspondence for many years, had not been recovered. The Davis letters may have been destroyed because of their content, along with Halleck's torn letter to Maria that physically detailed his first meeting with Drake and his letter relating Drake's death. In July 1845, Davis wrote Halleck a campy letter from Glasgow, promising: "When I take you by *the hand* (a dangerous thing coming from Scotland), I'll tell you all." [16] The affection would only be dangerous if "the hand" is somehow suggestive. Since 1736, Scottish medicine and poetry deemed effeminacy a key component of homosexuality and Scottish manners discouraged physical affection between men; American homosexuals were not stereotyped in the same way until the late nineteenth century.[17] "Hand" has other associations with the penis (for example, the notion that hand size, finger length or width, or distance between digits betrays penis size). Halleck's manipulation of hands in Drake's elegy and "Marco Bozzaris" was more than adequately rivaled by other homosexual writers. Whitman blatantly versified "hand jobs," writing: "The pulse pounding through palms and trembling encircling fingers, the young man all color'd, red, ashamed, angry; The souse upon me of my lover the sea, as I lie willing and naked."[18] The foreboding manual embrace in Davis's letter may have been a similar metaphor for mutual masturbation.

Davis also puns on "lay," which may have referred to the same activity: David Auld "kens all about you, and regards your lay, though on a 'rose,' the best since Burns. I told him you did that with your left hand, and when he came to read other matter, done with t'other hand, he would go into a fit." The forward prose charms Halleck with the news that his "Burns" was now displayed in the Scot's cottage and that this honor was "a *clincher,* 'a real hug-me-tight' (but that is not 'a merry thought')." "Merry," as in Byron's Merry Monks, may have been a positive code word for same-sex affection, as would be the later term "gay." Davis mentions favorite, but anonymous, rural and city haunts to which Halleck and himself "held equal titles" and closes obscurely: "I am quite sure I have seen much more than any other 'living critter,' and what I have not seen I can *talk* of quite as well as others." Davis anticipates Halleck's embrace and thanks him "for the pleasure your pen has given me."[19] Given the overall tone of the letter, Davis may have intended this compliment to be a phallic pun as well. Separated by an ocean, Davis could not have known that Halleck had put down his pen that often revealed more than he cared to risk. Instead, he picked up his sherry and launched more verbal attacks on the press.

By 1846, Halleck was frequently spotted with the painter Henry Inman at Frank's (No. 5 Barclay Street) and probably met Herman Melville at such watering holes about this time. Halleck caroused at the Italian immigrant's bar with Louis Clark, George P. Morris, and Edgar Allan Poe. A drinker's reputation shadowed Halleck from this establishment to a French café on Warren Street, where he "was fond of maintaining unexpected opinions."[20] Here, Henry Tuckerman heard Halleck claim that divine history was interrupted twice, once by the Reformation and "once when printing was invented," and saw that Halleck's "humanity made him recoil, with disgust and dismay, at the license of the press."[21]

Halleck relished Cooper's successful lawsuits against numerous newspaper editors who attacked the values expressed in *Homeward Bound* (1838) and *Home as Found* (1838). Cooper bragged that he had "beaten every man I have sued who has not retracted his libels" following the extensive litigations brought against the papers.[22] Not finding the victor home, Halleck wrote: "Allow me to congratulate you upon your success thus far in combating the spirit of Evil, . . . a defense of 'the liberty of *unlicensed* printing.'"[23] In addition to finding himself caught between the desires to publish and to avoid punishment, Halleck faced civil contradictions regarding personal freedom and sexuality.

The New York of 1846 was starting to look like the Guilford of 1646, the year of William Plaine's sodomy trial. Exactly one year to the date of the founding of the New York City Police Department in 1845, Edward McCosker was forced to resign from the First District following a public hearing before the mayor on charges of homosexuality.[24] Throughout the 1840s, Halleck demonstrated a "fear of the present" in New York.[25] At the same time, he felt that North-South relations were strained beyond the potential for peaceful reconciliation. No peace was to be had in the city or in the nation.

Halleck's literary supporters hoped he might "Wake from thy voiceless slumbers" and "Sing! For our country." Meanwhile, female admirers remained plentiful; Valentine's Day of 1847 found married and single women alike writing poems to Halleck and requesting more poetry. Halleck's Bible inscription for another DeKay bride in 1840 was typical of his platonic praises for woman "as a daughter and a sister" in roles "as a wife and a mother."[26] But Halleck did not respond to women or to editors and vigorously avoided politics. The literary hiatus continued to puzzle the press. The *Knickerbocker*'s "Epistle to the Editor" scolded a certain millionaire for chasing off Halleck's muse. The *New Mirror* hoped to pry "Halleck from his ledger" on September 2, 1843, and berated Astor for enslaving Halleck on June 15, 1844.

In 1848, Halleck's future course was once again determined by another man's death. Astor left a fortune of roughly twenty million dollars when he died late that March at the age of eighty-five. His will was printed on the front page of the *Herald,* which had previously criticized Astor's earnings in real estate. The *National Magazine* (1852) continued to polarize profit and poetry even four years after Astor's death, lamenting "the merchant [Astor] has swallowed the poet [Halleck]." Astor's will had proven "a shabby affair" for Halleck,[27] causing Halleck's regrets about his many years serving Astor in a confidential capacity to be more financial than artistic.

Halleck's sense of humor had gotten the best of him. The wealthiest businessman in the United States repaid his private secretary with a "ridiculous annuity."[28] Daniel Embury, Astor's former clerk and Halleck's good friend, explained that the inheritance provided some "bitter satire" for Halleck, who frequently teased his boss by asking, "Of what use is all this money to you? I would be content to live upon a couple of hundreds a year for the rest of my life."[29] Astor had the last laugh. Halleck would receive an annuity of just two hundred dollars per year. Ironically, the gold rush had begun drawing young men west as Halleck headed east to poorer prospects.

Halleck's readership was incensed and pressured Astor's son into adding a lump sum to the retirement. Adkins shows that William B. Astor was rumored to have provided between fifteen hundred and ten thousand dollars to Halleck's annuity; however, most sources agree with the larger figure.[30] Halleck maintained his characteristic dignity and objected to any criticism of the will. He expressed only gratitude at having been remembered at all by Astor, whose will also named Halleck one of the original trustees of the Astor Library. Although Halleck had reacted negatively to a paper's attack on the annuity,[31] his private feelings may have caused him to resign the honor he shared with Irving and three other trustees of the New York Public Library. Halleck had failed to secure his own financial future despite a career scrupulously caring for other people's money. In time, he lost his income, executive status, and New York lifestyle.

The practical effects of Astor's death were devastating. Passport in hand, Halleck canceled a trip to Europe that he had planned for the spring of 1849. Old ailments reappeared as he realized that retirement in a New York City suburb was beyond his means. Adkins concludes that Halleck "would have retired to Fort Lee. But the state of his resources undoubtedly prevented such an indulgence," and Everett Gleason Hill called Halleck's decision wise since his annuity, though small for New York, was "a fortune for Guilford."[32] He could not prevent his return to Guilford, though he did protest it.

Putnam's printed Halleck's letter concerning a sketch to be illustrated with a scene from Guilford:

You must pardon me for begging that [the illustration] may not be carried into effect; for although born here in Connecticut, where, as Lord Byron says of England, "men are proud to be," I shall never cease to "hail," as the sailors say, from your good city of New York, of which a residence of more than forty years made me a citizen. There I always considered myself at home, and elsewhere but a visitor. If, therefore, you wish to embellish my poem with a view of my country-seat . . . let it be taken from the top of Weehawk Hill, overlooking New York.[33]

In Bryant's words, Halleck's "end was like that of the rivers of his native state, which, after dashing and sparkling over their stony beds, lay themselves down between quiet meadows and glide softly to the Sound."[34] But Halleck's stringent request and windy explanation verged on indignation and made Bryant's attempt to romanticize Halleck's retirement to Guilford seem ludicrous. Halleck's cool attitude toward his hometown was

Thomas Hicks's 1855 oil on canvas of Fitz-Greene Halleck at age sixty-five. Though Halleck patiently sat for the portrait, he was not pleased by its smirking mouth. The painting was done for Benjamin R. Winthrop, a fellow clerk and friend from Halleck's early years at Jacob Barker's firm. (Collection of the New-York Historical Society.)

well known. He slunk back into town on a quiet June day like an apprehended fugitive returned to the prison yard.

Guilford had only lowered its regard for Halleck since 1808 when he had "caught the fever" of New York. No one doubted that he felt at home there and "out of New York he was out of his element, . . . virtually unproductive."[35] Charles Lewis Biggs claims that Halleck reappeared as a "weak, doddering, spent man" and admonishes, "He deserves a better remembrance."[36] Joel E. Helander understates the problem when he observes that Halleck seemed "a little bored with Guilford." Halleck's fame, however, continued in anthologies and public school curricula through the 1850s and 1860s.

The *Poetical Writings of Halleck* (1852) and D. Appleton's republication of that 1847 collection in 1858 (issuing two reprintings that year) marked new milestones in Halleck's canonization. *Croakers* was expanded into a complete edition by the Bradford Club in 1860, and Appleton produced *Young America* in 1865. In 1862, Halleck was featured in Evert Duyckinck's *Portrait Gallery of Eminent Americans* and James Wynne's "Fitz-Greene Halleck" in *Harper's New Monthly* in April. In 1866, W. L. Andrews published a third edition of *Fanny* and "Lines to the Recorder." Halleck's minor poem "Strong as That Power" was printed by the *New York Times*, February 2, 1868, and Wilson's *Poetical Writings* appeared in 1869. A western state purchased Halleck's anthology for district-wide use in 1858, and his works appeared in primers like *Reader of the School and Family Series* in 1861. His 1858 edition "enjoyed a wide circulation," purchased by the thousands for use in public schools, and Halleck's works remained in many school readers into the twentieth century. His major poems became "familiar to every school-boy and school-girl in the land" and "Marco Bozzaris" was "spouted by two generations of school-boys."[37] According to David Baillie, the attention only served to isolate him as Guilford's "locally neglected genius and literary world-leader."

Guilford residents seemed agitated by Halleck's lingering fame, and "he lived withdrawn from active and social life, dwelling in the most frugal isolation."[38] He managed to import some pleasure whenever friends dropped in town. *Harper's New Monthly* gave a rather queer account of two female friends. One was

a gay and highly-accomplished lady, who often startled the sober villagers of Guilford by her daring feats of horsemanship, and would frequently whirl through their quiet streets upon a mettled steed at a speed on the jockey side of three minutes. Both . . . were the frequent subject of the village gossips, who were astonished on one occasion to observe her, accompanied by another lady, remarkable for great personal beauty, rein up at the door of the bachelor poet.[39]

Halleck hosted selected old friends, reviewed the past, read voraciously, and took a great number of countryside walks. As in his youthful days, he walked alone.

Halleck took long and frequent excursions to New York City. Walking "alone and unobserved" to seedy bars, he was spotted by a New Yorker who said Halleck "did not shun the haunts of men among 'publicans and sinners'" but "shunned notoriety."[40] In July 1850, *Fraser's* questioned Halleck's recent years of refusing all solicitations to write. Instead of writing, Halleck headed for New York in order to help commemorate another author; Cooper had died in September 1851. Halleck and Rufus Griswold served as cosecretaries for the memorial project chaired by Irving, but the Cooper Monument Association failed to raise the necessary funds for a New York monument. Perhaps the loss of Cooper reminded Halleck that he had little time left to write. Breaking a long calm spell, he set out to denounce the American body politic once and for all.

In 1852, a second section for the poem "Connecticut" ended Halleck's literary exile and condemned the blind patriotism that had characterized the poem's earlier version. "Connecticut" was published under the Croaker signature H., which bid Halleck's older readers to recognize humor in the dark poem. But Halleck's twist on American history unnerved many of his readers. He could risk this now for he was growing too old to mind the consequences and he believed that his fame was already secure. Plans were in the works for a statue commemorating him. As early as 1852, Charles A. Davis proposed two huge bronze statues of Halleck and Irving for Gramercy Park.

"Connecticut" was intended as a section of a three-canto national epic on the Revolutionary War, tentatively titled *Minute-Men*. The poem was subtitled "From *Minute-Men,* an Unpublished Poem." *Minute-Men* became a target of gossip as numerous papers asked Halleck to complete the ambitious project of 1826.[41] In 1834, the *New York Mirror* sarcastically remarked that Halleck had "almost made up his mind to commence his long-talked-of poem, 'The Minute-Men.'"[42] The poem was announced as forthcoming by the *Southern Literary Messenger* in November 1841, when *Richardsiana* published an anonymous parody of "Connecticut" entitled "Extract from an Unpublished Poem." The first eleven stanzas of "Connecticut" were composed over a two-year period and were originally published in the *New York Review* and *Athenaeum Magazine* for March 1826. The finished poem did not appear for another twenty-six years, and the twelfth stanza connecting the two halves was never completed. The final version contained thirty-seven stanzas. The completed "Connecticut" appeared in the *Knickerbocker,* in May 1852, and held up the perverse morality of colonists as a ghastly deterrent from emulating their social tyranny. The expanded poem maintained the Byronic *ottava rima* form of the first half. All consistency ended there.

"Connecticut" opens in awe of a regional geography as unyielding and harsh as its inhabitants. The "conquered" sea "crouches" at the foot of towering cliffs for "'tis a rough land." Its "stubborn race" builds a "'fierce democracie,' / where all are true / To what themselves have voted—right or wrong." The inhabitants discharge priests and declare their own omniscience. The state's attributes are positive in 1826's version, but "Connecticut" is a tough neighborhood.

The poem's second section turns hostile:

> They burnt their last witch in CONNECTICUT
>   About a century and a half ago;
> They made a school-house of her forfeit hut,
>   And gave a pitying sweet-brier leave to grow
> Above her thankless ashes; and they put
>   A certified description of the show
> Between two weeping-willows, craped with black,
> On the last page of that year's almanac.

Stanza thirteen provides the transition from singing the state's beauty to chastising America's forefathers. Trees weep over the burnt offering, partly covered by a sympathetic bush. Nature personified (Halleck's favorite metaphor for emotion) continues to mourn the unnatural crime committed by a society oblivious to its culpability. A fading rose hears the "warning and well-meant remarks" of those who have "executed—the lady and the law."[43] Violets mourn the victim's muted ashes, displaced to the rear of the Almanac, and express grief over the duplicity of her perpetrators. In ironic contrast to her oppressors, the witch wins the reader's heart.

Whitman would also empathize with witches. His narrator longs for "my excrementitious body to be burn'd" and stands with "a witch burnt with dry wood . . . All these [martyred] I feel or am."[44] One cannot know if Halleck was aware of historical parallels between convicted sodomites and witches.[45] However, as early as 1625, *Theologia Moralis* connected sodomy to witchcraft, and Thomas Shepard's 1640 sermon lumped together "all atheism, sodomy, blasphemy, murder, whoredom, adultery, witchcraft, and buggery."[46] Single or widowed women were often associated with sodomy, as in the case of the childless Eunice (Goodie) Cole who was convicted of witchcraft in 1656 and 1672 for taking on a variety of forms in order "to entice a young woman, named Ann Smith, to live with her."[47] But lesbianism contradicted the puritanical denial of female sex drive and colonial America generally excluded women from sodomy laws. Even so, Elizabeth Johnson was severely whipped and fined in December 1642 for making sexual advances on another woman.[48] John Cotton's rejected proposal of 1636 included women with women, but the provision was edited out in his adopted New Haven Colony proposal of 1656.

Puritans in "Connecticut" are further compared to "the fiends of France, whose cruelties decreed / Those dextrous drownings in the Loire and Rhone, / [and who] Were at their worst, but copyists second-hand / Of our shrined, sainted sires, the Plymouth pilgrim band."[49] Worse than the French they were inclined to condemn, America's colonists were fiendish murderers. "Connecticut" specifically berates Cotton Mather.

Although Halleck's ancestors and the Mather families were old associates, Halleck labels Mather a religious hypocrite and political tyrant. Halleck's great-great-grandfather, John Eliot, was a friend of Cotton Mather, who wrote a long sketch of Eliot in *Magnalia Christi Americana*. Of Halleck's poetical sketch, Duyckinck summarized, "No finer study of Mather has appeared . . . alongside of the bitterest denunciation of evil doing."[50] Mather's harshness and bigotry are reprehensible, and the narrator argues that history has been distorted by "the folios of one COTTON MATHER, / A chronicler of tales more strange than true" and an arrant liar. The "venerable Cotton" rages "where meek religion wears the assassin's knife" and rules Indians "by sprinkling earth with blood." The perverse baptism-communion runs off Mather's altar built over "indignant bones / Of murdered maidens, wives, and little ones."[51]

The Puritan-sanctioned holocaust of dissenters forces the reader to side with the condemned witch and the Indian.

> HEROD of Galilee's [Mather's] babe-butchering deed
> Lives not on history's blushing page alone;
> Our skies, it seems, have seen like victims bleed,
> And our Ramahs echoed groan for groan.

Pointedly, Halleck employs biblical characters to counterattack the Puritan fathers. The narrator wishes Mather's "folios, followers, facts, forgot" even while the same witch hunts were still going on. Although "the Christian-sponsored and the Christian-nursed, / Clouded with crime the sunset of their day," the speaker hopes the "stain" and "guilt" on the "pilgrim axe" will teach America to do better.[52]

A second volley is launched against religious conformity:

> And our own MATHER'S fire-and-fagot tale
> Of Conquest, with her "garments rolled in blood,"
> And banners blackening, like a pirate's sail,
> The Mayflower's memories of the brave and good.

Diametric sodomitical allusions in Mather's "fire-and-fagot tale" confuse the image of burning social outcasts and smudging the *Mayflower* with pirate hues. Significantly, the moralist (Mather) is reincarnated as the criminal (pirate), as the witch has been resurrected as a saint. His "sour grape-juice" disposition symbolizes a spoiled holy communion of unholy crime. The ironic use of grapes serves as a backlash to sermons preaching against same-sex activity. Exactly one hundred years after Bradford's outbreak of sodomy in 1642, Jonathan Edwards's "grapes of Sodom" needed to be squashed.[53] The inversion of right and wrong is inherent in the irony of Mather's famed eulogies to his adversaries. His pen is personified as a widow grieving the same "darling husband" she "scolded up from earth to heaven" in his lifetime.[54]

Halleck risked a great deal with his harsh appraisal of New England's past. The assault on popular ideals once again divided his readers. The valiant and vicious lines of "Connecticut" showed a "clashing of moods" and were typical of his "peculiar character."[55] Halleck was demoralized by his country's record of attaining freedom only to abuse it. Adkins believed that the poem was written "with the detachment of an outsider" and suggests that Halleck remembered "humorously in his verses on 'Connecticut' what he deemed the narrowness and bigotry of his native state."[56] But Wilson, who was Halleck's guest in Guilford, felt that the poem attacked only the town.

Its moral integrity insulted, Guilford fought back. Contemporary critics supported the town's negative reaction, whereas later critics reacted somewhat more favorably. The *National Magazine* said "Connecticut" "was unworthy of living. . . . If [Halleck] has any more of the same sort left, we advise a bonfire somewhere in his neighborhood."[57] Nevertheless, the poem was added to the new edition of Halleck's works. Adkins placed "Connecticut" among Halleck's best work and Stanley Williams defended it, calling Halleck "the most distinguished Connecticut poet."[58] *Literary History* also praised the poem. If Halleck won his fight against American Puritanism, he surrendered his opportunity for local citizenship. Emphasizing the maniacal theology and sexual hysteria of Guilford's elders did not endear Halleck to his townsmen. Residents retaliated by depicting him as a wealthy, lazy, crazy, Catholic, drunken, bachelor monarchist. Sodomitical associations linked all these accusations.

For starters, Halleck's white-collar wardrobe offended neighbors. Ironically, his clothes were his only material assets from years of hard work. Even generations later, a town historian declared Halleck "the wealthiest inhabitant of Guilford" and claims were made that his annuity left him "plump and unworried."[59] *Fraser's* also reported that Halleck lived on a "handsome annuity," when in truth Halleck was in a "low state" of "meager financial resources."[60] At age seventy-five, he was forced to move with his sister Maria from the family house on the town green to rooms on an off street. Despite fifty years' income and a purported seventeen thousand dollars in literary earnings, Halleck was "cramped by insufficient means" and accepted an "end chilled by poverty and neglect" with stoicism.[61] Whatever Halleck's actual income may have been, Guilford saw him as an aristocrat and, apparently, considered sodomy a luxury item.

Halleck rejected the town's value of frugality and "had no idea of this glorification of poverty."[62] He was in no position to spend lavishly but strongly objected to the attitude "that any single man who spent more than five hundred dollars a year would be drummed out of the town."[63] Kenneth R. Lee concluded that Halleck was unpopular "because he had no visible means of support, had never made a crop or brought in a boatload of fish."[64] The very target of "Connecticut," Cotton Mather had preached a sermon called "The Sin of Sodom" in 1701, warning: "The sin of Sodom was, Abundance of Idleness. All the Sins of Sodom will abound, where Idleness is countenanced." Mather was joined by others in this belief.[65]

In 1644, Edward Coke reinstituted the death penalty for sodomy caused, in part, by idleness. William Bradford of Pennsylvania claimed there were no sodomites in his state by 1786 because its youth "worked hard and married early, thus eliminating the problem."[66] Even Halleck's early "A View of the United States" emulated the Puritan work ethic, warning: "Toil, toil, my lads, to purchase honest gain; / Shun idleness, shun pleasure's tempting snare."[67] By the time of Halleck's generation, the Puritan work ethic had become inseparably meshed with the Puritan sex ethic. Sodomy continued to be associated with an absence of physical labor. Halleck's work as a millionaire's secretary and poet was Guilford's idea of a life spent in folly or worse.

Halleck was an American artist "when less sympathy was felt with artistic endeavor" and residents were "disturbed" by his "bohemian ways."[68] Hawthorne's humorless recollections in "Artist of the Beautiful" of his kinsmen's distrust aptly described Halleck's situation. Hawthorne's lack of humor and asocial behavior annoyed Halleck, who once commented wryly, "Last night Nathaniel Hawthorne and I sat together at dinner and talked for an hour, although Hawthorne said nothing."[69] As late as 1976, Guilford's Reverend Charles Biggs was critical of Halleck's "sweatless work."[70] Halleck only chastized himself for intellectual sloth, writing to a friend: "I find myself fast becoming as ignorant of books and their writers as the President of a College or the Regent of a University."[71] If Halleck felt that his mind was slipping, Guilford was quick to agree.

Sodomy had also become linked to insanity. Although nineteenth-century American cases of sodomy dwindled radically while British executions persisted, the United States emulated England's jumbling of sexuality, gender norms, and mental health. Britain carried out over fifty

sodomy executions in the first third of the nineteenth century,[72] while sodomy laws carrying the death penalty were abolished beginning with Pennsylvania in 1786, New York and New Jersey in 1796, Rhode Island in
1798, for free persons in Virginia in 1800, Massachusetts in 1805, New
Hampshire in 1812, Connecticut in 1821, and Delaware in 1826.[73] While
legal changes created some relief for same-sex partners in America, the
homosexual caricature was imported, and subsequently:

Mid-nineteenth-century American texts began to inscribe sodomitical acts within
a sphere that allowed an association of emotional context with the act, making
the anxious leap from notions about the individual sodomite to speculations
about a species marked by effeminacy and mental instability.[74]

The new sodomite was turned on the British who created him. American
Federalists like Royall Tyler described American characters as manly
compared to Red Coats,[75] while English pamphlets such as *Plain Reasons for the Growth of Sodomy in England* (1730) and *Satan's Harvest
Home* (1749) had illustrated the evolving British sodomite's effeminate
nature.[76]

Guilford's gossipers assured themselves that Halleck was "quite out
of his mind."[77] In retirement, he would compose poetry aloud on walks
and punctuate new thoughts with a swing of his umbrella so that townspeople "became perfectly satisfied in their own minds that poor Halleck
had gone mad, and that he should accordingly be confined in a safe
place."[78] His declaration of British loyalty a century after the American
Revolution did not help his case for mental competency.

Halleck's claim of being a monarchist further alienated him from his
humorless neighbors. In the collective Puritan mind-set, the British monarchy had evolved into sodomy's greatest advocate. Early Stuart England
was fairly tolerant of homosexuality, and for six decades after the passage
of 5 Elizabeth, c. 17, sodomy trials were both scarce and politically motivated.[79] Laxity of the law was ensured by rumors of King James's own
homosexuality.[80] Further, James I harbored strong anti-Puritan sentiments, so the preservation of Puritan faith from royal defilement was
promoted by public convictions of sodomitical Laudian clergymen like
Reverend John Wilson who was made infamous for coveting male parish-
ioners.[81] Guilford's belief that Halleck really was a monarchist was both
a civil and a moral insult. A persistent rumor that he had secretly converted to Catholicism while in New York only fanned the flame.

American Puritanism abhorred Catholicism. The American sermon
"Danger of Desertion" claimed that England was in "captivity and bond-
age under the blindness of popery."[82] Halleck had made a one-hundred-
dollar donation, one-half of his annual retirement annuity, to help rebuild
Christ Protestant Episcopal Church, which would later be the setting

for his own funeral. But such philanthropy could not hush the "often-repeated, but groundless statement" that Halleck was a Roman Catholic.[83] Adkins's claim that Halleck leaned toward Catholicism because of his words—"It is a church which saves you a deal of trouble"—missed Halleck' sarcasm.[84] Halleck proposed that "the great masses of the people of all countries believe as their fathers believed before them. Not one in a thousand ever chooses his religious faith."[85] Halleck in fact rarely attended any type of church service, so Duyckinck rightly realized that Halleck's defense of Catholicism, like the "maintenance of his monarchical theory in republican America," was "mere intellectual sport."[86] Halleck showed no partiality for creeds: Catholic and Protestant were alike to him. This was not the case, however, for Maria.

Maria Halleck was so distressed by the rumors of her brother's Catholicism that she convinced her minister to write a long letter to *Putnam's* categorically refuting the allegation in order to "rescue [her brother's] memory."[87] Rector Lorenzo T. Bennett responded to *Putnam's* obituary notice, contradicting the rumors and declaring Halleck a devout, model parishioner, who only stayed away from services because of his hearing loss.[88] Bennett vehemently argued that Halleck had an unshakable devotion to his church and that he would have attended the Catholic services within yards of his own door if he had converted. Bennett also documented Halleck's religion with a letter from the rector of St. Stephen's Church in Ridgefield, Connecticut. Maria read and approved the defense before its submission. But Guilford's allusions to Halleck's outsider status did not drive him out of his mind or into the Catholic church. They drove him to drink.

Praise for Halleck's "champagne-talk" was not merely metaphorical.[89] Noting that old memories and literature comforted the aged poet, Charles F. Johnson professed that Halleck "is to be forgiven if he sometimes resorted to temporary means of artificial forgetfulness." While J. H. Monroe would honor Halleck with the New Hotel Halleck in 1902, Halleck's drinking "frequently shocked the Puritan sensibilities of many of the villagers, who often failed to respond to the poet's addresses."[90] One of Halleck's chums recalled "the grace of [Halleck's] brow, as our wine glasses touched each other."[91] An account in the *New England Magazine* adds that Halleck was "one of the merriest souls that ever chirped over a winecup."[92] Gabriel Harrison also recollected drinking with Halleck in New York.[93] Among others, Evert Duyckinck recalled an intoxicated Halleck: "I met Halleck returning from the spot [a Brooklyn pub], redolent of its cheer. Anticipating my movement, he hailed me with some rollicking intimation of the crisping duck. . . . he was too genuine a poet in his anacreontics to despise the generous vintage."[94] One town elder who recalled

Halleck's funeral said that people "kept away back in the grave yard at the dedication services, because they thought they had not ought to honor Halleck because he drank whiskey!"[95]

To Puritan forefathers, poetry had been the "Devil's wine,"[96] and Guilford's later citizens felt that Halleck's indulgence quelled his poetic fire: "If [Halleck] was lighted up occasionally, it was not with the fire divine. He rusted out, and that not gloriously."[97] The *Knickerbocker*'s article on Halleck also juxtaposed alcohol and poetry: "Various are the devices invented by human ingenuity . . . from the miserable excitement of alcoholic drinks up to the refined and intellectual pleasures of poetry."[98] But the *New England Magazine* saw no trace of alcoholic debilitation in his verse: "Indeed there is a very healthy tone about everything he has written; nothing seems the fruit of unnatural excitement; he evidently does not belong to the gin-and-water school of poetry."[99]

Even while living in the big city, Halleck had been confounded by the New York City Temperance Society, founded 1829, and the immensely popular Washingtonian movement, which moved tens of thousands to pledge abstinence. New York's chapter was established in 1841. The New York melodrama *The Drunkard* (1850) broke all previous performance records, and Whitman had not been above capitalizing on these movements with his popular novel *Franklin Evans the Inebriate*. For himself, Halleck used the issue of prohibition to point out religious hypocrisy. In 1864, he wrote a friend that he was shocked to hear a "Maine-law man" speak against Christ's miraculous wine-making miracle, claiming, "Were He [Christ] now on earth He would not dare to outrage public opinion to such a degree."[100] But moral opposition against Halleck ran as late as 1970, when Guilford's citizens decided against naming a room in the public library after Halleck because he drank too much.[101] His bachelorhood only compounded the problem.

Halleck's decision never to marry carried a high social price. America has simultaneously forbidden same-sex marriage and condemned a perceived lack of homosexual commitment within relationships right into the twentieth century. Halleck's lifestyle was as far outside of mainstream rural America as his lack of interest in women must have seemed to his coworkers and female admirers. Because of the conspicuous absence of women in his life, some assumed that Halleck had no feelings at all. The unsigned "Halleck's Monument" reconsidered his poetry by the heterosexual standards that the *Broadway Journal* had used in 1845:

In that crucial test of poetry, the treatment of Love and Women, Mr. Halleck was wholly deficient. If he had never made any attempt in that direction it might have been claimed for him that he had the power, if he had chosen to use it; but he tried, and utterly failed.[102]

M. B. Brady's undated print of Fitz-Greene Halleck. Halleck reluctantly allowed himself to be photographed by Brady, probably during the Civil War. (Portrait File, Miriam and Ira D. Wallach Division of Art, Prints, and Photographs, The New York Public Library: Astor, Lenox, and Tilden Foundations.) Another Brady daguerreotype dated 1855 also depicts a debilitated Halleck depressed by heavy drinking and by his forced retirement to Guilford. The New York Public Library also holds a Civil War portrait of Halleck after an engraving by Perine and Giles used in *Eclectic Magazine* (February 1868) and Horatio Greenough's 1868 bas-relief-style drawing of Halleck.

Revealing no interest for the opposite sex, Halleck's verse was further described as bad sex: "His entire treatment of the subject [heterosexual romance] is so passionless, so dry and mechanical . . . that it is clear he had no feeling to express nor imagination to conceive the sweet passion." Additionally, critics discounted his love for Drake. Ironically, they also condemned Halleck's bachelorhood but praised its presumed virtue.

Halleck was chastised for not producing children as well as for his "literary sterility" in retirement.[103] One twentieth-century critic thought trade had "sterilized Halleck's creative power," while another took Halleck to task as a decadent "priest and devotee of culture" who never married and "did not envision children, with all they mean in human life. Nor had he any civic sense."[104] In sharp contrast, William Allen Butler, orator at the statue's commemoration, publicly praised Halleck's "pure youth" and "unsullied manhood" and regarded his poetic power as "the bright consummate flower of a virgin soil."[105] Halleck could not win by the rules of his hometown in his retirement anymore than in his adolescence.

Despite all of the barbs tossed his way, Halleck remained a congenial figure who never left home without his green umbrella and whose "silk hat was always doffed when a lady passed."[106] In the year of his death, a friend told Halleck, "'Your courtesy seems to be thrown away on those boors,' 'Yes, perhaps 'tis so,' he replied, 'but yet, that's no reason why I should be a boor.'"[107] Although Halleck maintained a stiff upper lip, Guilford's daily acts of rejection were deeply felt. In 1852, Halleck gladly returned to New York, even if it was only to give away another bride.[108]

Two years later, Halleck wrote "To Louis Gaylord Clark, Esquire," editor of the *Knickerbocker,* to help celebrate Clark's marriage. The poem appeared on the final page of *Knickerbocker Gallery* (1855), a collector's volume of over five-hundred pages. The book included works by Bayard Taylor, Henry Tuckerman, George P. Morris, Henry Longfellow, Frederick S. Cozzens, N. P. Willis, and Rufus Griswold. Clark was deeply moved by the "unusually personal" poem and wrote Halleck, "My heart is in my mouth, and most grateful tears are in my wife's eyes."[109] Halleck had also sent Clark a copy of his portrait by Charles Loring Elliott.

Halleck had attended Clark's wedding in the same manner as a guest in the poem: "A stranger, mateless and forlorn, / Pledged bachelor and hermit sworn." The first-person narrator is witness to the "sanction of approving Heaven" and nearly forgets "my anti-nuptial vow" and is tempted to propose to one of the bridesmaids. But the lure of family life is fleeting. Halleck was much more interested in flattering young men.

Halleck responded to a male admirer's request for an autograph two years after Clark's wedding, warning him that the poet's handwriting was not that of "a poetess." Halleck's letters grew increasingly campy as he aged. In 1867, Halleck asked Frederick S. Cozzens to burn a part of the letter he had sent him as soon as he had read it. Adkins found the opening paragraph "an enigma," and the subsequent prose was no more transparent. Halleck feigned surprise at a "Golden wedding" "indebted to a third person! How shocking!" and joked, "You were very fortunate in being absent when I called twice upon you lately in New York."[110] Adkins failed to see the letter's humor and claimed that Halleck was "lost in a world growing daily more subtle and scientific," whereas Richard Henry Stoddard more astutely observed that Halleck's frequent stays in the city were the direct result of his banishment to Guilford and his lifelong lure to "the sweet security of the streets."[111]

By 1857, Halleck seemed to be visiting more dead people than live ones in New York. That September he joined Wilson to see the new comedy *Married for Money,* which starred his friend, Charles Mathews. Halleck talked Wilson into a grave-hopping expedition the next morning. They visited the resting places of numerous associates such as actor George Frederick Cooke, whose tomb was inscribed with Halleck's words in 1821, and Alexander Hamilton. Wilson claimed that Halleck showed him many graves during this visit as well as during an 1866 visit to New York.[112]

As he approached his seventieth year, Halleck met George Canale, Greek translator of "Marco Bozzaris," in New York and began to identify himself as a "stranger and sojourner" in the city.[113] He was, nevertheless, among familiar faces for Burns's centenary dinner held at the Astor House Hotel in 1859. Halleck and Bryant were again touted as America's greatest living poets, the competition having been eased by Irving's death. In May 1859, Halleck had written a private poem to Bryant. That poem personified spring as an adolescent boy who "has blossomed on his wandering way," meandering through nature and life. The carefree youth is eternal and charms plants from their "mortal doom."[114] Bryant maintained his friendship with Halleck and often called on him while he was incapacitated by a severe cold in April 1860. Halleck felt so ill that he gave directions for funeral services and burial in New York City in case of his death. Although he was facing his own mortality, Halleck was always sure to return to New York for July 4th, his favorite day. He personified the holiday as "him" who was "as noisy and as merry as ever" in an 1858 letter.[115]

The nation, in turn, had not forgotten Halleck. In 1852, Lydia Huntly Sigourney sent a long epistolary poem hoping that Halleck would once again "startle the mermaids from their slumbers." More praise from his literary friends followed. He was persuaded to attend a festival for American writers in September 1853. Two months later, an honorary dinner was planned at the Century Club. Halleck claimed a scheduling conflict but was prevailed upon to attend the January 18, 1854, gala. Bryant presided at the Halleck dinner, which was described in detail by the *Journal of Commerce* (January 19, 1854). Halleck reciprocated the honor by serving on a committee planning Thackeray's dinner during his visit to the United States in 1855–1856, but at that dinner, during the guest of honor's speech denouncing George IV, Halleck walked out declaring, "I can't listen any longer to his abuse of a better man than himself."[116]

Halleck was also honored by friends who planned to name their next son after him. His November 1859 letter requested that they delay doing so until he was dead, though he was "highly flattered" and wrote of his "own monotonous and uneventful life" in Guilford. But he told Wilson that such gestures were in truth annoying. He complained:

I am favored by affectionate fathers with epistles announcing that their eldest-born has been named after me, a calamity that costs me a letter of profound gratefulness, the correspondence usually terminating with a gentle hint that the illustrious poet's namesake's parents would greatly prize a copy of his poetical writings, with the dear child's name inscribed in the book, etc., etc.[117]

His cynical view of public adoration knew no boundaries.

An increasingly irritable Halleck also feigned shock at inaccuracies in the explanatory notes of the Bradford Club's *Croakers* (1860) for which he had not been consulted.[118] He was also pestered by "frequent appeals for letters to hard-hearted editors" and of requests for money by "a Bohemian." Others sought his influence in obtaining jobs at the Astor Library or solicited criticism for their own poetry. Halleck scoffed at lecture-circuit committees in sixteen different states that offered him fifty dollars to speak. He laments in a letter to Wilson: "I have been persecuted by autograph-hunters, those 'mosquitoes of literature.'" Perfect strangers begged for manuscript copies, and innumerable applications poured in not only for his own autograph but also for those of Astor and Drake. The same letter tells of numerous universities and clubs hounding Halleck with honorary posts and of others who hoped their dearly departed would be honored with a poem from Halleck "similar to the one beginning 'Green be the turf above thee,' etc.," for which they would gladly pay.[119] But a price could not be placed on that elegy.

In 1866, Halleck was contacted by John Williamson Palmer, who was planning a new edition of "the most elegant collection [of poetry], internally and externally, ever published in this country." Palmer wanted an autographed copy "of the Lines on the death of the Poet Drake." He pleaded, "I cannot account for the oversight by which a poem so universally admired was omitted from the first editions."[120] Halleck never replied. The public was so insensitive to his love for Drake that he could never sign the dead Drake's name or prostitute his lines on Drake's death.

In another letter to Wilson (January 28, 1861), Halleck asked his future biographer to pass along a poem that he did not write to a female admirer who had requested an original poem from him. He asked Wilson to "ask her if the inevitable destiny of woman, that of 'falling in love,' sooner or later, has ever been more beautifully expressed" than in the enclosed poem.[121] Halleck also refused requests for poems on the Civil War. Not even Abraham Lincoln's praise moved Halleck to write on that subject. In 1860, Lincoln wrote a mutual friend: "I am greatly obliged for the volume of your friend, Fitz-Greene Halleck's poems," adding, "Many a month has passed since I have met with anything more admirable than his beautiful lines."[122] Halleck could not support either side of the Civil War and wrote Mrs. John Rush on November 21, 1861, that both sides were at fault. Given his pacifism, Halleck would probably have objected to the inclusion of his works in Frank Moore's *Civil War in Song and Story* (1882).

Halleck's poetry reflected the low social status of free blacks but accentuated their good qualities. "To the Baron Von Hoffman" mentions a black servant, "Carlo, beloved of thy bosom." Halleck joked to Drake's daughter that slaves had belonged to Southerners ever since they had been "stolen."[123] Although he never joined the abolitionists, Halleck generally conveyed a kind sentiment in polished manners that extended across racial boundaries. A Northern friend was startled while walking with Halleck on Broadway "when he stopped, turned back, took off his hat to, and shook hands with, this negro."[124] In his last conversation with Joel Benton, Halleck expressed relief that "'the crime of Slavery'" had been "cured" by the war.[125]

Halleck's own patriotic dilemma paralleled Harriet Jacobs's sentiment: "It is a sad feeling to be afraid of one's native country."[126] Chances are that he both identified with the plight of slaves and took offense at the homophobic content of American abolitionist literature. The relationship between sodomy and slavery was one of tremendous contradiction. Although homosexuality existed in many African cultures, some black critics argue that homosexuality is a white habit and "a remnant of slavery."[127] This contradiction has begun to be addressed, yet Wayne Dynes asserts that "although abundant evidence now exists for a variety of homosexual social patterns in black Africa, the notion that the behavior is somehow distinctively white lingers."[128] Even today, African homosexuality is denied by some African Americans.[129] Still, both the North and South used sodomy to their own advantage. Slave owners argued that Africa was a haven of sodomy, and a Southern editorial claimed that New York was worse off than Sodom.[130]

One critic claims that colonists perpetuated white supremacy by seeing African sodomy as "an index to the viciousness of . . . barbaric societies."[131] Another cites African eunuchs, tribal sodomy, and "religious transgenderal homosexuality" in more than ten African countries and claims that "slaves brought from Africa persisted in the homosexual practices they'd learned [there]."[132] In American law, black men were frequently judged to be more sexually threatening than white men and New England trials were often racially biased.[133] Juxtaposed to this racial-sexual position, abolitionist literature relied on the colonial model of sodomy as rape.

The correlation between homosexual rape and slavery was established by works like Harriet Beecher Stowe's *Uncle Tom's Cabin,* which compared slavery to the vices of Sodom and Gomorrah and created anxiety over the situation of the "remarkably beautiful" Jim Crow, a slave-boy "petted and noticed by his master."[134] Although Harriet Beecher Stowe is not considered an abolitionist because of her novel's embrace of colonization, Frances E. W. Harper and Harriet Jacobs were certainly abolitionists. Harper's poem "Bible Defence of Slavery" also connects slavery with Sodom, and her "Lessons of the Street" depicts a young black homosexual prostitute.[135] Jacobs's narrative has a subplot about a male slave who is "not allowed to wear any thing but his shirt" for bedroom floggings. The master's hand grew palsied as he became "a mere degraded wreck of manhood" construing "the strangest freaks of despotism": "Some of these freaks were of a nature too filthy to be repeated."[136] The slave-owning sodomite's physical disability provides poetic justice for his sexual sins. The exiling of America's sodomites by colonists foreshadowed removal policies prescribed for Indians and colonization proposed for blacks.

As a metaphor, slavery was well suited to those keeping their sexuality under lock and key and who were also persecuted by their own nation's government. Recurringly, Halleck's narrators are hostages in undeserved chains, but Rush's request for a lyric on the war was nonetheless deflected by Halleck's rhetorical response:

Is this Southern, this sin-born war of ours, worthy of a poet's consecration? . . . On the contrary, it is but a mutiny, a monstrous mutiny, whose ring-leaders are a dozen crime-torn politicians, determined to keep themselves in power, and will sooner or later find its Nemesis in the blood and tears of a servile insurrection.[137]

Halleck did agree to write on "a war with England," which was one possible consequence of the Union navy's Captain Charles Wilkes's capture of John Slidell, a Southern leader taken from the British steamer *Trent* while on his way to Europe as a minister plenipotentiary of the Confederate government. Halleck told Rush that he would sing "the wrath of John Bull for the captivity of John Slidell, . . . as Homer won his laurels by singing the wrath of Achilles for the loss of his sweetheart." Even Halleck's comments on the entrapment of Slidell end with a return to the comic, though.

An 1863 letter to Maria Van Sickle was a response to her request for a picture of Halleck, who hoped that a mutual female acquaintance could "entrap the 'millionaire.'" Since war contracts had sent wealthy men "flying in our cities," Halleck promised to spread his "net over a brace of them and have them bagged to her address. She can choose the eldest first, and reserve the youngest for future choosing."[138] But it was Halleck's more familiar theme of a man marrying for money that served as the punch line of his last major poem, "Young America." As though he had been storing up the mischief that still glittered in his face, he wrote just as soon as peace was imminent.

Nearly seventy-five years old, Halleck sent his last poem off for publication in the *New York Ledger*. Having once observed, "Ere the dolphin dies / Its hues are brightest," Halleck had saved his best for last.[139] Although America grew more homophobic after the Civil War when a conservative backlash reestablished the pursuit of sodomites,[140] Halleck felt a new freedom in his final years and transformed a popular political phrase into a pederastic spoof on marriage. "Young America" was a popular phrase that had served as the title of a newspaper in 1845 and as a slogan for New York Democrats in 1852. Mortimer Thompson's 1856 parody of "Hiawatha," "Plu-Ri-Bus-Tah," attacked Halleck's capitalistic "Yunga-Merrekah." Halleck's "Young America" is a three-hundred-line poem of rhymed iambs described as "rather a series of lyrics in varied measure, held together by a running comment."[141] However, Halleck was satisfied with the composition. In late November 1865, he pushed his publisher for "the project of a new volume or volumes, embracing the Young America."[142]

At the pedagogical level, the poem reviewed American history from its religious foundation (personified by a preacher) to its independence (personified by a Revolutionary War soldier). "Young America" extended Halleck's use of a boy figure who had represented spring in a private poem to Bryant five years earlier. This time, an eroticized fourteen-year-old boy symbolizes the nation at a new point of maturity after the Civil War. The subtext could have been titled "Young Halleck." Although his lids are closed in sleep, the protagonist is blessed "with eye-delighting eyes / Sparkling as stars, and blue as summer's skies" reminiscent of Halleck's "Forget-Me-Not" poem to Drake and their cowritten "The American Flag." The boy is an effeminate figure with the "sweetest tone" and "bright gold hair / In thick curls clustering round his even brow, / And dimpled cheek." Like a sexual cherub, he sleeps in a garden ripe for plucking. Miltonic images (of the honeymooners in *Paradise Lost*) surface as they had in Halleck's adolescent poem to Carlos Menie. The boy sleeps "cradled on rose-leaves, curtained round with vines, / And canopied by branches of a tree" in an Edenic bower. Nature plays the spouse as "the youth reclines" basking in her "fond caressing glow" and "wedded love-clasps," until a Gospel teacher stumbles upon the boy in "a moment's mute surprise" but with "grateful eyes."

Delighted with the boy's "loveliness," the preacher is reminded of his own lost son and whispers, "Would that I might wake, / And woo, and win him, for his soul's sweet sake, / To make my home his cloister, and entwine / All his life's hopes and happiness with mine." The preacher has visions of a blessed domestic life with a boy who will turn away from "gay sportive dreams." The clergyman essentially desires to reproduce himself in the boy who will grow up to be the shepherd of the flock when he is gone. But he flees at the approaching sound of the bugle, fife, and drum, and the boy sleeps on.

A military officer also attaches himself to Halleck's boy in wedlock imagery. He nicknames the boy "the young Endymion"[143] and sings a "mental song" while spying on the sleeping teenager. Meanwhile, the soldier's troops pay "heart-homage" with "each saluting eye" as they file past the boy and his admirer by the thousands. The military band is "plaintively breathing partings" in music that moves "the soldier's heart beat quick and gay" as he tears himself from the object of his adoration. Like the preacher, he wishes he could keep the boy in a lifelong commitment: "Ah me! What delight it would give me to wake him, / And lead him wherever my life-banners wave." He envisions the boy as an envoy of peace, bearing the olive branch after battle. The soldier also hopes to reproduce himself in the mutable figure.

In short, Halleck had come full circle. "Young America" returned to his teenaged poem "The Fortunate Family" in which a boy receives his surrogate father/husband. Both poems seek escape from ordinary society by presenting an alternative family. Children are set free in "gay delight" from "their school-room cages" in the next section of "Young America." The boy wakes after a whispered song "from lips unseen, unknown" and the vision of a fairy who "was not at all inclined to marry." He rises from the familiar "green turf" of Halleck's elegy to Drake and decides, since he was once rejected, that "he is happiest who had never loved," repeating the philosophical conclusion of Halleck's earlier poem "Love." Although he is yet a child, his "veiled" and "hidden" grief does not allow him to forget "painful memories" as he bids his vanished muse adieu.[144]

The poem concludes, "Farewell to Rhyme! and welcome Reason!" as the boy rejects being adopted by preacher or soldier. A month shy of being fifteen, he emerges from his trance as a man who has given up on love.

Then the poem turns comic as its hero submits to true American values, and the final lines vow:

> There but remains one promise to fulfil,
> I bow myself obedient to its will,
> And am prepared to settle down in life
> By wooing—winning—wedding A RICH WIFE.[145]

Among others, Duyckinck found the above stanza a "most lame and impotent conclusion," although Adkins felt that the critic seemed "largely to have missed the satiric touch with which the poem concludes."[146] Yet Adkins himself described the ending as "obviously forced and incongruous." Lathrop found it "hard to discern any purpose, artistic or otherwise" in the entirely "weak performance."[147] Evaluating his own dreams of adolescent men and his actual experience with Drake, Halleck decided that nothing serious had come of his long fight for personal freedom.

Having failed to find the egalitarian model of same-sex love he had sought, Halleck reconsidered the classical model. But in doing so, his eye was actually on the future generation. The pederast gaze, tamed by platonic and paternal affirmations, does not profess Halleck's acquired taste for man-boy sexual relations but infuses his mature insights into the collective body of future homosexual poets who would carry on the cultural war. Halleck did not want others to suffer the same isolation, confusion, and unhappiness that his own early sense of difference had caused. His disillusionment with democracy was almost as bad as his disappointment with love. America did not, and would not, see its homosexual children.

Colonists, shocked by the young age at which Indians wed, were even more offended by the identification of preadolescent berdaches by tribal members. Walter L. Williams's "Inborn Character and Childhood Activities" discusses the identification of berdaches throughout the nineteenth century among various tribes at ages three to five, six, twelve, and fourteen.[148] Late twentieth-century homophobic campaigns, such as California's Proposition 6 against gay teachers and Anita Bryant's religious campaign, "Save the Children," posit a single model of asexual or exclusively heterosexual child development in America. Hence, the Boy Scouts of America continue to ban gay leaders who might only be scouting for boys.

Shortly after Halleck's poem appeared, Horatio Alger, Jr., who would become famous for *Ragged Dick,* a novel about an adolescent New York street urchin, admitted to participating in "unnatural crimes" with the young boys of his parish.[149] About the same time, Halleck found himself taking an apologetic stand regarding his poem. He responded to Mrs. John Rush's year-long silence on "Young America" by admitting, "I cannot expect [it] to be liked, or even tolerated."[150] Frederick Cozzens joined other critics who were perplexed and could not compare the poem "to anything else for it is not like anything else. . . . Something that may be enjoyed but cannot be defined."[151] The end of the Civil War coincided with the resolution of Halleck's internal battle. Unable to realize his own dream of male marriage, he surrendered to an earlier and highly sexualized view of homosexuality. Like the protagonist in "Young America," Halleck had finally awakened.

Halleck's other poem of 1864 was "Charade." The unpublished poem lived up to its title. Superficially about the modern soldier, it focused on death. The "screaming trumpet" calls young men to die in the opening lines and by the midpoint of the poem the narrator-poet sings "beneath the silent night" over a corpse with a wreath on its head and a cross upon his breast. The dutiful tear of the surviving poet is shed before the final lines in which Halleck drops the charade:

> Yea call him by his name
>   No fitter hand may crave
> To light the flame of the Soldier's fame
>   On the turf of a Soldier's grave.

Halleck often complained to friends of his struggle to keep the word "turf" in his Drake elegy against numerous editorial suggestions.

At seventy-five, Halleck still challenged death and hated marriage. He sarcastically congratulated James H. Hackett who was remarrying: "May your marriage destiny be the long life of the one, and the long purses of the other!"[152] Halleck had met Hackett in 1818, and Hackett's second marriage was to a bride more than forty years younger than himself. Halleck skipped the wedding but visited New York City three times in 1867, the year of his death. His April trip was hampered by a serious cold which made him quite irritable. He had fully recovered in time for a June return when he attended an author's dinner. He wrote his ideas about literature down in several letters before returning to the city in autumn.

In early September 1867, Halleck struggled to define American poetry in a long correspondence to James Grant Wilson. As if Halleck knew death was quickly approaching, he prepared a final summary of his thoughts. In a letter written at the same time to a lifelong friend, he recorded his observations on democracy and marriage. Because of bipartisan bickering, he estimated the vote at "no value" in a party system and claimed that he had never voted in a political election, although he had cast two social votes: "once for an assistant alderman, and once for a ten-dollar bill, both of which proved counterfeit."[153] Halleck spent the first two weeks of October 1867 in New York with another cold. While in the city, he first confided to Wilson that he believed death was drawing near.

Halleck's faculties remained intact up until his death. On October 26, he wrote in a final letter, "An Author knows his own meaning better and can better express it than his critic can. Critics like noxious weeds do but cumber the ground they spring up on."[154] In fact, such weeds had never understood the green turf that Halleck had metaphorically used to blanket Drake's grave. During their final interview, Halleck directed Wilson as though recalling the opening of "On the Death of Joseph R. Drake": "If we never meet again, come and see me laid under the sod of my native village." Among Halleck's private papers near his deathbed, Wilson discovered several unpublished verses written by Drake at the ages of five and ten years old.

Halleck made preparations for his own grave, clearly conveying his final wishes to his sister. On the day he died, November 19, 1867, Halleck had walked to his doctor's house and then sat up talking to Maria. Around eleven o'clock that Tuesday night, he called out, "Marie, hand me my pantaloons, if you please."[155] By the time she turned around with his underwear, her brother had died without making a sound.

Three days after his death, Halleck's coffin, adorned with a silver plate, was buried in Guilford. He was not laid beside Drake as he had once hoped. Instead, Halleck and his father were exhumed in August 1868 and placed under the new Halleck monument at the center of the cemetery. *Harper's New Monthly Magazine* described the graveyard as puritanical,[156] and Adkins observed that the funeral was underattended due to the town's "indifference and prejudice." A final resistance to Guilford's puritanical superstition and local tradition against naming the dead may well have been Halleck's last request. When Maria was reminded that it was customary in Guilford to ring out the departed's age on the church bell so that townspeople might guess who had died, she declined. Guilford may have possessed the oldest town clock in America, but the night air remained locked in silence.

6

Halleck and His Friend

Why should I subscribe money to build some hero's statue? . . .
He does not know what fear is.

Walt Whitman, Leaves of Grass

WITH DRAKE and Halleck both dead, the story of their friendship could finally be told. That task was taken up by Bayard
Taylor. Halleck had met both his biographer James Grant Wilson and Taylor at Bixby's Hotel in New York City in 1851. Bixby's was
defined by *Harper's* as "just the place for a bachelor, and certainly it is
for a poet," and it was a Bixby resident who recorded Halleck's obscr-
vations of the changes in the "moral physiognomy" of New York City.[1]
Bixby's provided a space where the artistic and genteel could come together. Although the hotel catered to the bachelor, Taylor, who was a
married man, found himself there. Taylor had remarkable insight into
both the expression and oppression of homosexuality in nineteenth-
century America. Taylor's widow did not give Wilson the impression that
her husband had been happy, and Taylor's sexuality has been questioned
by at least three scholars who treat him as homosexual.[2] An influential
editor and prolific writer, Taylor commemorated Halleck's Guilford monument in July 1869.

Taylor was preparing his dedicatory address for that ceremony and
was writing his version of Goethe's *Faust* when he arrived in Guilford.
Taylor was also outlining his manuscript for America's first homosexual
novel, *Joseph and His Friend* (1870). Taylor was at the height of his influence, but his designation as the "right and suitable"[3] orator for the
Halleck dedication was appropriate for reasons other than his literary
status. Halleck had had an excellent friend in Taylor, who also attended the
unveiling of Halleck's statue eight years later. As a confident seventeen-

year-old, Taylor had solicited Halleck's autograph. The teenaged Taylor apologized for his boldness and closed his letter, "By sending [your auto-graph] with the bearer you will confer a lasting favour on yours truly."[4] The favor was repaid with interest: Taylor would fictionalize Halleck's love for Drake.

Taylor also served as a link between Halleck and Walt Whitman at another liberal establishment. Robert K. Martin believes that Halleck and Whitman met through Taylor as regular clients of Charles Pfaff, whose restaurant bar catered to a homosexual clientele.[5] Pfaff's was patronized by "writers, whores, queens and street-car drivers" as well as by editor Henry Clapp, Whitman's "friend and companion in the Pfaff's restaurant coterie."[6] Whitman frequented Pfaff's bohemian bar between 1857 and 1861, where he doted over his "'darlings and gossips,' who gathered at Pfaff's Restaurant on Broadway near Bleeker Street in Greenwich Vil-lage."[7] Whitman supposedly read "Beat! Beat! Drums!" to an audience at Pfaff's, and his uncollected poem "The Two Vaults" was based on the underground establishment. The poem reflects the "bright eyes of beauti-ful young men!" strutting the bar in an unreal "pageant"; the hungry narrator longs to "arrest" one of them "as they flit along" in the literal and figurative underground bar.[8] Pfaff's joins the list of New York sites (bathhouses, wharves, and parks) where homosexuals met and returned to boarding houses for sex or patronized male prostitutes throughout the 1840s and 1850s.[9]

Whitman certainly knew Halleck informally long before Taylor's prob-able introduction. Whitman's journals mention seeing Halleck at the the-ater and running into Halleck on Broadway.[10] Whitman and Taylor had been good friends before their 1876 estrangement that was possibly caused by Whitman's professional jealousy of Taylor.[11] They shared Halleck's be-lief that American democracy was severely limited. Like Halleck, Taylor and Whitman were attracted to urban life, foreign eroticism, and the arts.

Whitman also shared Halleck's great love of the opera. Halleck was seated between the deposed king of Spain (Joseph Bonaparte) and James Fenimore Cooper at the Park Theater for the October 1825 premiere of New York's first Italian opera. Halleck enjoyed the opera so much that he determined to take Italian lessons from opera librettist Lorenzo Da Ponte, who became a close friend. After the performance, Halleck frol-icked about with the former king in uninhibited horseplay resulting in the "raciest and most amusing" evening that Halleck would ever recall.[12] Other charms of city life were also held in common by Halleck and Whitman.

The sheer variety of urban living appealed to both poets. Whitman used lengthy detailed catalogs to show that national unity was formed from the diversity within America. Halleck initiated this ironic technique

Bayard Taylor, author of *Joseph and His Friend* and key speaker at Fitz-Greene Halleck's Guilford commemoration. (From Ralph Trautmann's steel-plate portrait in the author's private collection.)

of lyrical listing to show that multiculturalism—rather than social purity or conformity—was essential to true national representation. Whitman's "First O Songs for a Prelude" and "Drum-Taps" very literally list Manhattan scenes, as does Halleck's "Lines to the Recorder" with its compilation of New York sites:

At Bellevue, on her banquet-night,
  Where Burgundy and business meet,
On others, at the heart's delight,
  The Pewter Mug in Frankfort Street;
From Harlem bridge to Whitehall dock,
  From Bloomingdale to Blackwell's Isles,
Forming, including road and rock,
  A city of some twelve square miles,
O'er street and alley, square and block,
  Towers, temples, telegraphs, and tiles,
O'er wharves whose stone and timbers mock
The ocean's and its navies' shock.[13]

Whitman also had literary strategies in common with Taylor.

Whitman's *Leaves of Grass* and Taylor's *Lands of the Saracens* and *Poems of the Orient* were all published in 1855 and attempted to expand the social consciousness of their audiences. Like other uninhibited authors, including Byron and Wilde, Taylor used travel for "the expression of ideas that were inconceivable at home."[14] Like abolitionist and feminist works that employed countercultural anecdote, such as Lydia Maria Child's *Appeal in Favor of That Class of Americans Called Africans* or Margaret Fuller's *Woman in the 19th Century,* American homosexual advocates used the Arcadian tradition to idealize foreign homosexuality in support of their own cause.[15] International motifs confronted national mores and emphasized the acceptance of same-sex affection in other cultures. Taylor's homoerotic description of young Turkish bath attendants reinforced Byron's sodomitical description.[16] Unlike Halleck, however, Taylor traveled to see people, not things. His interest in personal relations and dislike of tourist attractions led an acquaintance to comment, "Taylor has traveled more and seen less than any man I ever met!"[17]

Taylor's *Lands of the Saracens* also criticized Americans who "meekly hold out our wrists for the handcuffs of Civilization. . . . Our progress is nervous, when it should be muscular."[18] Taylor's participation in the American cult of masculinity paralleled Whitman's celebration of maleness. Both poets were influenced by the cultural anxiety accompanying a dissolution of separate spheres for men and women, especially in the urban workplace. Taylor projected this concern in his dedication of Halleck's monument, which identified Halleck as the child of "a healthy, masculine race!" and remarked that his "intercourse with men, has suggested to others the epithet 'courtly'—but I prefer to call it *manly*"—a term used twice more in Taylor's tribute to Halleck.[19] Manhood was also emphasized in Taylor's *North American* article on Halleck. Whitman believed that his vision of masculine lovers was prophetic. The comradeship he envisioned between men would be the natural expression of democratic love. Such love would annihilate the artificial dictates regarding same-sex affection in earlier epochs.

Whitman amplified Halleck's protest against American social, military, and religious institutions that restrained his love. Rather than mocking marriage, Whitman's "States!" (which appeared only once in 1860's *Leaves of Grass* as part of "Drum-Taps") directly challenged married couples: "Were you looking to be held together by the lawyers? / By an agreement on a paper?" Whitman shared Halleck's lack of conventionalism regarding military service as well as marriage. Whitman, too, elevated the soldier while preaching pacifism, proclaiming, "Away with themes of war! away with war itself!" and offered this commentary on a historic victory: "It sickens me yet." Whitman's narrator kisses an enemy's corpse in "Reconciliation," and, as Halleck recalled Perth Amboy's platoon kissing, Whitman praises homoerotic relations in the army: "The chief encircles their necks with his arm and kisses."[20] Whitman responded to war by nursing strangers; Halleck responded to the threat of death by nursing Drake.

Whitman's theological liberalism also emulated Halleck's God who stood outside of creed and church. Edwin Haviland Miller endorses Thomas G. Couser's opinion that "Whitman's 'final union with God' is presented 'in images that legitimize, by spiritualizing, his homoerotic impulses.'"[21] In addition to the critical attitude toward marriage, patriotism, and God, Halleck's metaphors also resound in Whitman's symbolism. Halleck borrowed, generated, and inspired poetic expressions of same-sex love that appeared to undermine his culture's most sacred rites of passage. Whitman shared Halleck's fascination with "manly" love[22] but carefully distanced himself from earlier poetics. While Halleck credited influential predecessors, Whitman obscured them.

Whitman never admitted indebtedness, even for poems that came close to paraphrase of others' published work. Apparently, he was "less of a unique phenomenon and an anomaly" than previously supposed or self-declared.[23] Both Whitman's "Red Jacket" and "Twilight" had similarities to Halleck's own, earlier "Red Jacket" and "Twilight." While these were popular topics, Whitman's geographical proximity to Halleck suggests the possibility of influence. Whitman's free verse may have been intuited, as some argue, or influenced by an English poem published around 1851;[24] it may also have been inspired by a French movement as Sculley Bradley and Harold W. Blodgett argue. Halleck's experimental "The Field of the Grounded Arms," and the controversy it raised, however, was a much closer source of inspiration.

Joining others who latched onto Halleck's "The Field of the Grounded Arms," Whitman plagiarized a phrase from the poem in an early sketch that remained private.[25] Another writer used a stanza of "The Field of the

Grounded Arms" for the motto of "Fall of the Alamo" in the *Knicker-bocker* (September 1836), and Prosper M. Wetmore's *Lexington with Other Fugitive Poems* (1830) borrowed Halleck's title phrase, "plain of the grounded arms," which Wetmore acknowledged in a footnote. The *New York Evening Post* (October 5, 1830) even commented on Wetmore's "delicious compliment to Halleck." By contrast, Whitman's use of Halleck's poem went unacknowledged. But Halleck's and Whitman's verse did cross paths, and critics would draw connections between the two poets.

Halleck's "A Poet's Daughter" was anthologized in *American Poems* (1872), which William Rossetti dedicated to Whitman, and Whitman copied a line from the poem.[26] John Greenleaf Whittier also provided a literary link between Whitman and Halleck. Whittier wrote a poem honoring Halleck, and Whitman wrote "As the Greek's Signal Flame" to honor Whittier. Charles F. Johnson dreamed, "If we could unite the virile qualities, the breadth, force and flashes of insight, of Whitman, to the taste, melody and elegance of Halleck, then we should have the great national poet, whose words a million men would carry in their hearts."[27] Such a literary collaboration would not have pleased Whitman, who would have judged Halleck as a poet of the elite and who worked even harder than Byron to create the myth of poetic autonomy. But William Carlos Williams's criticism of Whitman's *Leaves of Grass* is perfectly suited to Halleck's "Field of the Grounded Arms." Williams credits Whitman's "so-called 'free verse'" as "an assault on the very citadel of the poem itself; it constituted a direct challenge . . . that still holds good after a century of vigorous life during which it has been practically continuously under fire."[28] This revolution against traditional form had already been ignited by Halleck's earlier work.

"The Field of the Grounded Arms" presents imagery based on grass and leaves. The twenty-four quatrains about the Battle of Saratoga are addressed to strangers who see the "wakened leaf" of the vacant valley. The narrator takes in the scope "o'er sleepless seas of grass" and "leaves upon the bough" before taking the reader beyond "the music of to-day," floating "far up the stream of time" from the present spring to an era when "the forest-leaves lay scattered cold and dead, / Upon the withered grass." After describing an honorary surrender and fade of glory, "a foe is heard in every rustling leaf," and "the field of death" becomes a "couch of happy dreams" as warriors glow with their "sons' proud feelings."[29]

As with the theme of future generations in "Young America," "The Field of the Grounded Arms" owed much to its transcendental element. Halleck's favorite metaphor to describe his love for Drake was the plant, tree, or flower. A leaf or leaves dominate much of his poetry, as does his favorite color green and the combination of green and grass. The use of green as a central symbol of homosexuality throughout the nineteenth century has been well documented.[30] From Halleck's own green umbrella (an "inseparable companion") to Wilde's trademark green carnation, the color was associated with plant life that can exist without heterosexual birth. As natural symbols of self-creation, plants inverted the view of homosexuality as unnatural and also suggested self-determination.[31] Lavender flowers accompanied the allusion.

Bluish and especially lavender flowers, like Halleck's forget-me-nots, signified gender disruption, as when the color results from crossing blue with pink. Halleck preferred the violet, whereas Whitman favored the heart-shaped lilac. Halleck may have known that in sixteenth-century England violets were worn by men and women who did not plan to marry, and he might have been aware of the association of same-sex love with lavender, which dates to ancient times.[32] Pansy was slang for homosexual since at least the late nineteenth century, and flowers represented homosexual beauty through 1900 when Stephen Crane began his novel on a New York homosexual prostitute, *Flowers of Asphalt* (1901). In New York and other cities, blue eye shadow identified "he-harlots" who wore red ties about the neck, referred to as "wearing one's badge."[33]

Whitman blended plant symbolism with Greek homoeroticism in the "Calamus" section of *Leaves of Grass.* A. L. Rowse observes, "The symbols and signs are there for the perceptive. The calamus plant was a sweet-smelling flag with a phallic bloom and stiffly erect leaves."[34] Sasha Alyson agrees that "the calamus plant [was known] as a symbol of homoerotic love," and Wayne R. Dynes traces the homosexual history of the term "Calamites" (e.g., Ganymede).[35] Whitman scholars used "calamus" rather than "homosexual" to describe Whitman's erotic poetry through the last quarter of the twentieth century. Bradley and Blodgett believe that "To What You Said" is "unmistakably a 'Calamus' poem in sentiment"; its narrator "kisses his comrade lightly on the lips." The editors also note that "the 'Calamus' sentiment" was dropped from the final stanza of "Starting from Paumanok" in all editions after 1860. Whitman responded to J. A. Symonds's homosexual reading of "Calamus" with emphatic denial that his poetry espoused same-sex relations with claims "alleging his normal sexuality." ("Normal" is Blodgett's term.) Whitman's self-editing qualified his claim: "I will not reject any theme or subject because the treatment is too personal. As my stuff settles into shape, I am told (and sometimes myself discover, uneasily, but feel all right about it in calmer moments) it is mainly autobiographic."[36] Charley Shively identifies Fred Vaughan as the inspirer of the "Calamus" poems, although he is not even mentioned in Justin Kaplan's 1980 *Whitman.*

Whitman concealed his sources in order to promote his own reputation, and he diluted and retracted his same-sex content in the face of criticism. His omissions effaced vital historical sexual contexts, even though he thanked "poets of old lands" and communed with "poets unnamed."[37] Whitman freely borrowed the form, ideas, and symbols of oppression, silence, and self-creation from previous writers. He had also learned a great deal from his employment by New York newspapers and printers during the peak of Halleck's popularity (ca. 1840). Whitman was employed by the *New World* in 1841, shortly before its reprinting of Lawson's *Southern Literary Messenger* review of Halleck. Whitman worked for papers such as the *Columbia* (sporadically) and the *New York Mirror* (in 1844), both of which regularly published Halleck's works. Between 1846 and 1847, Whitman served as editor of the *Brooklyn Eagle,* which printed a letter to the editor concerning *Fanny.* From 1841 until 1848, Whitman also contributed to the *Broadway Journal,* which published its homophobic review of Halleck in 1845.

Significantly less humble than Halleck, Whitman realized that if one did not like what critics had to say, one could anonymously review oneself. Byron had been destroyed by the media, Halleck had evaded it, and Whitman manipulated it to an unconscionable degree. Whitman's undated and private lines about another man's statue may well have referred to Halleck. No other mid-century poet would have been a rival for such a major project as the Halleck statue—a project underway while Halleck was still living. Among poets, Halleck was rare for

receiving his bays while "he's alive to wear them." In the maturity of his prime, he finds his poetry thoroughly "endenizened in the national heart," and his fame ever brightening. . . . his strikes us as a condition to be envied. Nor is his high reputation confined to his own country.[38]

Whitman would have resented Halleck's unwanted fame just as he had envied Taylor's success.

Whitman may have seen the *New York Times* solicitation of contributions for Halleck's statue in 1869 and could not have avoided hearing about the spectacle of the Central Park unveiling ceremony. Following the fundraisers for the statue, Whitman wrote the three-line poem found among his *Notes and Fragments* in which he rejected the anonymous American hero honored with a statue. He argued that a common blue-collar boy was equal in greatness. Whitman decided that he should not spend money on some hero's statue, adding, "He does not know what fear is," as if referring to a man whom Whitman knew personally.[39] If the reference is to Halleck, it demonstrates Halleck's fundamental differences from Whitman.

Halleck was perceived as a wealthy member of the literary establishment who took his good fortune in stride. Whitman struggled with class, editors, a resistant audience, and notoriety. Although Halleck was never counted among Whitman's friends, their messages of same-sex love are similar underneath vastly different exteriors. Whitman's "eventual success in incorporating his potentially disruptive homosexuality into his republican poetics" was, in part, possible because of earlier attempts.[40] Halleck helped construct the genteel tradition that gave rise to the view of homosexuals as "superior beings, who nonetheless purchased their superiority at the price of physical expression."[41] Whitman sacrificed a great deal, such as his government job, in marching to his own drum beat. But Halleck also overcame daunting obstacles. Halleck never justified his love through shame or apology. He, too, knew fear.

About the time that Taylor's *Joseph and His Friend* was serialized, Whitman began to edit homoerotic content out of his own writings. As Halleck had done during the peak of his writing career, Whitman entered a phase of personal defense as his work was increasingly scrutinized for its sexual content. Bradley and Blodgett agree that significant changes in the final meanings of Whitman's poetry occurred about 1871, a year after *Joseph and His Friend,* which had fallen slightly behind schedule. Whitman also declined Mrs. Anne Gilchrist's marriage proposal in 1871. Numerous alterations shifted Whitman's content as new social and medical approaches to same-sex desire emerged in antebellum America.

American society had been slow to recognize consensual homosexual behavior, but quick to punish it. The criticism of the Halleck statue's effeminate pose—even a century after its dedication—points to at least one cultural facet added to the sodomitical type following the Civil War.[42] Increasing unrest in the American urban same-sex subculture, homosexual emancipation movements in Europe, and the rise of the New Science were rapidly opening the self-constructed cages of homosexual writers. By mid-century, psychological sexual theories were in the air. Arno Karlen writes a compelling history of the effect science, social Darwinism, and the birth of psychiatry had on the awareness and treatment of homosexuality. Carroll Smith-Rosenberg also finds that "beginning at mid-[nineteenth] century, medical and scientific discussions of male homosexuality began to increase in number."[43] With these new curves thrown at the homosexual, Whitman straightened out his meaning.

Whitman's compulsive editing of the text of *Leaves of Grass* demonstrates growing discomfort with earlier sexual disclosure. Three poems open to homophobic criticism were dropped in 1860 along with "Hours Continuing Long," the most blatant of the "Calamus" poems, and the homoerotic "States!" Such changes increased after 1871 when the overtly homosexual "Now Lift Me Close" was cut. "Mannahatta" (1881) dropped seven lines describing the "friendly young men," whom "I swear I cannot live happy without I often . . . sleep, with them!" Whitman also declared "A Font of Type" too personal and deleted lines from "I Have

Wood engraving by A.R.W. (actual identity unknown), which captures the effeminate pose of J. W. MacDonald's bronze statue of Fitz-Greene Halleck. (Portrait
File, Miriam and Ira D. Wallach Division of Art, Prints, and Photographs, The
New York Public Library: Astor, Lenox, and Tilden Foundations.) The American
public increasingly associated homosexuality and effeminacy in the decades between Byron's death and the commemoration of Halleck's statue.

Appeared" as well, which closed: "Do you fancy there is some water in the semen of the perpetual copulation / Do you suppose the laws might be reformed and rectified?" Whitman also took on a female persona in several poems to obscure their homosexual content.

Like Halleck, Whitman began to fear the law and the American press. Neither man felt at home in his homeland. Halleck, who was more socially timid than Whitman, was mortified by the realization that he would die in Guilford. Taylor tried to salvage Halleck's personal reputation in a dedication speech that defended Halleck before his harshest critics—his townsmen. Taylor left New York with Richard Stoddard, a homosexual. The two men traveled by train together sharing a "delightful" day despite the occasion.[44] Taylor, who has been called "the most outspoken advocate of 'the other [homosexual] love' in mid-century America," argued Halleck's worth passionately.[45] Taylor remained convinced through 1877 that "the first distinction" of American letters fell upon Halleck rather than Cooper, Hawthorne, or Poe.[46] His dedicatory address answered the charge that Halleck "was afraid of the shadow which his own fame cast before him" by explaining that his "honest and honorable silence" merely reflected the modesty of a "true priest of the human heart."[47] That pure heart was broken by the twisted morality of an ignorant populace.

Taylor blamed American society for the suppression of Halleck's aesthetics. Taylor baited his Guilford audience by suggesting that the celebration of Halleck's life might "symbolize the intellectual growth of the American people" and that the future might result in "the creation of an appreciative and sympathetic audience" for Halleck's verse.[48] While Taylor called the ceremony "'a red letter day' in the history of Guilford," it was more like a scene of social rejection out of Hawthorne's *Scarlet Letter*.[49] But Taylor did not give up. If society would not swallow the truth about Halleck's heart, then he would spoon-feed it a fictional account. Taylor's formal tribute to Halleck was closely related to his novel by more than just timing. Taylor's art imitated Halleck's life.

Taylor had known Halleck intimately and professed: "I have never known a man so independent of the moods and passions of his generation."[50] A critic of the speech reversed Taylor's intended compliment, countering, "Never did a man less represent the age in which he lived."[51] That age presented the dawning of the modern homosexual who came out "into the light of day" from the 1860s until the last decade of the nineteenth century.[52] The commemorative speech closed with Taylor's condemnation of the rejection Halleck had experienced before and after the Civil War:

As our last prophetic hope, we look for that fortunate age, when the circle of sympathy, now so limited, shall be coextensive with the nation, and when even as the Poet loves his Land, his Land shall love her Poet![53]

Taylor's statement portrayed Halleck as a literary Christ scourged by the very people he was trying to redeem. The passage above ended his speech, and the graveyard was cleared of the crowd so that Halleck "was left to the sunny silence of the green field."[54] Peace finally settled upon the turf above him.

Guilford appeared mildly repentant of its mistreatment of Halleck by 1936 when a rumor surfaced that New York was scrapping the Halleck statue. Townspeople proposed that it be transferred to the town. David G. Baillie sermonized: "O Brothers—have we in Guilford been recreant or faithful to the solemn charge committed to us by John Greenleaf Whittier? We may have been neglectful—forgetful if not recreant; but it is not yet too late to make amends." The attempt to preserve the statue may have soothed Guilford's collective conscience, but it could not atone for Halleck's pain.

Taylor's defense was as bold as his next novel was daring. Robert K. Martin claims that Taylor "enjoyed an immense advantage over" Halleck because homosexual literary circles and supportive audiences had been established by the middle of the nineteenth century.[55] Even so, it seems remarkable that Taylor had contracted *Joseph and His Friend* for publication in the *Atlantic Monthly* in 1869, more than a century before Gore Vidal's *Burr* (1973), which barely alludes to Halleck's homosexuality at all. *Joseph and His Friend* was published in book form by *Putnam's* in New York and London in 1903. In addition to Taylor's and Vidal's novels, Melville's *Mardi* also fictionalized Halleck as Bardianna's scribe, Marko, in an allusion to "Marco Bozzaris." In reference to Astor's humorous will, Bardianna leaves his faithful accountant three milk teeth, "as a very slight token of my profound regard."[56] One Melville biographer states plainly that Marko represented Halleck.[57]

Vidal presented Halleck and Drake as minor characters in *Burr* and embellished their relationship in ways fitting the genre of historical fiction. Halleck and Drake live and work together in Vidal's novel. Regarding himself as an enemy of the people, Vidal's Halleck acknowledges his outsider status, telling a young admirer that he is a monarchist and a Catholic. After Halleck departs from one scene, Irving gossips to an attractive young man: "You look so much like his friend Joseph Rodman Drake [who died fifteen years ago] . . . Halleck has not recovered to this day." Later, Irving refers to the poetic duo as Jonathan and David. A teary, rum-soaked Halleck recalls the Croaker project with Drake and makes a reference to his membership in the Ugly Club.[58] As with biographies of Halleck, the earlier novel discloses his sexuality more forthrightly, and like Wilson, Taylor knew his subject personally.

Joseph and His Friend, considered the first American gay novel, was produced a century before Stonewall would mark the rise of America's modern gay rights movement and was introduced by lines from a Shake-spearean sonnet: "The better angel is a man right fair" (Sonnet 144). In spite of Coleridge's editing of pronouns in Shakespeare's sonnets, they have long served as a rich source for homosexual allusion. Halleck, who was "a close student of Shakespeare," did not believe that Shakespeare wrote the sonnets, arguing that they were "quite out of his straightfor-ward character." [59] Taylor's novel may have inspired Richard Meeker's *Bet-ter Angel* (1933), republished as *Torment,* in which the plot echoes the brother-sister motif of Taylor's *Joseph.* Hubert Kennedy's estimation of *Better Angel* as the first homosexual American novel with a positive gay character and a happy ending does not account for *Joseph and His Friend.* [60] In time, the word "angel" came to connote a masculine male who kept a more effeminate male partner. [61]

Taylor's preface was more blunt than his Shakespearean motto and dedicated *Joseph and His Friend* to those

who believe in the truth and tenderness of man's love for man, as of man's love for woman: who recognize the trouble which confused ideas of life and the lack of high and intelligent culture bring upon a great portion of our country popula-tion,—to all such, no explanation of this volume is necessary. Others will not read it.

Taylor's novel pitted individual sexual freedom against mob morality. The novel's protagonist, Joseph Asten, is an innocent, twenty-three-year-old man who is associated with cherry-time and cherries, which symbolize his sexual naiveté. Joseph Asten takes Joseph Drake's first name while his surname is reminiscent of Astor, Halleck's famous employer and friend, whom Taylor accused of hindering Halleck's artistic development. [62] (Tay-lor's father was also named Joseph.) Joseph has several flirtatious ex-changes with men, especially Elwood Withers who may be modeled on Halleck's friend, Daniel Embury, before being seduced by a deceptive woman, ironically named Julia Blessing. She prefers intellect to wealth, but her father does not. It is probable that Henry Eckford fathered both Halleck's Fanny and Taylor's Julia.

One of Julia's first taunts is to envision her future fiancé, Joseph, with an effeminate headdress: "Wouldn't a wreath of flowers look well on Mr. Asten's head?" The incident conjures up Halleck's desire to weave Drake's hair in "On the Death of Joseph R. Drake." Julia is masculine and squeezes "maiden secrets of his own" out of Joseph, who is unprepared to resist her wiles since "his bringing up has been fitter for a girl than a boy." Joseph's failure to recognize his innate difference is blamed on his overprotective mother who steered him from "lustier sports." As Guil-ford's citizens had instructed Halleck, Joseph's disapproving neighbors teach him that any variation is to be suppressed. [63] Like the real Drake,

Joseph is more romantically nebulous than his friend and engages in heterosexual activity.

An exhilarating horseback ride unleashes Joseph's "jailor of thought" beyond the boundaries that had prohibited personal freedom:

> With one strong, involuntary throb, he found himself beyond the line, with all the ranges ever trodden by man stretching forward to a limitless horizon. He rose in his stirrups, threw out his arms, lifted his face towards the sky, and cried, "God! I see what I am!" [64]

Cloaked in Halleck's metaphor of criminal as hero, Joseph embarks on his sexual awakening. The horseback ride, a common romantic metaphor for sex, had figured as well in Drake's poem "To Croaker, Junior." Taylor's wording is also suspiciously close to that of Whitman's "Hours Continuing Long" wherein the narrator abandons self-doubt and shame, declaring, "I am what I am."

Taylor probably read Wilson's *The Life and Letters of Fitz-Greene Halleck* (published in 1869) as a source for his Guilford speech. Joseph's monologue in Taylor's *Joseph and His Friend* echoes Halleck's early New York letters to Maria confessing his fear that he was unique and would never find a compatible partner. Joseph "wondered whether other men shared the same longing" and pondered the social injustice of reformed drunkards being praised while a man discovering all the possibilities of passion "is kept more secret than sin. Love is hidden as if it were a reproach; friendship watched, lest it express its warmth too frankly." Coming out to himself, he is baffled by the revelation: "I am lonely, but I know not how to cry for companionship; my words would not be understood, or, if they were, would not be answered. Only one gate is free to me,—that leading to the love of woman." [65] Joseph arrives at the same conclusion that his real-life model, Joseph Drake, had drawn.

As the last guests leave Joseph's "coming-out" party, he is "conscious of a tenderer feeling of friendship than he had ever before felt, and begged [Elwood] to stay for the night." Elwood reluctantly agrees and the two swap secrets about women before "Joseph stole back to his bed, and lay there silently." "Stole" hints at sexual crime in this silent bedroom scene. Later, on his way to ask for Julia's hand, Joseph is perplexed by a chest pang that "mysteriously resisted his errand." The pain is temporarily relieved by the sight of sailors and blue-collar men. [66] The omen is not heeded and Joseph's marriage is set for October, the same month as Drake's real-life wedding.

Joseph's introduction to the friend of the book's title, Philip Held, immediately establishes him as a Halleck figure. Joseph literally falls into the arms of Philip, who is studying hieroglyphics, an interest that suggests words must be open to interpretation. Philip Held's initials echo Fitz-

Greene Halleck's initials and *Held* is "hero" in German, a language with which Taylor was well acquainted. Like Fitz-Greene Halleck, Philip Held alone never submits to marriage. In addition to his name, other details establish Philip as the reincarnation of Halleck.

Philip is twenty-eight, five years older than Joseph. Halleck was five years Drake's senior.[67] Philip is allowed to act on the private feelings that Halleck had conveyed to his sister and attempts to talk Joseph out of his engagement, refusing the honor of best man, as Halleck had also wished to do. The similarity extends to physical appearance. Philip has "a smooth, frank forehead," hands "graceful without being effeminate," and dark gray eyes that provide contrast to Joseph's sparkling blue pair. The description fits the gray-eyed Halleck who was smitten by "the light of [Drake's] young blue eyes."

Joseph bashfully beholds Philip. Experiencing the equivalent of contemporary gaydar, an instinctive gaze of recognition between gay men, Joseph eyes the stranger who provides a resolution to his self-doubt. Whitman also noted this phenomenon, writing: "O Manhattan—your frequent and swift flash of eyes offering me love." One narrator celebrates the "curious questioning glances—glints of love!" as he cruises Broadway, which is one big "unspeakable show," and another speaker finds "one picking me out by secret and divine signs" in the anonymous multitude in which "some are baffled, but that one is not—that one knows me. Ah lover and perfect equal, . . . to discover you by the like in you."[68] In Taylor's novel, Philip "felt his [Joseph's] gaze," "answered it," and Joseph "dropped his eyes in some confusion" until a "momentary flash" of self-recognition strikes.[69] The narrator comments that Philip's gaze carries the nonverbal response: "'We are men, let us know each other!' [which] is, alas! too rare in this world." The words mimic Halleck's exclamation that he and Drake must know each other, allegedly blurted out upon their first introduction. Joseph is "fighting the irresistible temptation to look again" when the train they are riding in crashes. Knocked unconscious, Joseph literally awakens to a new life with his head in Philip's lap.[70]

In one of the most romantic scenes ever devised, Joseph is baptized into a new love by fire and ice: the cold water of a cloth Philip presses to his forehead as Philip's hot tears simultaneously drop on Joseph's cheeks. Discovering new power, Joseph finds familiarity in Philip's face and "the hand which had rested on his heart was warm with kindred blood." Philip insists on nursing Joseph, lifts him up, and takes the hand involuntarily offered by the injured man "with a silent assurance which he felt needed no words."[71] Philip nurses Joseph, a role that Halleck in life fulfilled with "more than a brother's love" in Drake's last days.

Like Halleck, Philip is a proud outsider who does not belong to the general class of men. As the ancients cited homosexuality as a sign of higher civilization precisely because it was unnecessary for procreation, Taylor also develops this idea throughout the text. Recovering over several days, Joseph's "thoughts dwelt much more on Philip Held than on Julia Blessing" and "his heart sprang with an instinct beyond his control" toward his new friend. Philip supersedes Joseph's fiancée, just as Drake seemed to obscure Walter Franklin's fiancé. Joseph's recuperation is interrupted by a visit from the Reverend Chaffinch who is annoyed by Joseph's new freedom from fear of judgment and damnation. Joseph loses his homosexual virginity by staying over at Philip's apartment, where their friendship is symbolically (at least) consummated. The opening sentence of the following chapter sums up the previous night's events: "There was not much of the happy bridegroom to be seen in Joseph's face when he arose the next morning."[72]

Taylor's description of Joseph's marriage parallels Halleck's view of Drake's wedding. First, Elwood tearfully declines the request to be Joseph's best man, then Philip, too, refuses the office, and the wedding proceeds as scheduled without a groomsman. Joseph's "mechanical" dressing is assisted by Philip who repeatedly urges Joseph to call off the wedding. Instead, Joseph "mechanically" exchanges his marriage vows. Still, he is haunted on his honeymoon by the "more than brotherly love" Philip transmits from afar.[73] The situation parallels the poetic energy between Halleck and Drake during his honeymoon when the two poets were unknowingly writing poems to one another. Like Joseph Drake, Joseph Asten is quickly bored with married life and reestablishes his friendship with Philip.

Joseph welcomes Philip and his masculine sister, Madeline Held, to move closer to him. Philip's sister Madeline reflects her brother's beauty while providing a masculine twin figure for Joseph to legitimately marry. She has the same hair and "frank, firm face" as Philip and is "about as stubborn" with an interest in botany and geology. Joseph confides his wish that he had such a sister. Philip describes her as a lemon, "acid and agreeable," and credits her intellect with solving the mysterious death of Joseph's wife. *Joseph and His Friend* also has minor characters named Maria and Fitzwilliam, further suggesting the Halleck siblings.

Confiding his despair over the "dishallowed marriage-bed," Joseph is led by Philip's hand to a river bank: "The silence and the caress were more soothing to Joseph than any words." As in the case of Halleck and Drake, the two fictional men have their most intimate moments along the water's edge. Julia tells Joseph that Philip is in love with a married woman, Mrs. Hopewell. Joseph starts "as if he had been shot." Actually, the appropriately named Hopewell confesses to being in love with the indifferent Philip, not unlike Flanner's publicized infatuation with Halleck. When Philip learns of Hopewell's feelings for him, he leaves her to search for

Joseph, who whispers, "Philip, I want you!"[74] Taylor shatters Halleck's metaphorical representations.

Chapter 20, "A Crisis," provides the climax of homosexual emancipation in the novel. Like Walter Franklin, Joseph, who had considered suicide the day before his wedding, reconsiders self-destruction. Julia has convinced Chaffinch to reproach Joseph with blasphemy, but the tables turn on the startled minister. Joseph accuses him of "pious impertinence" by blackening "this most sacred part of his nature" and leaves "crying aloud: 'I will go to Philip! . . . I must have a word of love from a friend, or I shall go mad!'" He stumbles into the hemlocks of the forest where Philip intuitively finds him contemplating death. Reading Joseph's thoughts, "Philip took his hand, drew him nearer, and flinging his arms around him, held him to his heart."[75] Philip assures Joseph that rather than feeling inferior he can take absolute confidence that his special design places him above the average laws of the human race.

Philip rhetorically asks, "Is life to be so sacrificed to habit and prejudice?" and concludes his speech:

There must be a loftier faith, a juster law, for the men—and the women—who cannot shape themselves according to the common-place pattern of society,—who were born with instincts, needs, knowledge, and rights—ay, *rights!*—of their own![76]

Philip's speech expresses Halleck's indignation at public morality and popular opinion.

Joseph responds with cautious temptation and with Halleck's familiar metaphor: "to snap my chains, break violently away from my past and present life, and surrender myself to will and appetite. O Philip, if we could make our lives wholly our own! If we could find a spot." Philip assures Joseph that there is a place for "fettered outlaws," namely Greece or another Near East clime of olives and oranges. As the sun sets and birds twitter, they join hands and Taylor's plot fulfills Halleck's fantasy:

Each gave way to the impulse of his manly love, rarer, alas! but as tender and true as the love of woman, and they drew nearer and kissed each other . . . happiness was not yet impossible.[77]

Unlike Halleck's unfulfilled wish to remove Sarah Eckford Drake, Philip's desire for Julia Blessing Asten's death is granted.

At the news of Julia's death, "Philip's heart gave a single leap of joy." Joseph is as numb at the funeral as he was at his wedding and finds relief "when night came [and] only Philip was beside him." As he had rescued Joseph in the train wreck, Philip again saves Joseph, who is put on trial for murdering Julia. After the truth emerges that Julia's death was neither murder nor suicide but accidental, Julia's father apologizes "even as

David rent his garments," a public toast that only Philip and Joseph understand.[78] The allusion to Jonathan and David, subjects of Halleck's earliest homosexual verse, give new meaning to old religion.

Like Whitman, Philip seeks "a new code of ethics" for the world while Joseph strikes a compromise with the status quo. However, Joseph discovers a new masculinity with a trip to the West and in a letter from San Francisco entreats Philip not to run from "perversions of the world": "the freedom we craved is not a thing to be found in this or that place. Unless we bring it with us, we shall not find it."[79] Joseph is as transformed by his travel adventures as Halleck had been by his 1821 trip to the West after losing Drake and as Taylor had been by his eastern journeys. Joseph's return provides an uneasy resolution, however, because he marries Philip's sister. As James Gifford notes, Joseph acts unbelievably here; Madeline is only "a more acceptable female Philip."[80] As a mirror figure of her sibling, a popular Romantic image, Madeline fails only to symbolize Philip's feminine side. She seems too masculine, even though she is emotionally sensitive. When her brother and Joseph entwine hands in front of her, she plans "arrangements solely for his and Philip's intercourse" and leaves the two alone.[81] Wilson, who knew Maria Halleck quite well, said that she very strongly resembled her brother "in disposition as well as in personal appearance," as does the sister in Taylor's novel.[82]

Philip feels "a little sting of pain somewhere" when Joseph and Madeline announce plans to wed and believes that "they have destroyed my life." As Halleck had been unable to do for Drake and Sarah Eckford, Philip pledges to be "vicariously happy" for the newlyweds but warns couples that "God's wonderful system is imperfect." He claims his place in society by adopting their future offspring: "myself in their children, nay, claiming and making them *mine* as well."[83] The scene reminds the reader of Halleck's namesake, Janet Halleck Drake, and his role as godfather to Drake's grandchild.

Halleck's use of silence and secrets emerge in *Joseph and His Friend*'s imagery as well. Taylor's fiction also puns on "crime" and "straight." Although the prosecutor for Julia's alleged murder says that "the growth of [Joseph's] free-love sentiments" leads to "crime," Julia remains the novel's criminal figure. Like Sarah Eckford, Julia is guilty at the wedding altar. Reversing the euphemism for sodomy, her false charm is "a crime for which there is no name."[84] Joseph's father-in-law orders his drinks, "Straight, if you please," as if reprimanding Joseph upon his arrival at the bar. The reader is advised that there is nothing like a vigilant wife "to set a man straight."[85] It is not Taylor's puns but the novel's compulsive study of natural acts and human nature that implores the reader to invert the social-sexual hierarchy.

Taylor lauded Halleck's "cleverness of allusion," but their fifteen-year friendship during Halleck's years of silence gave Taylor reasons to believe that "a delicate natural instinct told [Halleck] that he did not belong" to the culture.[86] That instinct is thoroughly depicted. However familiar Halleck's code of silence may have been to Taylor and to Whitman, the technique of humoring an audience was uniquely Halleck's own.

Halleck's letter reminding a friend that "one true use of language" is "to conceal our thoughts" is paraphrased by Whitman's line that "in what is written or said, for-get not that Silence is also expressive."[87] Whitman's tongue "begins to be loosen'd" as his poetry encourages "all the hapless silent lovers" to remove their gags. Whitman's "Says" urges disciples: "There can be no salvation for These States without innovators—without free tongues, and ears willing to hear the tongues."[88] Whitman himself had listened to earlier calls for sexual liberation.

Though having common goals, Halleck and Whitman used very different strategies. Halleck had tried to humor his audience in both senses of the word. He emulated the traditional heterosexual marriage motif and then poked fun at it. He came to laugh at himself and the absurdity of his social situation in a heterosexist nation. Though he mourned Drake for the rest of his life, Halleck dwelled on "those happy days when we only lived to laugh."[89] But he did more than grumble privately about life's unfairness. His satires on marriage undermined life's pain and seriousness with camp.[90] When he sent an original portrait of himself to a Mr. Andrews, Halleck wrote as if offering a modest gift to "a kind-hearted bride" who

always assures her husband that, for his dear sake, she prefers his simple bridal-ring to the expensive *trousseau* that other friends have presented her. Let me hope that you will be toward me equally civil and more sincere.[91]

For Halleck, another man is more earnest than a wife.

Although the sun would never shine as brightly as it had before Drake's death, Halleck did smile again. He provided his public and private audiences with the humor they had discovered in *Fanny* and *Croakers*. He often associated himself with the female sex, signing off in one letter that he was "unveiling, womanlike, in my postscript the real purpose of this letter."[92] Disconcerted at having found a male acquaintance out one afternoon, he left his name on a scrap of paper, "adding 'in bridal phrase', 'no cards.'"[93] One bookseller recalled Halleck's response to seeing himself etched in mourning beside Drake's grave in an illustrated collection of poetry that included his famed elegy. Halleck "objected in a most whimsical but decided manner to the 'shocking bad hat' that he wore on the occasion."[94] Whitman once claimed, "I pride myself on being a real humorist under everything else," but he was certainly not a humorist in the popular vein.[95] That was Halleck's gift.

Halleck's comic poems sugarcoated the message that Whitman would continue to present in his own style of sexual and poetic revelation. Taylor's effort to idealize the Halleck-Drake affair likewise advanced Halleck's queer constructs. As Halleck had done for Byron, Taylor liberated Halleck's sexual content from the metaphor. These writers changed American sexuality and art, but Halleck did not know the breadth of his own achievement.

Whitman might never have been able to envision his homosexual theology without the previous work of Halleck and others. Reversing the Puritan's universal moral typology, poets like Whitman perceived three distinct phases of homosexual evolution: in ancient Greece, in the German emancipation movement, and (they hoped) in the future of democracy in the United States. Whitman saw social progress "come for thrice a thousand years" and addressed his readers one by one: "My comrade! For you to share with me two greatnesses, and a third one rising inclusive and more resplendent, The greatness of Love and Democracy." Having studied the Greek and Germanic social orders, Whitman links German philosophers to Plato and Socrates and places hope in "those Greek and Germanic systems" evident in "to-day's" Christian virtue: "the dear love of man for his comrade."[96] Havelock Ellis's radical arguments to decriminalize homosexuality ultimately backfired, and Nazism eventually spread from Berlin, which had been Europe's homosexual mecca in the late nineteenth century. Whitman's "To a Foil'd European Revolutionaire" coincidentally describes a failed emancipation movement.

Byron and Taylor had reached the actual Greece, which Halleck and Whitman only visited in their imaginations. Halleck's last poem returned to the classical pederast model as did Whitman's poetry and prose. Whitman's "scholar kisses the teacher and the teacher kisses the scholar" and he praises "a youth who loves me and whom I love." "O Tan-Faced Prairie-Boy" also suggests boy worship as did the amended poem "We Two Boys Together Clinging." One narrator confesses to "coming home with the silent and dark-cheek'd bush-boy."[97] Michael Moon's persuasive essay on Whitman's "The Child's Champion" deconstructs the short story as homosexual allegory.[98] Like Halleck's soldier in "Young America," Whitman's sailor pursues metaphorical marriage with an adolescent boy. The child is rescued from another drunken sailor by his champion as Taylor's Held had rescued Joseph from his female seducer. Moon holds that the boy and his rescuer reproduce each other in symbolic maternal ways, just as Halleck's preacher and soldier want to form themselves with the boy in "Young America." In *Joseph and His Friend*, Philip initiates Joseph, who then literally provides the children.

Whitman's sexual prophecy was intertwined with his political vision of the third great democracy. This sexual-political view was reinforced by religious movements from ancient philosophy to Protestant reform in German Lutheranism to the homosexual humanistic ideal of Christian love in America. Whitman's bold depiction of Christ as homoerotic models "the dear love of man for his comrade, the attraction of friend to friend."[99] Whitman's secularized Christ is a close relative of Halleck's predominant narrative voice, a criminal outsider misunderstood and persecuted by the people he has come to enlighten.

Whitman used historical descriptions of sodomites as insane, diseased, or criminal to remind readers that Jesus was the "brother of rejected persons—brother of slaves, felons, idiots, and of insane and diseas'd persons." Whitman also empathized with the lunatic, the sick and the criminal. Like Christ, homosexuals in America were tried for blasphemy, cultural defiance, and opposition to the religious stronghold. Whitman's narrator imagines mounting the scaffold and takes pride in being a "Comrade of criminals." "To Him That Was Crucified" mourns the execution of "brethren and lovers as we," adding, "I belong to those convicts and prostitutes myself."[100] Gay theologians have pointed out Christ's homoerotic aspects, such as his platonic friendships with promiscuous women and his relationship to John, "the disciple he loved," who repeatedly reclined on Christ's chest.[101] Whitman's unwilling disciple, Gerald Manley Hopkins, a priest alarmed by his own homoeroticism, plagiarized Whitman but fought his attraction to Whitman's "essentially Greek character."[102] In fact, Whitman's very name became a signifier of homosexuality for Hopkins and Swinburne.[103]

Unlike Whitman, Halleck rejected his own homosexual idealism and saw his effort to advance American society as a complete failure. Adkins writes that Halleck's poems reveal his tragic personality, concluding, "They are seen as the inevitable struggles of a mind seeking rest and finding none."[104] Yet gay pride eventually embraced and overturned Halleck's criminal identification. The pink triangle, emblematic of homosexuals jailed and executed by the Nazis, became an American banner of homosexual liberation. However, as many late twentieth-century gays have found, the United States remains a country whose cultural institutions retain the colonial belief that heterosexuals fall in love and homosexuals have sex.

It has been suggested that heterosexual romance is taken at face value in literature, whereas "writings descriptive of homosexual love are metaphors for something completely different."[105] Halleck, whose decanonization has often been blamed on his romanticism, was very much the realist. He did not merely recollect his feelings in a state of repose but used his imagination to suggest the muted position he held as a negated citizen of the democracy. When Taylor visited Halleck in Guilford, the elderly poet could not believe that Taylor was still having difficulty defining poetry.

Halleck did not let him struggle unnecessarily and blurted out that poetry is "simply the opposite of reason!" elaborating, "A poet has nothing to do with the facts of things, for he must continually deny them!"[106] His was the voice of experience.

In Halleck's poems and collected letters, Taylor heard Halleck's "repressed sobs."[107] His criminal act of officiating as Drake's best man was turned upside down in Taylor's novel. Unlike Halleck, Philip does not compromise his integrity by acting as Joseph's groomsman. Joseph's wedding is itself the criminal act. Philip insists that Joseph's last full day as a single man be shared alone with him in the city. There, Philip begs Joseph not to marry and articulates what Halleck could not say fifty years before. The words free the American reader from centuries of sexual policing and take Joseph's breath away:

"This!" Philip exclaimed, laying his hands on Joseph's shoulders,—"this, Joseph! I can be nearer than a brother. I know that I am in your heart as you are in mine. There is no faith between us that need be limited, there is no truth too secret to be veiled. A man's perfect friendship is rarer than a woman's love, and most hearts are content with one or the other: not so with yours and mine! I read it in your eyes, when you opened them on my knee: I see it in your face now. Don't speak: let us clasp hands." But Joseph could not speak.[108]

Although Philip stoically accepts Joseph's second marriage because it will make his sister happy and because he can vicariously father Joseph's children, he breaks his sexual silence. Philip's quiet self-sacrifice parallels the homosexual content of Halleck's own muted poetry. That same unspeakable love was also on Whitman's looser lips.

Whether national or universal in their scope, both Halleck and Whitman contemplated an inclusive canon. Halleck confessed:

I have never been able to define what "American Literature" means. Must its author live at and speak the language of Canada or Cape Horn? Must he write in Portuguese in the Brazils? in Spanish at Havana? in French at Quebec? or Cherokee among our Indians?[109]

Whitman's rhetorical verse presented the same paradox of what constitutes an American: "Is he some Southwesterner rais'd out-doors? is he Kanadian? / Is he from the Mississippi country? Iowa, Oregon, California? / The mountains? prairie-life, bush-life? or sailor from the sea?"[110] Unlike many of his readers and admirers, Halleck felt that rule by the majority was more oppressive than rule by a monarchy. Democracy's treatment of minorities remains a measure of its success, yet Halleck's decanonization suggests its failure.

Halleck's body is still represented by J. Wilson MacDonald's heavily criticized statue. The complaint made by *Harper's Weekly* was reiterated

Fitz-Greene Halleck (ca. 1865) about the time "Young America" appeared. (From Ralph Trautmann's steel-plate portrait in the author's private collection.) A similarly lionized Halleck also appeared in Christian Schussele's *Washington Irving and His Literary Friends* completed in 1864 and currently in the Smithsonian Institution's National Portrait Gallery's collection.

by Taylor who found the statue too theatrical to represent his friend. Now, as postmodern critics begin to decipher the sexuality in Halleck's poetry, some editors are still questioning his place in the American literary canon. As Halleck's poetry was followed by Taylor's prose, Taylor's novel preceded Fred W. Loring's *Two College Friends* (1871). Loring's novel climaxes with the premature death of one friend. Its sentiments are familiar:

O my darling, my darling, my darling! please hear me. The only one I have ever loved at all, the only one who has ever loved me . . . don't forget it. If you knew how I love you, how I have loved you in all my jealous morbid moods.[111]

Loring speaks as Halleck could not upon the loss of Drake. Halleck lived in another time, before Joseph's friend, before Loring's friends. Except for these few novels, the canon remained unfriendly to gay readers. For another century, the inclusion of homosexual poetry would remain distinctly un-American.

As much as Halleck's verse added to the homosexual tradition in world literature, it also made a contribution to heterosexual ideology. Halleck invited his readers to question the value of art, government, and marriage. Perhaps more than beauty, value is in the eye of the beholder. While Drake judged his own poetry "valueless,"[112] Halleck had scraps of Drake's childhood poems within arm's reach of his own death bed a half century later. In 1845, the *Broadway Journal* condemned Halleck's effort to put love into verse, while the *Knickerbocker* wrote, "We rejoice to see [Halleck's works collected] because we believe they will do more than any thing we can effect, toward convincing men that *there is value in poetry.*"[113] In effect, Halleck's poems freed all Americans to reconsider ideals they had taken for granted for centuries. Halleck's proud chains linked him to other cultural prisoners who heard his pocket flute. Through subdued metaphors, he gradually unveiled himself and his nation. Halleck's love for another man, like his image in MacDonald's incapable hands, endures.

Notes

Bibliography

Index

Notes

INTRODUCTION

1. *Memorial* 43; Wilson, "Recollections" 175; Anderson, "From These Roots." The *New York Tribune* estimated only thirty thousand in attendance ("Halleck Statue" 17).

2. In Wilson, *Letters* 494–96; in Adkins 408.

3. In "Halleck Statue," *Harper's Weekly* 42e5.

4. Curtis 422.

5. Taylor, "Fitz-Greene Hallock," *North American Review* 60.

6. In *Memorial* 51.

7. In Duyckinck, "Fitz-Greene Halleck" 238; in Adkins 337.

8. In Adkins 354; in Wilson, *Letters* 558.

9. These and numerous other regrets are reproduced in *Memorial* 39, 40, 35, respectively.

10. Lee, "150 Years" 1.

11. "Halleck Monument," *New Haven Palladium* 19; *Memorial* 13.

12. Rutherford 153.

13. Dunning C19. Lee's "Famed Local Poet Snubbed" was a rebuttal to the *Times*'s minimizing Halleck's fame.

14. Tierney 18. Warren Reiss's letter refuted Tierney and asserted Halleck's significance (8).

15. See Poe's reputation in Parks 4; Moss 55. Poe, "The Literati" 14.

16. Stevens 484, emphasis in original; Poe, "Fitz-Greene Halleck" 160.

17. Bryant, "Fitz-Greene Halleck" 520.

18. "American Poetry," *New York Times* 5, col 1; Hutchinson 6.

19. "Poetry of Fitz-Greene Halleck" 553–54; Lathrop 721. Halleck's second edition of *Fanny*, expanded by fifty stanzas, was published in 1821.

20. A. Quinn 261.

21. Adkins 231.

22. Poe, "The Literati" 14.

23. Lawson 348.

24. Lathrop 726.

25. In Adkins 339.

26. In Wilson, *Letters* 536.
27. Stevens 484.
28. In Wilson, *Letters* 525.
29. Ibid. 5–6.
30. Adkins 219.
31. Katz, *Almanac* 45; Halperin, *Hundred Years* 17.
32. Burrows and Wallace 58–59, 797.
33. R. K. Martin, *Tradition* 91. Martin defines Halleck and other premodern homosexual poets with this phrase.
34. Taylor in *Memorial* 60.

CHAPTER 1. SHEPHERDS OF SODOMY

1. Greenberg, *Construction* 148; Dynes 961. Also see Greenberg, *Construction* 141–52; Dover; Sergent; Percy, *Greek Pederasty* and *Pederasty and Pedagogy*.
2. See Bray's landmark study as well as Bredbeck; Goldberg, *Sodomtries* and *Queering the Renaissance;* Norton, *Mother Clap's;* B. Smith; and Summers, *Homosexuality.*
3. Bray 82.
4. Norton, *Mother Clap's* 103, 100–102; also Dynes 826–27.
5. See Boswell, *Same-Sex Unions in Premodern Europe.*
6. Bray 81, 86; Norton, *Mother Clap's* 99–102.
7. Dynes 127–29; Roscoe, *Zuni* 5.
8. W. Williams 9.
9. Roscoe, *Zuni* 5; P. Allen 3; W. Williams 87.
10. W. Williams 31; Abelove 505.
11. Boughner 74.
12. Dynes 128; W. Williams 4, 31, 45–46, 69, 83, 92, 107. Katz provides a dozen additional accounts of American berdachism from 1801 to 1897 (*History* 292–317).
13. W. Williams 166–67.
14. Roscoe, *Zuni* 70.
15. In Wilson, *Letters* 561.
16. Bradford 339; Bray 29. America's religious zealots connected droughts with homosexual activity as late as 1976 (Dynes 870).
17. Orgel 21.
18. Norton, *Mother Clap's* 9; Bray 81–114; Dynes 827–28.
19. See Coote 162–67, 173; Fone, *Hidden* 138–39.
20. B. Smith 26; also Bray 49.
21. Katz reproduces capital antisodomy laws passed in 1613, 1632, 1636, 1641, 1642, 1647, 1648, 1650, 1656, 1661, 1663, 1665, 1668, 1671, 1672, 1676, 1680, 1683, 1691, 1697, 1700, 1702, 1706, 1712, 1718, 1719, and 1732 (*Almanac* 68–133).
22. Bill Number 64 (Katz, *History* 24).
23. Bradford 351.
24. Arend H. Huussen, Jr., in Maccubbin 169–78; Dynes 899.

25. Block 14; M. Hyde 11.
26. Burg, "Ho Hum" 69; also B. Smith 52.
27. See McIlwain 20; Dynes 630–31; Greif 109; Rowse 48–69.
28. Greenberg, "Socio-Sexual" 94; Rousseau, "Introduction" 58.
29. Bradford 351.
30. Katz, *Almanac* 74, 76, 35.
31. Bradford 351–52, 356–57.
32. In Katz, *Almanac* 73; Powers 43.
33. Bradford 351.
34. *Newsweek*'s front-page article, "Bisexuality . . . A New Sexual Identity Emerges" (July 17, 1995), lacks historical perspective, whereas *The Making of Victorian Sexuality* acknowledges that the English notion of exclusive homosexuality remains a "cultural rarity" (Mason 4).
35. In Katz, *Almanac* 108–11.
36. Weidenfeld 29; Delbanco and Heimert 102.
37. Bradford 329, 354.
38. In Katz, *Almanac* 80–81.
39. Dynes 1333; Trumbach, "Transformed" 105.
40. Trumbach, "Birth" 136; see Trumbach, "Transformed" 109; Norton, *Mother Clap's* 53.
41. In Katz, *Almanac* 97. Katz provides vital excerpts and a concise medical history from primary sources and includes Edmund S. Morgan's decoding of Wigglesworth's private accounts (*Almanac* 94–100).
42. Kane 23.
43. Winthrop 2: 324.
44. Frantzen 454.
45. See Katz, *Almanac* 64, 70.
46. Winthrop 2: 324.
47. In Fone, *Road* 1.
48. Hill 383.
49. In Kane 34.
50. Poe, "Fitz-Greene Halleck" 160. Stevens upheld the error (482). See Adkins 14–15n. 2.
51. Hallock 9–10.
52. Told to Bryant in Stoddard 888.
53. Hill 386.
54. Eliot, *Biographical* 177, 174.
55. In Wilson, *Letters* 27.
56. See Jennings 223–34, 245, 248, 251–52.
57. Bryant, "Fitz-Greene Halleck" 516.
58. Bradford 227; also Morton 87. Morton was also guilty of writing secular poetry, and some suggest his colony's name, Merrymount, may have been a pun on sodomitical activity (Kane 14). John Endecott ordered Morton's maypole brought down, an event Hawthorne fictionalized in "Maypole of Merry Mount."
59. In Wilson, *Letters* 56.
60. Sullivan G35; Wilson, *Letters* 33. Mary Eliot Hallock was thirty when

she married in 1875, the same year Jeremy Bentham produced an astounding sixty-page essay refuting negative beliefs about homosexuality (Crompton, *Byron* 19–57).

61. Adkins 12.

62. James Wynne claims the population of Guilford remained at 2,000 in 1862, more than ten years after Halleck had retired there. This stagnation was probably due to Civil War fatalities (634).

63. Hugh Walpole's observation can be found in Rowse 300.

64. Mitchell 706; Stoddard 888.

65. In Biggs, "Son" 23.

66. Steiner 411.

67. Poe, "The Literati" 13; Bryant, "Fitz-Greene Halleck" 516.

68. Halleck, *Writings* 245.

69. Duyckinck, "Fitz-Greene Halleck" 246; in Adkins 397.

70. Wilson, "Recollections" 171; Hill 384. Joel E. Helander's letter to me, September 9, 1990, verifies Halleck's use of "Hallock" through at least 1801.

71. Wilson, *Letters* 51.

72. "Poet Halleck's Great Scrap Book" 17. Halleck's copy of "Not to Them" (in *Churchmaus Magazine* under "Greene Halleck") shows exquisite penmanship (Halleck, Folder 1).

73. In "Fitz-Greene Halleck—Son of Guilford," Biggs calls the poet Guilford's greatest son (23), a title echoed verbatim by Baillie. *A Modern History of New Haven*'s subtitle refers to Halleck as one of "Two Sons of Guilford" (Hill 383), and the *New Haven Palladium* distinguishes him as "Guilford's most eminent son" ("Halleck Monument" 19).

74. Undated, "Invocation to Sleep" was written during Halleck's adolescence, sometime before he left Guilford at the age of nineteen. The poem is in Adkins's appendix of Halleck's hitherto unpublished poetry (425–26).

75. Not much later than Halleck, Whitman may have used the term in its modern, homosexual meaning (Shively, *Drum* 40).

76. Ironically, Halleck was rumored to have written a paper delivered in Guilford that argued the right of women to propose matrimony to men. See Adkins 271 n. 82.

77. In Wilson, *Letters* 70–71, 59, 68–70, 100.

78. Moon, "Disseminating" 247.

79. Kaplan 303, 131.

80. Panati 5–6.

81. In Wilson, *Letters* 50–51.

82. Bradford 383; Burg, *Pirate* 16; Fone, *Road* 11–20, 49–52, 57–61. Robert K. Martin's *Hero, Captain, and Stranger* more fully develops Melville's nautical homoeroticism.

83. W. Williams 154.

84. Dynes 998. See also Agnos; Burg, *Sodomy and the Pirate Tradition* and *American Seafarer*; Cordingly, *Terror* 39, 229, 215; and Cordingly, *Black Flag* 100–103, 134–35.

85. Boughner 90; Greenberg, *Construction* 345.

86. Dynes 296. See Boswell, *Christianity* 252; E. Cooper 27–28; Fone, *Road* 45; Horner.

87. R. K. Martin, *Tradition* 96.

88. In Wilson, *Letters* 81–82.

89. Hill 386–87.

90. Wilson, *Letters* 65. The poem is in *Letters* 66–68.

91. R. K. Martin, *Tradition* 96. See Summers, *Heritage* 707–9.

92. In Halleck, *Writings* 99; Duyckinck, "Fitz-Greene Halleck" 237; Wilson, *Letters* 534; Adkins 201.

93. In Wilson, *Letters* 175; Lawson 343.

94. In Wilson, *Letters* 93–98.

95. "Fitz-Greene Halleck and the Village Belle" 132.

96. The pen name Y.H.S., used by Halleck in publishing three poems in 1814 and another in 1867, has never been deciphered; he also rearranged his own initials, F.H.G., in a personal letter "for concealment." (Adkins 37n. 45; "Poet Halleck's Great Scrap Book" 17).

97. In Greenberg, *Construction* 335; Norton, *Mother Clap's* 54. Margaret or Mother Clap's was perhaps the most famous molly house. "Margeries" were synonymous with mollies until the mid-nineteenth century.

98. Bergmann 137.

99. Crompton, *Byron* 37, 61; see also Porter and Teich 147, 257.

100. In Rousseau, "Introduction" 74.

101. See Katz, *History* 25–26.

102. Mather 1.

103. Byron 6: 207.

104. Bercovitch 137; see also Weeks, "Inverts."

105. Paglia 22; Greenberg, *Construction* 346.

106. Homberger 39. See Kates for a similarly notorious French transvestite.

107. Lee, "150 Years" 2; Hill 387.

108. Mitchell 706; Hutchinson 6.

109. Pattee 377.

110. In Adkins 24.

111. In Lawson 341.

112. Taylor, "Fitz-Green Hallock," *North American Review* 66.

113. Lathrop 729.

114. Tuckerman 214.

115. Hillard 155.

116. Saslow 100.

117. In *Memorial* 18.

118. In Katz, *History* 37, 48, 39.

119. In Wilson, *Letters* 134, 132.

120. Dynes 899.

121. In Wilson, *Letters* 134–35.

122. Morton 151.

123. In Kane 29.

124. In Duyckinck, "Fitz-Greene Halleck" 242, emphasis in original.

CHAPTER 2. LOVE AND WAR

1. Halleck to his sister, Maria (in Wilson, *Letters* 184).
2. In Howe 312; Poe, "The Literati" 15.
3. Hill 387.
4. In Wilson, *Letters* 121.
5. Helander 88–89. Helander's wording of 1969 is coincidental; he assures me that he was shocked to learn of Halleck's homosexuality (personal communication, September 9, 1990).
6. Fullerton 124.
7. In H. Smith 202.
8. In Wilson, *Letters* 213, 104–5.
9. Burrows and Wallace 483–84.
10. Adkins 27; in Wilson, *Letters* 119.
11. In Wilson, *Letters* 106–7.
12. Ibid. 123–24.
13. Ibid. 138.
14. Ibid. 108, 112.
15. R. K. Martin, *Tradition* 97.
16. Adkins 267.
17. A network of New York boarding houses concentrated single men and joined "recognized cruising grounds" and male clubs in assisting a "cognitive transition" of American homosexuality during the early nineteenth century (Greenberg, *Construction* 355, 337). These boarding houses allowed homosexual transients privacy and freedom from police (Chudacoff 91).
18. In Wilson, *Letters* 117–20.
19. Ibid. 130–31.
20. Embury and his sister, poet Emma Catherine (Manley) Embury, frequently wrote Halleck (ca. 1814–1815). The Embury-Halleck letters are in Box 1 of Emma Embury's papers in the New York Public Library's Rare Manuscripts Department.
21. Charles F. Heartmen had thirty-one copies of this long and remarkable letter printed by Rutland in 1921.
22. Adkins 34–35.
23. In Wilson, *Letters* 158.
24. In Katz, *History* 40–44. See also Dynes 899; Karlen 310.
25. Halleck, Untitled lines, *Holt's Columbian.*
26. Halleck, "Lines," *Holt's Columbian.* The poem reappeared in *Appleton's Journal* on May 8, 1869. Yale's collection preserves a manuscript.
27. In Adkins 429.
28. In Wilson, *Letters* 155–56.
29. Ibid. 122.
30. Ibid. 140.
31. Ibid. 153; Halleck in a letter to Edward Greene, dated May 5, 1863, reproduced in Wilson, "Halleckiana."
32. In Embury.
33. In Wilson, *Letters* 146. Irving's *Life and Letters of Washington Irving*

relates this anecdote by Governor Tompkins in a letter dated September 26, 1814. The Knickerbocker school of writers, including Bryant, Child, Drake, Halleck, Irving, James K. Paulding, and others, took its name from Irving's *Knickerbocker's History of New York* (1809).

34. Wilson, "Halleckiana."
35. Halleck, *Writings* 313.
36. In Wilson, *Letters* 152.
37. In Katz, *History* 24.
38. "American Poetry," *New York Times* 5.
39. Halleck, *Writings* 326–27.
40. Ibid. 183, 181.
41. In Adkins 401.
42. Lee, "150 Years" 2; Tuckerman 216.
43. In *Memorial* 46.
44. Taylor, "Fitz-Green Halleck," *North American Review* 61.
45. In Wilson, *Letters* 141.
46. Ibid. 164–65. Wilson dates the surviving fragment of this letter to summer 1815. The lines describing Drake have since been torn off the letter.
47. In Wilson, *Bryant* 395.
48. Biggs, "Son" 23.
49. Duyckinck, "Fitz-Greene Halleck" 234.
50. Lathrop 718.
51. Stoddard 890; Howe 313.
52. Wilson, "Drake" 66.
53. Adkins 32, see n. 34.
54. E.g., Bergmann 136.
55. Pleadwell 67; Trent 280.
56. In Wilson, "Drake" 66.
57. Brooks 245; Wilson, "Drake" 67.
58. In Wilson, *Letters* 184.
59. Karlen 309; Dellamora 193–217.
60. Ward 499; Helander 87.
61. Pleadwell 66.
62. In Wilson, *Letters* 184.
63. Stoddard 890. See Drabble regarding the use of "Benedick" as a code for a "sworn bachelor" (87).
64. In Wilson, *Letters* 184.
65. *National Portrait* 148; Pleadwell 44.
66. "Drake" *New York Daily Tribune* 6.
67. In Pleadwell 67.
68. Ibid.
69. Wilson, "Drake" 65; Wilson, *Bryant* 282.
70. Halleck, *Writings* 299.
71. Wilson, "Drake" 66; "Drake" *New York Daily Tribune* 6; Stoddard 890; Howe 314.
72. *National Portrait* 148.
73. Adkins 47.

74. Lathrop 726.
75. Norton, *Mother Clap's* 189.
76. In Wilson, *Letters* 165.
77. Ibid. 175.
78. Adkins 41.
79. See Duberman, "Writhing Bedfellows" 85–101.
80. In Wilson, *Letters* 177, 181.
81. Bryant, "Fitz-Greene Halleck" 519.
82. In Wilson, *Letters* 171.
83. Ibid. 173.
84. Stoddard 889.
85. In Wilson, *Letters* 174.
86. "Drake's Poems," *New York Mirror* 165.
87. In Pleadwell 269.
88. Ibid. 276.
89. In Wilson, *Letters* 183.
90. In Wilson, "Drake" 68.
91. Not published for another fifteen years, the poem finally appeared in the *New York Mirror* (March 4, 1832) and was reprinted in the *New York Evening Post* (March 22, 1832). It was republished in Drake's *The Culprit Fay and Other Works* (1835) under the title "To a Friend."
92. Adkins 46.
93. See Wilson, *Letters* 191–93; Adkins 43n. 72. As with the Menie materials, Wilson reprints the letter and comments on the self-destruction; Adkins omits the event except for a brief footnote. Drake's original letter is preserved in Drake, *Miscellaneous Papers*.
94. In Wilson, *Letters* 193–95.
95. Dynes 789, 791; see also Laqueur.
96. Karlen 186, 184; Porter and Teich.
97. Dynes 791; Katz, *History* 135–37.
98. In Porter and Teich, 358; see also Rosario.
99. See Katz, *History* 37–39; Bullough and Bullough.
100. In Wilson, *Letters* 196.
101. Ibid. 201–7.
102. Greif 109.
103. Dynes 944.
104. Bradford 275; Gigeroff n. 21.
105. In Wilson, *Letters* 211–12.
106. Stedman 40–41.

CHAPTER 3. THE WIDOW HALLECK

1. In Pleadwell 95.
2. Wilson, "Drake" 70.
3. Biggs, "Son" 23; R. K. Martin, *Tradition* 93.
4. Spiller 736.
5. Biggs, "Prime."

6. In Halleck, *Writings* 255–56.

7. Ibid. 296–97.

8. Ibid. 272, 295.

9. In Wilson, *Letters* 215, 217; in Stoddard 892.

10. In Halleck, *Writings* 268–69, 258.

11. "Drake" *New York Daily Tribune* 6.

12. Halleck, *Writings* 266, 382, 329.

13. Ibid. 266–67.

14. Wilson, "Halleck and His Theatrical Friends" 217–18.

15. Stevens 482.

16. *Memorial* 60.

17. In Adkins 63.

18. Wilson, *Letters* 218; *Memorial* 61.

19. Adkins 63n. 58, 60; in Adkins 63.

20. In Wilson, *Letters* 219.

21. Stevens 486.

22. Halleck, *Writings* 304–5.

23. Ibid. 340–41.

24. Howe 314.

25. Wilson, *Letters* 220; see also Howe 314; Lathrop 719.

26. Wynne 638.

27. See Wilson, *Letters* 221, 223.

28. Ibid. 231.

29. Lathrop 721; Wilson, *Letters* 234. A pirated edition dated 1819 could not have been published before 1821 (Blanck 356).

30. Pattee 375–76.

31. In Wilson, *Letters* 236–38; Wilson, "Poet Halleck" 516.

32. Steiner 492; see Adkins 110–11.

33. In H. Smith 202; "Talk of the Town" 33.

34. Adkins 122.

35. Ibid. 107.

36. Dynes 292–94; see also Halleck, *Writings* 270, 304, 305, 313, 314, 317.

37. "Halleck Monument," Folder 1.

38. Lawson 344.

39. From "Horace in New York" (1826), quoted at length in Wilson, *Letters* 308–12.

40. In Wilson, *Letters* 228, 230.

41. Ibid. 236.

42. In Wilson, "Drake" 70; Wilson, *Letters* 246.

43. "American Poetry," *Foreign Quarterly Review* 308.

44. Hendrickson 58.

45. Pleadwell 260–61, 277, 269.

46. Drake, *Culprit* 42–43, 45. Drake's biographer explains Drake's use of pronoun gender as various errors in other works (Pleadwell 205n. 118, 215n. 68).

47. Pleadwell ix.

48. Wilson, *Letters* 163.

49. Pleadwell 68, 90.

50. Ibid. 95.
51. Wilson, *Letters* 242.
52. Halleck, *Writings* 34.
53. Poe, "The Literati" 14; Poe, "Critical Notices" 336.
54. Stoddard 893.
55. Halleck, *Writings* 34–35.
56. Poe, "Critical Notices" 336; Felleman 539.
57. Lewisohn 49; C. F. Johnson 257.
58. Tuckerman 215.
59. Adkins 118n. 8.
60. Lathrop 729, 727.
61. Halleck, *Writings* 213–14.
62. "Poet Halleck's Great Scrap Book" 17. The owner of Halleck's famous scrapbook said he obtained the hodgepodge at a "ruinous price" and published "To * * *" for the first time (Halleck, Folder 1).
63. Halleck, *Writings* 40.
64. Ibid. 222–23.
65. This undated poem had been in Halleck's scrapbook. Adkins offers a history of the lost scrapbook and contrasts versions of the poem which was first published in the 1869 edition of Halleck's works (435–36nn. 108–22).
66. Halleck, *Writings* 62–63.
67. Ibid. 85, 39, 38.
68. Ibid. 51–52.
69. Ibid. 208.
70. Adkins 242.
71. Child, *Letters from New York* 105, 109. Child also recounts the practical joke played on Clarke (108).
72. Adkins 244.
73. Ibid. 430–32.
74. Ibid. 125–26.
75. In Wilson, *Letters* 248.
76. In Adkins 437.
77. Halleck, *Writings* 55–56. Mrs. Dash may have been a pun on Halleck's real confidant, Mrs. Rush.
78. Wilson, "Halleck and His Theatrical Friends" 219.
79. Howe 315.
80. Halleck, *Writings* 33.
81. Pleadwell 91, 111.
82. Halleck, *Writings* 349–50. Wilson verifies the identification in a note on this poem in ibid. 385n. 83.

CHAPTER 4. CONQUER AND DIVIDE

1. Pleadwell 68.
2. Steiner 493.
3. In Wilson, *Letters* 250.

4. In Wilson, *Letters* 251, see n. 1, 285, 265; in *New York Mirror,* May 6, 1837, 359.

5. In Wilson, *Letters* 257–58. See Adkins for a complete history of this poem (138nn. 119–23).

6. "Halleck Monument," Folder 1.

7. In Wilson, *Letters* 251.

8. Ibid. 257–58, 284; in Adkins 135.

9. In Wilson, *Letters* 305.

10. In Coote 194.

11. Hone 1: 44.

12. "Halleck and Bryant" 483; Nakamura 87.

13. Halleck, *Writings* 21–22.

14. Brooks 251.

15. Halleck, *Writings* 23–29.

16. Wilson, *Letters* 286.

17. Halleck, *Writings* 88, 87.

18. In Adkins 160; see also Adkins 159–63 for publication history.

19. In Tuckerman 214n; also in Taylor, "Fitz-Green Halleck," *North American Review* 62–63.

20. "American Poetry," *Foreign Quarterly Review* 312.

21. Biggs, "Prime"; Ward 499; also Anderson, *Roots* 32.

22. In Adkins 164.

23. Cooper, *Mohicans* 4, 288, 325; see also Cooper, *Mohicans* 40, 51, 86, 103, 138, 225, 298, 300, 382.

24. In Wilson, *Letters* 293–94.

25. Halleck, *Writings* 15–16.

26. In Wilson, *Letters* 302–3.

27. Brooks 244.

28. Adkins 147, 157.

29. In Wilson, *Letters* 305.

30. On Edlestone see Crompton, *Byron* 105, 175–78; on Chalandrutsanos 334; see Crompton, *Byron* 325.

31. In Quennell 308.

32. In Leonard 42.

33. Wilson, *Bryant* 273.

34. Halleck, *Writings* 363, 362, 46.

35. In Katz, *History* 27–28. Louis Dwight's 1826 broadside of convict interviews provided first-hand accounts of consensual homosexuality within the subculture of imprisoned males.

36. In Duyckinck, "Fitz-Greene Halleck" 237.

37. In Wilson, *Letters* 504.

38. Adkins 172.

39. Ibid. 178.

40. Bryant, Review of *Alnwick Castle* 9.

41. In Wilson, *Letters* 319–20; in Helander 89.

42. W. Clark 412.

43. "Fitz-Greene Halleck," *Emerald and Baltimore* 5.
44. In Adkins 233.
45. Ibid. 233–34n. 62.
46. Leggett 129.
47. In Wilson, *Letters* 350–51.
48. Bryant, "Writings" 1; Bryant, "Fitz-Greene Halleck" 522.
49. In Adkins 232; in Wilson, *Letters* 351.
50. Snelling 32.
51. Halleck, *Writings* 332.
52. In Adkins 228.
53. In Wilson, *Letters* 262–63.
54. Ibid. 345.
55. In Adkins 248, see also 157; also in Wilson, *Letters* 352.
56. Halleck, *Byron* xvi.
57. "Death," *Littell's* 639.
58. Halleck, *Byron* xvii, xviii, 101, xxi. Halleck was mistakenly referring to Edlestone for whom Byron's love has been well-documented by Crompton's *Byron and Greek Love.*
59. Ibid. xxiii, xxiv.
60. Ibid. xxviii, 18, 139, 116, 179.
61. Ibid. xxiv, xxi, xxiii, xvii, xx, xxii, xxiii.
62. Biggs, "Son" 23.
63. In Wilson, *Letters* 393.
64. Parton, *Famous* 462.
65. "American Poetry," *Foreign Quarterly Review* 314.
66. Burrows and Wallace 441.
67. In Wilson, *Letters* 353–54.
68. Ibid. 360.
69. Ibid. 463; in Duyckinck, "Fitz-Greene Halleck" 241.
70. Adkins 273; Lathrop 725.
71. W. Clark 415.
72. In Wilson, "Halleck and His Theatrical Friends" 221–22.
73. Halleck, *Writings* 227, 65.
74. Bryant, Review of *Alnwick Castle* 12; Bryant, "Fitz-Green Halleck" 521.
75. See Adkins 206n. 146.
76. Halleck, *Writings* 67.
77. Halleck, Folder 1.
78. Biggs, "Prime."
79. Ward 502.
80. In Wilson, *Letters* 479–80.
81. Ibid. 436.
82. Halleck, *Writings* 211.
83. Adkins 206.
84. Butters et al. 241.
85. Steiner 493.
86. Burrows and Wallace, 796–97.
87. In Wilson, *Letters* 349.

88. Coincidentally, the discarded "mad poet" McDonald Clarke died in the insane asylum on Blackwell's Island in the same year as Lawson's review.
89. Lawson 344–49.
90. In Ostrom 294.
91. In Thomas and Jackson 563.
92. In Burrows and Wallace 796.
93. Adkins 306.
94. Halleck, Folder 1.
95. Travelli 4; Adkins 267.
96. Adkins 268, see n. 72; Flanner's letters are in Wilson, *Letters* 377–90.
97. In Adkins 271.
98. Wilson, *Letters* 373.
99. Adkins 271–72.
100. In Wilson, *Letters* 289.
101. Ibid. 292.
102. Ibid. 473–75.
103. Ibid. 330.
104. Tuckerman 212–13.
105. In Wilson, *Letters* 565.
106. Ibid. 541.
107. Godwin 200.
108. Benton 243.
109. Lawson 344.
110. Tuckerman 213.
111. In Wilson, *Letters* 457.

CHAPTER 5. A RETURN TO GANYMEDE

1. Parker 465.
2. In Wilson, *Letters* 400.
3. In the *New York Evening Post* (April 3, 1837).
4. In Wilson, *Letters* 408.
5. Ibid. 442.
6. "Poet Halleck's Great Scrap Book" 18.
7. See Burrows and Wallace 682–83.
8. In Wilson, *Letters* 407; Benton 243.
9. See Elizabeth Barrett Browning's letter of surprise concerning Cushman's "female marriage" in Sherwood, *Hosmer* 41. See also Faderman 220–25; Kane 57–62.
10. In Adkins 433–34.
11. Halleck, *Writings* 244.
12. Ibid. 197–98.
13. In Wilson, *Letters* 404–5.
14. See Halleck's March 1863 letter in Wilson, *Bryant* 273.
15. Dickens 496.
16. Wilson, *Letters* 446; Davis's emphasis in Wilson, *Letters* 447–48.
17. Greenberg, *Construction* 335, 383.

18. Whitman 105; see also Whitman 120, 132, 159, 166, 313, 687.
19. In Wilson, *Letters* 447–48.
20. Bryant, "Fitz-Greene Halleck" 522.
21. In Wilson, *Letters* 458–59.
22. In Adkins 287n. 8.
23. In Cooper, *Correspondence* 490.
24. See Katz, *History* 29–33.
25. Adkins 285.
26. In Wilson, *Letters* 417.
27. Stevens 483.
28. Helander 88; Magnusson 654; Parton, *Life* 83.
29. In Wilson, *Letters* 477.
30. Adkins 311; see C. F. Johnson, "Fitz-Greene Halleck" 257; Steiner 493. Halleck, Special Collections, Item 5, shows a payment of only $600 to Halleck.
31. See Wilson, *Letters* 477.
32. Adkins 315; Hill 385.
33. In Duyckinck, "Fitz-Greene Halleck" 240.
34. Bryant, "Fitz-Greene Halleck" 515.
35. Hill 385, 384.
36. Biggs, "Son" 23.
37. Duyckinck 235; Pattee 376.
38. Tuckerman 209.
39. Wynne 635.
40. In Wilson, *Letters* 487–88.
41. Adkins 165–66, see 305n. 96.
42. "Literary Report" 39.
43. Halleck, *Writings* 70–75.
44. Whitman 182, 66.
45. See Karlen 199–212; Dynes 1395–98.
46. In Higgins 81.
47. J. Dow 80; see also Barstow; Evans.
48. G. F. Dow 44.
49. Halleck, *Writings* 77.
50. Duyckinck, "Fitz-Greene Halleck" 235.
51. Halleck, *Writings* 76–77.
52. Ibid. 77–79.
53. Edwards 152.
54. Halleck, *Writings* 81.
55. Lathrop 727; Duyckinck, "Fitz-Greene Halleck" 235.
56. Adkins 165, 28.
57. Stevens 484.
58. Adkins 214; in Lee, "150 Years" 3.
59. Baillie; Pattee 377.
60. "American Poetry," *Fraser's* 15; Adkins 359–60.
61. C. F. Johnson, "Fitz-Greene Halleck" 257.
62. Duyckinck, "Fitz-Greene Halleck" 240.

63. In Wilson, *Letters* 561.
64. Lee, "150 Years" 3.
65. In Katz, *Almanac* 124.
66. In Boughner 108.
67. In Wilson, *Letters* 47.
68. C. F. Johnson "Fitz-Greene Halleck" 257; Adkins 338.
69. In Lee, "150 Years" 2; Benton offers a slight variation in *Frank Leslie's* 243.
70. Biggs, "Son" 23.
71. In Duyckinck, "Fitz-Greene Halleck" 242.
72. Greenberg, *Construction* 354.
73. Katz, *Almanac* 104–31.
74. Fone, *Road* 42.
75. Tyler 246–48.
76. Cohen, "Legislating" 184–85; Rousseau, "Pursuit" 147–48.
77. Adkins 321.
78. Wilson, *Letters* 490.
79. Burg, "Ho Hum" 69; B. Smith 52.
80. Dynes 630–31; Rowse 48–69.
81. See Bray 69–70.
82. In Delbanco 65.
83. Wilson, *Letters* 432.
84. Adkins 290.
85. In Wilson, *Letters* 462.
86. Duyckinck, "Fitz-Greene Halleck" 242.
87. Bennett 262.
88. Ibid.
89. Duyckinck, "Fitz-Green Halleck" 243.
90. Adkins 338.
91. Ibid. 413.
92. Hillard 155.
93. In Thomas and Jackson 472.
94. Duyckinck, "Fitz-Greene Halleck" 241.
95. In Adkins 338n. 107.
96. Hillard 159.
97. Biggs, "Prime."
98. "Poetry of Fitz-Greene Halleck" 557.
99. Hillard 157.
100. In Wilson, *Letters* 535.
101. August 1996 interview with town historian, Joel Helander.
102. "Halleck Monument," Folder 1.
103. Pattee 377.
104. R. Halleck 108; Biggs, "Prime."
105. In *Memorial* 48–49.
106. Lee, "150 Years" 3.
107. Wilson, *Letters* 58.
108. Ibid. 417.

109. Adkins 324; in Wilson, *Letters* 501.
110. In Adkins 397, 399n. 31, 400.
111. Ibid. 190; Stoddard 895.
112. See Wilson, *Letters* 511–13.
113. Ibid. 515.
114. Special Collections, Item 1.
115. Ibid. Item 4.
116. In Wilson, *Letters* 493, 506.
117. Ibid. 420, 428.
118. See Adkins 336.
119. In Wilson, *Letters* 426–29.
120. In Adkins 423.
121. In Wilson, *Letters* 221.
122. In Wilson, "Recollections" 176.
123. In Pleadwell 406.
124. In Adkins 288n. 11.
125. Benton 243.
126. H. Jacobs 279.
127. Bergman, "African" 159; see Bergman, *Transfigured* 163–87.
128. Dynes 147; also see Dynes 19, 1207.
129. Poussaint 126, 131.
130. In Burrows and Wallace 872.
131. Orgel 20.
132. Greenberg, *Construction* 60–61, 342.
133. Katz, *Almanac* 61, 90, 128.
134. Stowe 220, 3.
135. Harper, *Brighter* 60, 89–90.
136. Jacobs 288–89.
137. In Wilson, *Letters* 524–25.
138. Ibid. 425.
139. Halleck, *Writings* 150.
140. Dynes 899.
141. In Adkins 347.
142. Special Collections, Item 3.
143. Halleck, *Writings* 186. Endymion also figures in "Lamentings" (*Writings* 333).
144. Ibid. 185–91.
145. Ibid. 192.
146. In Adkins 348; Adkins 347.
147. Lathrop 725.
148. W. Williams 49–54.
149. In Burrows and Wallace 978.
150. In Wilson, *Letters* 533.
151. In Adkins 346.
152. In Wilson, *Letters* 495.
153. Ibid. 566.
154. In Adkins 418.

155. "Funeral," Folder 1.
156. Wynne 634.

CHAPTER 6. HALLECK AND HIS FRIEND

1. Wynn 638; in Wilson, *Letters* 486.
2. Wilson, *Bryant* 371–72; Duberman, *Hidden* 170; R. K. Martin, *Tradition* 97–109; Summers, *Heritage* 28.
3. "Halleck Monument," Folder 1.
4. In Wilson, *Bryant* 361, 348.
5. R. K. Martin, *Tradition* 93, 98.
6. Shively, *Drum* 11; Whitman 246n.
7. E. Miller, *Letters* 18.
8. Whitman 660–61; see Whitman xlvi.
9. In Burrows and Wallace 796.
10. In Holloway, *Uncollected* 20; in Cowley 12, 13.
11. R. K. Martin, *Tradition* 104.
12. In Wilson, *Letters* 520.
13. Halleck, *Writings* 169.
14. R. K. Martin, *Tradition* 98.
15. Fone, *Road* 17; Gifford 9.
16. Taylor, *Lands* 150–60.
17. In Wilson, *Bryant* 358.
18. Taylor, *Lands* 310.
19. In *Memorial* 20–21, 23, 25.
20. Whitman 608, 201, 297, 321, 429.
21. Miller, *Song* 128.
22. See "manly" in Halleck (*Writings* 27, 27, 72, 166, 183 [manlier], 241 [manfully]) and Whitman (*Leaves* 19, 181, 185, 195, 222, 229, 282, 316, 325, 405, 523, 623, 694). Leverenz studies Whitman's model of masculinity as does Fone, *Landscapes*.
23. G. Allen, *Handbook* 44.
24. Ibid. 208, 218.
25. Mabbott; Holloway, *Uncollected* 96; see Adkins 233n. 58.
26. Holloway, *Uncollected* 45; see Adkins 245n. 106.
27. C. F. Johnson, "Fitz-Greene Halleck" 258.
28. In Whitman 903.
29. Halleck, *Writings* 41–45.
30. Alyson 99; Gifford 131.
31. See Dynes, "Color Symbolism" 249–50 and "Flower Symbolism" 411–12.
32. Alyson 100.
33. Dynes 249.
34. Rowse 290.
35. Alyson 99; Dynes 186.
36. Whitman 681, 28, 112, 770.
37. Ibid. 2, 515; see ibid. 355, 514.
38. Review of *Poetical, Knickerbocker* 164.

39. Whitman 705.

40. Maslan 123.

41. R. K. Martin, *Tradition* 97.

42. Dunning C1+.

43. Karlen 181–98; Smith-Rosenberg 266–67.

44. Stoddard 896–97.

45. Duberman, *Hidden* 170.

46. Taylor, "Fitz-Green Halleck," *North American Review* 60.

47. In "Halleck Monument," *New Haven Palladium* 20.

48. Taylor, "Fitz-Greene Halleck" *Tribune* 20–21.

49. In *Memorial* 27.

50. Ibid. 25.

51. "Halleck Monument," Folder 1.

52. Porter and Teich 256.

53. In "Halleck Monument," *New Haven Palladium* 20.

54. Halleck, Folder 1, "Fitz-Greene Halleck: Dedication of the Poet's Monument at Guilford, Conn."

55. R. K. Martin, *Tradition* 106.

56. Melville Chapter 117, 584.

57. Parker 465.

58. Vidal 116, 324–25.

59. Duyckinck, "Fitz-Greene Halleck" 244.

60. Kennedy's Introduction in Meeker.

61. Karlen 307.

62. Taylor, "Fitz-Greene Halleck," *North American Review* 62.

63. Taylor, *Joseph* 18, 55, 48, 22, 26.

64. Ibid. 50.

65. Ibid. 51.

66. Ibid. 63, 65, 68.

67. There is some evidence that twenty-eight was a sexually significant number in nineteenth-century literature. Whitman's "Song of Myself," section 11, is one case in point; Kate Chopin's heroine in *The Awakening* is another.

68. Whitman 126, 521, 135.

69. Taylor, *Joseph* 91.

70. Ibid. 91–92.

71. Ibid. 93–94.

72. Ibid. 96, 98, 113.

73. Ibid. 113, 122.

74. Ibid. 156, 171, 165, 194.

75. Ibid. 210–11, 213.

76. Ibid. 214.

77. Ibid. 215–17.

78. Ibid. 270, 279, 333.

79. Ibid. 343, 355.

80. Gifford 28.

81. Taylor, *Joseph* 341.

82. Wilson and Fiske 48; "Halleck Monument," Folder 1.

83. Taylor, *Joseph* 360–61.
84. Ibid. 318, 168; see also ibid. 215, 255, 284.
85. Ibid. 202–3, 9; see also ibid. 10, 65, 104, 212.
86. Taylor, "Fitz-Greene Halleck," *North American Review* 61, 62, 64.
87. In Wilson, *Letters* 525; Whitman 586.
88. Whitman 85, 231, 106, 600.
89. In Wilson, "Drake" 70.
90. In *Camp: The Lie That Tells the Truth,* Philip Cove credits Susan Sontag and Christopher Isherwood as defining critics of homosexual camp. For other historical perspectives on camp see: Meyer; David Bergman, *Camp Grounds;* Chermayeff et al.
91. In Duyckinck, "Fitz-Greene Halleck" 239.
92. In Wilson, *Bryant* 271.
93. In Tuckerman 216.
94. In Wilson, *Letters* 468.
95. Whitman 894.
96. Ibid. 5, 21, 121.
97. Ibid. 433, 132, 64.
98. Moon, *Disseminating* 63–68.
99. Whitman 121.
100. Ibid. 590, 41, 46, 22, 71, 183, 444, 385–86.
101. See "Children of Lilith" in Gifford 24.
102. R. B. Martin, *Hopkins* 350–51.
103. Dellamora 86–93.
104. Adkins 215.
105. Lilly 6.
106. In Taylor, "Fitz-Greene Halleck," *North American Review* 65.
107. Tuckerman 215.
108. Taylor, *Joseph* 112.
109. In Wilson, *Letters* 263.
110. Whitman 73.
111. In Kane 52.
112. In Wilson, "Drake" 70.
113. "Poetry of Fitz-Greene Halleck" 559.

Bibliography

Abelove, Henry, Michèle Aina Barale, and David M. Halperin, eds. *The Lesbian and Gay Studies Reader.* New York: Routledge, 1993.

Abraham, Julie. "Criticism Is Not a Luxury." *Nation* December 3, 1990: 706–12.

Adkins, Nelson Frederick. *Fitz-Greene Halleck: An Early Knickerbocker Wit and Poet.* New Haven, Conn.: Yale University Press, 1930.

Agnos, Peter. *The Queer Dutchman: True Account of a Sailor Cast Away on a Desert Island for "Unnatural Acts" and Left to God's Mercy.* New York: Green Eagle Press, 1993.

Albro, John, ed. *The Works of Thomas Shepard.* Vol. 1. New York: AMS Press, 1967.

Allen, Dennis W. *Sexuality in Victorian Fiction.* Norman: University of Oklahoma Press, 1993.

Allen, Gay Wilson. *The New Walt Whitman Handbook.* 1975. New York: New York University Press, 1986.

Allen, Gay Wilson. *The Solitary Singer.* New York: New York University Press, 1967.

Allen, Paula Gunn. *The Sacred Hoop: Recovering the Feminine in American Indian Traditions.* Revised ed. Boston: Beacon Press, 1992.

Alyson, Sasha, et al., eds. *The Alyson Almanac.* Boston: Alyson Press, 1989.

"American Poetry." *Foreign Quarterly Review* January 1844: 291–324.

"American Poetry." *Fraser's* July 1850: 9–25.

"American Poetry: Poems by Bryant, Longfellow and Halleck." *New York Times* January 30, 1864: 5+.

"American Poets and Their Critics." *Knickerbocker* June 1834.

Anderson, Beverly. "From These Roots." *Shore Line Times* [Guilford, Conn.] November 16, 1980.

Anderson, Beverly. *Guilford Roots.* Guilford, Conn.: n. p., 1990.

"Announcement of the Death and Services for Dr. Joseph Rodman Drake." *New York Evening Post* September 21, 1820.

Armstrong, Hamilton Fish, ed. *Book of New York Verse.* New York: G. P. Putnam's, 1917.

"Attack on Alnwick Castle." Review of *Alnwick Castle and Other Poems,* by Fitz-Greene Halleck. *Broadway Journal* May 1845: 281–83.

Baillie, David G. "Guilford's Poet, America's Bard." *Shore Line Times* [Guilford, Conn.] July 23, 1936.

Barbour, Philip, ed. *The Jamestown Voyages under the First Charter, 1606–69.* Vol. 2. London: Cambridge University Press, 1969.

Barnhart, Clarence, ed. *New Century Cyclopedia of Names.* Vol. 2. New York: Appleton-Century-Crofts, 1954.

Barret-Dvcrocq, Françoise. *Love in the Time of Victoria: Sexuality and Desire among Working-Class Men and Women in Nineteenth-Century London.* Trans. John Howe. New York: Penguin, 1991.

Barstow, Ann Llewellyn. *Witchcraze: A New History of the European Witch Hunts.* London: Pandora, 1994.

Bawer, Bruce. *A Place at the Table: The Gay Individual in American Society.* New York: Poseidon Press, 1993.

Behn, Aphra. *Oroonoko: Or, the Royal Slave.* 1688. Introd. Lore Metzger. New York: Norton, 1973.

Bennett, Lorenzo T. "Fitz-Greene Halleck—Was He Catholic?" Letter. *Putnam's* February 1854: 262.

Benton, Joel. "Some Reminiscences of Fitz-Greene Halleck." *Frank Leslie's Illustrated Paper* January 4, 1867: 243.

Bercovitch, Sacvan. *The Puritan Origins of the American Self.* New Haven, Conn.: Yale University Press, 1975.

Bergman, David. "The African and the Pagan in Gay Black Literature." *Sexual Sameness: Textual Differences in Lesbian and Gay Writing.* Ed. Joseph Bristow. New York: Routledge, 1992. 148–69.

Bergman, David. *Camp Grounds: Style and Homosexuality.* Amherst: University of Massachusetts Press, 1993.

Bergman, David. *Gaiety Transfigured: Gay Self-Representation in American Literature.* Madison: University of Wisconsin Press, 1991.

Bergmann, Harriet F. "Fitz-Greene Halleck." *Dictionary of Literary Biography.* Vol. 3: *Antebellum Writers in New York and the South.* Ed. Joel Myerson. Detroit: Gale Research, 1979. 136–37.

Berube, Allan. *Coming Out under Fire: The History of Gay Men and Woman in World War Two.* New York: Free Press, 1990.

Biggs, Charles Lewis. "Fitz-Greene Halleck—Son of Guilford." Reprinted in the *Shore Line Times*'s *Guilford Bicentennial Pages* March 1976: 23.

Biggs, Charles Lewis. "Halleck in His Prime." *Shore Line Times* [Guilford, Conn.] July 22, 1926.

"Bisexuality: Not Gay. Not Straight. A New Sexual Identity Emerges." *Newsweek* July 17, 1995: 44–50.

Blake, William. *William Blake: A Selection of Poems and Letters.* Ed. J. Bronowski. New York: Penguin, 1983.

Blanck, Jacob Nathaniel. *Bibliography of American Literature.* Vol. 3. New Haven, Conn.: Yale University Press, 1959. 356–65.

Bliss, Carman, ed. *Oxford Book of American Verse.* New York: Oxford University Press, 1927.

Block, Ivan. *History of English Sexual Mores.* Trans. William F. Fostern. London: Francis Alector, 1936.

Bibliography

Boorstin, Daniel J., and Ruth F. Boorstin, eds. *Hidden History.* New York: Vintage, 1989.

Boswell, John. *Christianity, Social Tolerance and Homosexuality.* Chicago: University of Chicago Press, 1980.

Boswell, John. "Revolutions, Universals, and Sexual Categories." Duberman, Vicinus, and Chauncey 17–36.

Boswell, John. *Same-Sex Unions in Premodern Europe.* New York: Villard, 1994.

Boughner, Terry. *Out of All Time: A Gay and Lesbian History.* Boston: Alyson Press, 1988.

Bowden, Henry W., and James P. Ronda, eds. *John Eliot's Indian Dialogues: A Study in Cultural Interaction.* Westport, Conn.: Greenwood Press, 1980.

Boyer, Paul, and Stephen Nissenbaum. *Salem-Village Witchcraft: A Documentary Record of Local Conflict in Colonial New England.* Boston: Northeastern University Press, 1993.

Bradford, William. *Of Plymouth Plantation: 1620–1647.* New York: Random House, 1981.

Bray, Alan. *Homosexuality in Renaissance England.* London: Gay Men's Press, 1982.

Bredbeck, Gregory W. *Sodomy and Interpretation: Marlowe to Milton.* Ithaca, N.Y.: Cornell University Press, 1991.

Bristow, Joseph, ed. *Sexual Sameness: Textual Differences in Lesbian and Gay Writing.* New York: Routledge, 1992.

Brodie, Janet Farrell. *Contraception and Abortion in Nineteenth-Century America.* Ithaca, N.Y.: Cornell University Press, 1994.

Brooks, Van Wyck. *The World of Washington Irving.* New York: E. P. Dutton, 1944.

Bryant, William Cullen. "Fitz-Greene Halleck." Address to New-York Historical Society. *Littell's Living Age* February 27, 1869: 515–23. Reprint of "Fitz-Greene Halleck." *New York Evening Post* February 3, 1869.

Bryant, William Cullen. Review of *Alnwick Castle and Other Poems,* by Fitz-Greene Halleck. *United States Review and Literary Gazette* April 1827: 8–13.

Bryant, William Cullen. "Writings of Fitz-Greene Halleck." *New York Mirror* September 24, 1836: 1.

Bryant, William Cullen, and George Palmer Putnam. *Memorial of James Fenimore Cooper.* New York: G. P. Putnam, 1852.

Buell, Lawrence. *New England Literary Culture: From Revolution through Renaissance.* 3d ed. New York: Cambridge University Press, 1989.

Bullough, Bonnie, and Vern Bullough. *Sin, Sickness and Sanity.* New York: Garland, 1977.

Burg, B. R. *An American Seafarer in the Age of Sail: The Erotic Diaries of Philip C. Van Bushkirk 1851–1870.* New Haven, Conn.: Yale University Press, 1994.

Burg, B. R. "Ho Hum, Another Work of the Devil: Buggery and Sodomy in Early Stuart England." Licata and Peterson 69–78.

Burg, B. R. *Sodomy and the Perception of Evil.* New York: New York University Press, 1983.

Burg, B. R. *Sodomy and the Pirate Tradition: English Sea Rovers in the Seventeenth-Century Caribbean.* New York: New York University Press, 1984.

Burke, W. J., and Will D. Howe. *American Authors and Books: 1640–1940.* New York: Gramercy, 1943.

Burrows, Edwin G., and Mike Wallace. *Gotham: A History of New York City to 1898.* New York: Oxford University Press, 1999.

Butters, Ronald R., John M. Clum, and Michael Moon, eds. *Displacing Homophobia: Gay Male Perspectives in Literature and Culture.* Durham, N.C.: Duke University Press, 1989.

Byron, Lord. "To John Murray." August 12, 1819. *Byron's Letters and Journals.* Ed. Leslie A. Marchand. Vol. 6. Cambridge, Mass.: Harvard University Press, 1973–1982. 207.

Caldwell, Patricia. *The Puritan Conversion Narrative.* Cambridge: Cambridge University Press, 1983.

Canale, George D. "A Memorial of the American Poet Fitz-Greene Halleck." Athens [Greece]: n. p., 1870.

Carman, Bliss, ed. *The Oxford Book of American Verse.* New York: Oxford University Press, 1927.

Carnes, Mark C. *Secret Ritual and Manhood in Victorian America.* New Haven, Conn.: Yale University Press, 1989.

Carpenter, Edward. *Selected Writings.* Vol. 1: *Sex.* Introd. Noël Greig. London: Gay Men's Press, 1984.

Carpenter, Edward. *Towards Democracy.* 1883. Foreword Gilbert Beith. London: Gay Men's Press, 1985.

Carruth, Gorton. *American Facts and Dates.* 9th ed. New York: HarperCollins, 1993.

"Catalogue of the Private Library of Fitz-Greene Halleck, Esq., to be sold by auction on Monday, Oct. 12, 1868." Vol. 8. New York: Leavitt-Strebeigh, 1868.

Chauncey, George. *Gay New York: Gender, Urban Culture, and the Making of the Gay Male World 1890–1940.* New York: Basic Books, 1994.

Chermayeff, Catherine, Jonathan David, and Nan Richardson. *Drag Diaries.* San Francisco: Chronicle, 1995.

Child, Lydia Maria. *An Appeal in Favor of That Class of Americans Called Africans.* 1833. New York: John S. Taylor, 1836.

Child, Lydia Maria. *Hobomok and Other Writings on Indians.* Ed. Carolyn L. Karcher. New Brunswick, N.J.: Rutgers University Press, 1988.

Child, Lydia Maria. *Letters from New York.* 1845. New York: Books for Libraries Press, 1970.

Child, Lydia Maria. "Willie Wharton." *Atlantic Monthly* March 11, 1863: 324–45.

Chopin, Kate. *The Awakening.* New York: Avon, 1972.

Christman, Henry M., ed. *Walt Whitman's New York: From Manhattan to Montauk.* 1963. New York: New Amsterdam, 1989.

Chudacoff, Howard P. *The Age of the Bachelor: Creating an American Subculture.* Princeton, N.J.: Princeton University Press, 1999.

Clark, Harry Hayden, ed. *Transitions in American Literary History.* Durham, N.C.: Duke University Press, 1953.

Clark, Louis Gaylord. "Charles Dickens." *Harper's New Monthly* August 1862: 376–80.

Clark, Willis. "Halleck's Poems." *American Quarterly Review* June 1837: 399–415.

Cohen, Ed. "Legislating the Norm: From Sodomy to Gross Indecency." Butters, Clum, and Moon 169–205.

Cohen, Ed. *Talk on the Wilde Side: Toward a Genealogy of a Discourse on Male Sexualities.* New York: Routledge, 1993.

Cohen, Patricia Cline. *The Murder of Helen Jewett: The Life and Death of a Prostitute in Nineteenth-Century New York.* New York: Knopf, 1998.

Coleridge, Samuel Taylor. *The Portable Coleridge.* Ed. I. A. Richards. New York: Penguin, 1984.

Cooper, Emmanuel. *The Sexual Perspective: Homosexuality and Art in the Last 100 Years in the West.* New York: Routledge, 1994.

Cooper, James Fenimore. *Correspondence of James Fenimore Cooper.* 1922. Vol. 3. Temecula, Calif.: Reprint Services, 1991.

Cooper, James Fenimore. *Last of the Mohicans.* 1826. New York: Dodd, Mead, 1951.

Coote, Stephen, ed. *The Penguin Book of Homosexual Verse.* New York: Viking Penguin, 1987.

Cordingly, David. *Under the Black Flag: The Romance and Reality of Life among the Pirates.* New York: Random House, 1995.

Cordingly, David, ed. *Pirates: Terror on the High Seas from the Caribbean to the South China Sea.* Atlanta: Turner, 1996.

Core, Philip. *Camp: The Lie That Tells the Truth.* London: Plexus, 1984.

Cowan, Thomas. *Gay Men and Women Who Enriched the World.* New Canaan, Conn.: William Mulvey, 1988.

Cowley, Malcolm, ed. *The Works of Walt Whitman: The Deathbed Edition.* Vol. 2. New York: Funk and Wagnalls, 1968.

Cozzens, Frederic[k] S. *Fitz-Greene Halleck: A Memorial.* New York: Trow & Smith Book Manufacturing, 1868.

Craft, Christopher. *Another Kind of Love: Male Homosexual Desire in English Discourse, 1850–1920.* Berkeley: University of California Press, 1994.

Crew, Louie, ed. *The Gay Academic.* Palm Springs, Calif.: ETC Press, 1978.

Crisp, Quentin. *Quentin Crisp's Book of Quotations.* New York: Macmillan, 1989.

Crompton, Louis. *Byron and Greek Love: Homophobia in Nineteenth-Century England.* Berkeley: University of California Press, 1985.

Crompton, Louis. "Don Leon, Byron and Homosexual Law Reform." *Essays on Gay Literature.* Ed. Stuart Kellogg. New York: Harrington Park Press, 1985. 53–71.

Curtin, Kaier. *"We Can Always Call Them Bulgarians": The Emergence of Lesbians and Gay Men on the American Stage.* 1987. Boston: Alyson Press, 1988.

Curtis, George William. "Halleck Commemoration." *Harper's Weekly* June 2, 1877: 422.

Davidson, Edward H., ed. *Selected Writings of Edgar Allen Poe.* Cambridge, Mass.: Riverside Press, 1956.

"Death of Fitz-Greene Halleck." *Littell's Living Age* December 7, 1867: 639–40.

Bibliography

"Death of Fitz-Greene Halleck." *New York Times* November 21, 1867: 5.

Delbanco, Andrew, and Alan Heimert, eds. *The Puritans in America: A Narrative Anthology.* Cambridge, Mass.: Harvard University Press, 1985.

Dellamora, Richard. *Masculine Desire: The Sexual Politics of Victorian Aestheticism.* Chapel Hill: University of North Carolina Press, 1990.

D'Emilio, John, and Estelle B. Freedman. *Intimate Matters: A History of Sexuality in America.* New York: Harper and Row, 1988.

Description of the Dedication of the Monument Erected at Guilford, Conn., in Honor of Fitz-Greene Halleck. New York: D. Appleton, 1869.

Dewey, Mary E., ed. *Life and Letters of Catherine M. Sedgwick.* New York: Harper and Brothers, 1871.

Dickens, Charles, ed. "Fitz-Greene Halleck." *All the Year Round* May 2, 1868: 496–98.

Dollimore, Jonathan. *Sexual Dissidence: Augustine to Wilde, Freud to Foucault.* Oxford: Clarendon Press, 1991.

Dorenkamp, Monica, and Richard Henke, eds. *Negotiating Lesbian and Gay Subjects.* New York: Routledge, 1995.

Dover, Kenneth. *Greek Homosexuality.* 1978. Cambridge, Mass.: Harvard University Press, 1989.

Dow, George Francis, ed. *Records and Files of the Quarterly Courts of Essex County.* Vol. 1. Salem, Mass.: Essex Institute, 1911.

Dow, Joseph. *History of the Town of Hampton, New Hampshire, from Its Settlement in 1638 to the Autumn of 1892.* Ed. Lucy E. Dow. Vol. 1. Salem, N.H.: Salem Press, 1893.

Dowling, Linda. *Hellenism and Homosexuality in Victorian Oxford.* Ithaca, N.Y.: Cornell University Press, 1994.

Drabble, Margaret, ed. *The Oxford Companion to English Literature.* 5th ed. New York: Oxford University Press, 1985.

Drake, Joseph Rodman. *The Culprit Fay and Other Works.* 1835. Ed. Janet DeKay. New York: G. Dearborn, 1859.

Drake, Joseph Rodman. Miscellaneous Papers. New York: New York Public Library Rare Manuscripts Department.

Drake, Joseph Rodman. "To Fitz-Greene Halleck." *New York Mirror* March 4, 1832: 1.

"Drake." *New York Daily Tribune* January 6, 1881: 4–6.

"Drake's Poems." *American Monthly* September 1835: 65–78.

"Drake's Poems." *New York Mirror* November 21, 1835: 164–65.

Duberman, Martin. "'Writhing Bedfellows': 1826 Two Young Men from Antebellum South Carolina's Ruling Elite Share 'Extravagant Delight.'" Licata and Peterson 85–101.

Duberman, Martin, Martha Vicinus, and George Chauncey, eds. *Hidden from History: Reclaiming the Gay and Lesbian Past.* New York: New American Library, 1989.

Dunning, Jennifer. "A Central Park Tour: Who's Who in Stone." *New York Times* November 21, 1980: C1+.

Duyckinck, Evert A. "Fitz-Greene Halleck: With a Portrait by Horatio Greenough." *Putnam's* February 1868: 231–47.

Duyckinck, Evert A. "Halleck's 'Young America.'" *New York Times* January 30, 1864: 5+.

Duyckinck, Evert A. *Portrait Gallery of Eminent Americans*. New York: Johnson, Fry, 1862.

Duyckinck, Evert A., and George Duyckinck. *Encyclopedia of American Literature*. Ed. M. Laird Simons. Vol. 1. 1875. Detroit: Gale Research, 1967.

Dyer, Kate, ed. *Gays in Uniform: The Pentagon's Secret Reports*. Introd. Gerry E. Studds. Boston: Alyson Press, 1990.

Dynes, Wayne R. *Encyclopedia of Homosexuality*. 2 vols. New York: Garland, 1990.

Eagleton, Terry. *The Ideology of the Aesthetic*. Cambridge: Basil Blackwell, 1990.

Edelman, Lee. *Homographesis: Essays in Gay Literary and Cultural Theory*. New York: Routledge, 1994.

Edwards, Jonathan. *Jonathan Edward's Basic Writings*. Ed. Ola Winslow. New York: New American Library, 1966.

Ehrlich, Eugene, and Gorton Carruth. *The Oxford Literary Guide to the United States*. New York: Oxford University Press, 1982.

Eliot, John. *A Biographical Dictionary: Containing a Brief Account of the First Settlers, and Other Eminent Characters among the Magistrates, Ministers, Literary and Worthy Men in New-England*. Boston: Edward Oliver, 1809.

Eliot, John. *Jews in America, or Probabilities, That Those Indians Are Judaical*. [England]: H. Brone, 1660.

Embury, Emma Catherine. Box 1, Papers. New York: New York Public Library Rare Manuscripts Department.

"Epistle to the Editor." Letter. *Knickerbocker* May 1844: 437.

Evans, Arthur. *Witchcraft and the Gay Counterculture*. Boston: Fag Rag, 1978.

Everest, Charles W., ed. *The Poets of Connecticut*. Hartford, Conn.: Case, Tiffany, and Burnham, 1843.

Faderman, Lillian. *Surpassing the Love of Men: Romantic Friendship and Love between Women from the Renaissance to the Present*. New York: William Morrow, 1981.

Felleman, Hazel. *The Best Loved Poems of the American People*. Garden City, N.Y.: Garden City Publishing Co., 1936.

Fiedler, Leslie A. *Love and Death in the American Novel*. 3d ed. New York: Stein and Day, 1982.

"Fitz-Greene Halleck." *Emerald and Baltimore Literary Gazette* January 10, 1829: 5.

"Fitz-Greene Halleck." *New Yorker* January 2, 1841.

"Fitz-Greene Halleck." *Our Album of Authors*. Philadelphia: Elliott & Beezley Press, 1877. 178–82.

"Fitz-Greene Halleck—Review of Poet's Life Prepared for Men's Club." *Shore Line Times* [Guilford, Conn.] December 15, 1932.

"Fitz-Greene Halleck and the Village Belle." *Harper's New Monthly* June 1878: 132–33.

Bibliography

"Fitz-Greene Halleck 1790–1943." *Shore Line Times* [Guilford, Conn.] July 8, 1943.

Fone, Byrne. *Masculine Landscapes: Walt Whitman and the Homoerotic Text.* Carbondale: Southern Illinois University Press, 1992.

Fone, Byrne. *A Road to Stonewall 1750–1969: Male Homosexuality and Homophobia in English and American Literature, 1750–1969.* New York: Twayne, 1995.

Fone, Byrne, ed. *Hidden Heritage.* New York: Avocation Press, 1980.

Fout, John C., and Maura Shaw Tantillo, eds. *American Sexual Politics: Sex, Gender, and Race since the Civil War.* Chicago: University of Chicago Press, 1993.

Franklin, Benjamin. *The Autobiography and Other Writings.* Ed. Kenneth Silverman. New York: Penguin, 1986.

Frantzen, Allen J. "The Disclosure of Sodomy in Cleanness." *Publications of the Modern Language Association of America* 3.3 (1996): 451–64.

Freud, Sigmund. *The Freud Reader.* Ed. Peter Gay. New York: Norton, 1989.

Fuller, Edmund, and B. J. Kinnick. *Adventures in American Literature.* New York: Harcourt, Brace and World, 1963.

Fuller, Margaret. *The Essential Margaret Fuller.* Ed. Jeffrey Steele. New Brunswick, N.J.: Rutgers University Press, 1992.

Fullerton, B. M. *Selective Bibliography of American Literature: 1775–1900.* New York: Payson, 1932.

"Funeral of Fitz-Greene Halleck." Folder 1, Halleck Papers. New York Public Library Rare Manuscripts Department.

Fuss, Diana, ed. *GLQ: A Journal of Gay/Lesbian Studies* 2.1–2 (1995).

Fuss, Diana, ed. *Inside/Out: Lesbian Theories, Gay Theories.* New York: Routledge, 1991.

"Gay for Life? Going Straight: The Uproar over Sexual 'Conversion'" *Newsweek* August 17, 1998.

Gerson, Oscar, ed. *Poetry for the Grades.* Vol. 7. Philadelphia: Franklin Press, 1918.

Gesner, George, ed. *Anthology of American Poetry.* New York: Avenel, 1983.

Giantvalley, Scott. *Walt Whitman: 1838–1939, a Reference Guide.* Boston: G. K. Hall, 1981.

Gifford, James. *Dayneford's Library: American Homosexual Writing, 1900–1913.* Amherst: University of Massachusetts Press, 1995.

Gigeroff, Alex K. *Sexual Deviations in the Criminal Law.* Toronto: University of Toronto Press, 1968.

Godwin, Parke. *A Biography of William Cullen Bryant with Abstracts from His Private Correspondence.* Vol. 2. 1883. Temecula, Calif.: Reprint Services, 1993.

Goldberg, Jonathan. *Sodomtries: Renaissance Texts, Modern Sexualities.* Stanford, Calif.: Stanford University Press, 1992.

Goldberg, Jonathan, ed. *Queering the Renaissance.* Durham, N.C.: Duke University Press, 1994.

Goldberg, Jonathan, ed. *Reclaiming Sodom.* New York: Routledge, 1994.

Goldsmith, Oliver. *Poems and Plays.* Ed. Tom Davis. 1975. London: J. M. Dent and Sons, 1990.

Graff, Gerald. *Professing Literature.* Chicago: University of Chicago Press, 1987.

Gray, Barry. "Fitz-Greene Halleck." *New York Evening Mail* January 9, 1868.

Greenberg, David F. *The Construction of Homosexuality.* Chicago: University of Chicago Press, 1988.

Greenberg, David F. "The Socio-Sexual Milieu of the *Love-Letters.*" Kimmel 93–103.

Greif, Martin. *The Gay Book of Days.* Secaucus, N.J.: Lyle Stuart, 1982.

Greven, Philip J. *The Protestant Temperament: Patterns of Child-Rearing, Religious Experience, and the Self in Early America.* New York: Knopf, 1977.

Griswold, Rufus. *Passages from the Correspondence and Other Papers of Rufus Griswold.* Cambridge, Mass.: W. M. Griswold, 1898.

Griswold, Rufus. *The Poets and Poetry of America, to the Middle of the Nineteenth Century.* Philadelphia: Carey and Hart, 1843.

Hackett, James H. "Reminiscences of the Poet Halleck." *New York Evening Post* January 31, 1868.

Haggerty, George E. "Literature and Homosexuality in the Late Eighteenth Century: Walpole, Beckford, and Lewis." *Studies in the Novel* 18.4 (Winter 1986): 341–52.

Hall, Richard. *Patriots in Disguise: Women Warriors of the Civil War.* New York: Marlowe, 1994.

Hallam, Paul. *The Book of Sodom.* New York: Verso, 1993.

Halleck, Fitz-Greene. *Alnwick Castle and Other Poems.* New York: G. and C. Carvill, 1827. 2d ed. New York: George Dearborn, 1836. 3d ed. New York: Harper and Brothers, 1845.

Halleck, Fitz-Greene. *Fanny.* New York: C. Wiley, 1819. 2d ed. New York: Wiley and Halstead, 1821; New York: W. L. Andrews, 1866.

Halleck, Fitz-Greene. *Fanny and Other Poems.* New York: Harper and Brothers, 1839.

Halleck, Fitz-Greene. Folder 1, Halleck Papers. New York Public Library Rare Manuscripts Department.

Halleck, Fitz-Greene. "The Indian Warrior." *Holt's Columbian* [New York] August 22, 1810.

Halleck, Fitz-Greene. "Joel Lewis Griffing, Esq'r." Letter printed for Charles F. Heartman. New York: Rutland, 1921. New-York Historical Society Manuscripts Room.

Halleck, Fitz-Greene. "Lines." *Holt's Columbian* [New York] July 22, 1814.

Halleck, Fitz-Greene. "Lines on the Late Doctor Joseph R. Drake; by a Friend." *Literary Gazette* February 24, 1821: 115.

Halleck, Fitz-Greene. *Lines to the Recorder.* New York: W. L. Andrews, 1866.

Halleck, Fitz-Greene. "Marco Botzares" ["Marco Bozzaris"]. Trans. George D. Canale. Cambridge, Mass.: Welch, Bigelow, 1859.

Halleck, Fitz-Greene. "Memory." *New York Times* February 2, 1868: 2.

Halleck, Fitz-Greene. *Poems by Fitz-Greene Halleck.* New York: Harper and Brothers, 1839.

Halleck, Fitz-Greene. *Poetical Works of Fitz-Greene Halleck.* New York: D. Appleton, 1847.

Halleck, Fitz-Greene. *Poetical Writings of Fitz-Greene Halleck: With Abstracts of*

Those from Joseph Rodman Drake. 1852. Ed. James Grant Wilson. New York: D. Appleton, 1869; New York: Greenwood Press, 1969.

Halleck, Fitz-Greene. Special Collections. Columbia University Rare Books and Manuscripts Library, New York.

Halleck, Fitz-Greene. "Strong as That Power . . . ." *New York Times* February 2, 1868.

Halleck, Fitz-Greene. Untitled lines on the Ugly Club. *Holt's Columbian* [New York] January 19, 1815.

Halleck, Fitz-Greene. *Young America.* New York: D. Appleton, 1865.

Halleck, Fitz-Greene, ed. *Selections from the British Poets.* 2 vols. New York: Harper and Brothers, 1840.

Halleck, Fitz-Greene, ed. *Works of Lord Byron: In Verse and Prose, Including His Letters, Journals, etc., with a Sketch of His Life.* 1834. 2d ed. New York: George Dearborn, 1836.

Halleck, Fitz-Greene, and Joseph Rodman Drake. *Croakers.* 1819. New York: Bradford Club, 1860.

Halleck, Reuben Post. *History of American Literature.* New York: American, 1911.

"Halleck and Bryant." *Literary Gazette* July 25, 1819: 483.

"Halleck Monument." Folder 1, Halleck Papers. New York Public Library Rare Manuscripts Department.

"Halleck Monument." *New Haven Palladium* July 9, 1869: 19–20.

"Halleck Monument." *New York Evening Post.* n.d. Folder 1, Halleck Papers. New York Public Library Rare Manuscripts Department.

"Halleck Monument." *New York Times* July 9, 1869: 5.

"Halleck's Monument." *Harper's Weekly* September 26, 1868.

"Halleck Statue." *Harper's Weekly* June 2, 1877: 425.

"Halleck Statue." *New York Tribune* May 16, 1877: 17.

Haller, John S., and Robin M. Haller. *The Physician and Sexuality in Victorian America.* Urbana: University of Illinois Press, 1974.

Hallock, Lucius H., ed. *A Hallock Genealogy.* New York: n. p., 1926.

Halperin, David M. *"One Hundred Years of Homosexuality" and Other Essays on Greek Love.* New York: Routledge, 1990.

Halperin, David M. *Saint Foucault: Towards a Gay Hagiography.* New York: Oxford University Press, 1995.

Halperin, David M. "Sex before Sexuality: Pederasty, Politics, and Power in Classical Athens." Duberman, Vicinus, and Chauncey 37–53.

Hansen-Taylor, Marie, and Horace E. Scudder, eds. *Life and Letters of Bayard Taylor.* Vol. 2. New York: Houghton Mifflin, 1884.

Hardman, Paul D. *Homoaffectionalism: Male Bonding from Gilgamesh to the Present.* San Francisco: GLB Publishers, 1993.

Harmon, William, ed. *The Oxford Book of American Light Verse.* New York: Oxford University Press, 1979.

Harper, Frances E. W. *A Brighter Coming Day.* Ed. and Introd. Frances Smith Foster. New York: Feminist Press, 1990.

Harper, Frances E. W. *Iola Leroy or Shadows Uplifted.* 1892. Introd. Hazel V. Carby. Boston: Beacon, 1987.

Harrison, James Albert, ed. *The Complete Works of Edgar Allan Poe.* 1902. Introd. Floyd Stovall. New York: AMS Press, 1979.

Hart, James D. *The Concise Oxford Companion to American Literature.* New York: Oxford University Press, 1986.

Haskins, George Lee. *Law and Authority in Early Massachusetts.* New York: Macmillan, 1960.

Helander, Joel E. *Guilford Long Ago.* Vol. 1. Guilford, Conn.: Joel E. Helander, 1969. 87–91.

Helminiak, Daniel A. *What the Bible Really Says about Homosexuality: Recent Findings by Top Scholars.* Foreword John S. Spung. San Francisco: Alamo Square Press, 1994.

Hendrickson, Robert. *American Literary Anecdotes.* New York: Facts on File, 1990.

Higgenson, Francis. *The Founding of Massachusetts.* Boston: Massachusetts Historical Society, 1930.

Higgins, Patrick, ed. *A Queer Reader.* New York: New Press, 1993.

Hill, Everett Gleason. Chapter 43. *A Modern History of New Haven and Eastern New Haven County.* Vol. 1. New York: S. J. Clarke Press, 1918. 383–88.

Hillard, George S. "Fitz-Greene Halleck: No. 1 in a Series of Literary Portraits." *New England* August 1831: 153–59.

Hollander, John, ed. *American Poetry: The Nineteenth Century.* Vol. 1: *Philip Freneau to Walt Whitman.* New York: Literary Classics, 1993. 97–109.

Holloway, Emory. *Uncollected Poetry and Prose of Walt Whitman.* Vol. 1. Garden City, N.J.: n. p., 1921.

Holloway, Emory. *Whitman: An Interpretation in Narrative.* New York: Knopf, 1926.

Homberger, Eric. *The Historical Atlas of New York City: A Visual Celebration of Nearly 400 Years of New York City's History.* New York: Holt, 1994.

Hone, Philip. *The Diary of Philip Hone.* 2 vols. Ed. Bayard Tuckerman. New York: Dodd, Mead, 1889.

Horner, Tom. *Jonathan Loved David: Homosexuality in Biblical Times.* Philadelphia: Westminster Press, 1978.

Howard, John R., ed. *One Hundred Best American Poems.* New York: Crowell, 1905.

Howe, M. A. Dewolfe. "Willis, Halleck, and Drake." *Bookman* June 1897: 304–16.

Hows, John A., ed. *In the Woods with Bryant, Longfellow and Halleck.* New York: J. G. Gregory, 1863.

Hutchison Percy. "A Knickerbocker Wit and Poet: Fitz-Greene Halleck, Whose 'Marco Bozzaris' Every American Schoolboy Used to Know." *New York Times* December 28, 1930: 6.

Hyde, Lewis, ed. *Rat and the Devil: Journal Letters of F. O. Matthiessen and Russell Cheney.* North Haven, Conn.: Archon, 1978.

Hyde, Montgomery. *The Love That Dare Not Speak Its Name: A Candid History of Homosexuality in Britain.* Boston: Little and Brown, 1970.

Irvine, Janice M. *Disorders of Desire: Sex and Gender in Modern American Sexology.* Philadelphia: Temple University Press, 1990.

Irvine, Janice M. *Sexual Cultures and the Construction of Adolescent Identities.* Philadelphia: Temple University Press, 1994.

Irving, Washington. *Life and Letters of Washington Irving.* 4 vols. Ed. Pierre M. Irving. New York: Putnam, 1862.

Jacobs, Harriet. *Incidents in the Life of a Slave Girl.* 1861. Introd. Valerie Smith. New York: Oxford University Press, 1988.

Jacobs, Robert D. *Poe: Journalist and Critic.* Baton Rouge: Louisiana State University Press, 1969.

James, Henry. "The Pupil." *Henry James: Selected Short Stories.* Introd. Quentin Anderson. New York: Rinehart, 1957. 167–214.

Jennings, Francis. *The Invasion of America: Indians, Colonialism, and the Cant of Conquest.* Chapel Hill: University of North Carolina Press, 1995.

Johnson, Allen, and Dumas Malone, eds. *Dictionary of American Biography.* New York: Scribner's, 1928–36.

Johnson, Allen, and Dumas Malone, eds. *Dictionary of American Biography.* Vol. 2. New York: Scribner's, 1958.

Johnson, Charles. *Middle Passage.* New York: Plume, 1990.

Johnson, Charles F. "Fitz-Greene Halleck." *Hartford Courant* September 9, 1889: 257–58.

Jones, Neal T. *A Book of Days for the Literary Year.* New York: Thames and Hudson, 1989.

Kane, Neal, ed. *Improper Bostonians: Lesbian and Gay History from the Puritans to Playland.* Boston: Beacon Press, 1998.

Kaplan, Fred. *Henry James: The Imagination of Genius, a Biography.* New York: William Morrow, 1992.

Karcher, Carolyn L. "Rape, Murder, and Revenge in 'Slavery's Pleasant Homes.'" *The Culture of Sentiment: Race, Gender, and Sentimentality in Nineteenth-Century America.* Ed. Shirley C. Samuels. New York: Oxford University Press, 1992. 58–72.

Karlen, Arno. *Sexuality and Homosexuality: A New View.* New York: Norton, 1971.

Kates, Gary. *Monsieur d'Eon Is a Woman: A Tale of Political Intrigue and Sexual Masquerade.* New York: Basic Books, 1995.

Katz, Jonathan. "The Early Nineteenth-Century Organization of Love." *The Invention of Heterosexuality.* New York: Dutton-Penguin, 1995. 40–47.

Katz, Jonathan. *Gay American History: Lesbians and Gay Men in the U.S.A.* New York: Harper and Row, 1985.

Katz, Jonathan. *Gay/Lesbian Almanac.* New York: Harper and Row, 1983.

Kearney, Patrick J. *A History of Erotic Literature.* London: Macmillan, 1982.

Keese, John, ed. *The Poets of America.* New York: Samuel Coleman, 1839. 3d ed. Detroit: Gale Research, 1976.

Kennedy, Hubert. *Ulrichs: The Life and Works of Karl Heinrich Ulrichs, Pioneer of the Modern Gay Movement.* Boston: Alyson Press, 1988.

Kenny, Maurice. "Tinselled Bucks: An Historical Study in Indian Homosexuality." *Gay Roots: Twenty Years of Gay Sunshine — An Anthology of Gay History, Sex, Politics and Culture.* Ed. Winston Leyland. San Francisco: Gay Sunshine Press, 1991. 113–23.

Kettell, Samuel, ed. *Specimens of American Poetry with Critical and Biographical Notices.* 3 vols. 1829. Boston: S. G. Goodrich, 1929.

Killingsworth, M. Jimmie. *Whitman's Poetry of the Body: Sexuality, Politics, and the Text.* Chapel Hill: University of North Carolina Press, 1989.

Kimmel, Michael S., ed. *Journal of Homosexuality.* New York: Haworth Press, 1990.

Koestenbaum, Wayne. *Double Talk: The Erotics of Male Literary Collaboration.* New York: Routledge, 1989.

Koestenbaum, Wayne. *The Queen's Throat: Opera, Homosexuality, and the Mystery of Desire.* New York: Vintage-Random, 1993.

Laqueur, Thomas W. *Making Sex: Gender and the Body from Aristotle to Freud.* Cambridge, Mass.: Harvard University Press, 1990.

Lathrop, George Parsons. "Fitz-Greene Halleck." *Atlantic Monthly* June 1877: 718–29.

Lauritsen, John, and David Thorstad. *The Early Homosexual Rights Movement: 1864–1935.* 1974. Revised ed. New York: Times Change Press, 1995.

Lawson, James. "Fitz-Greene Halleck: Moral and Mental Portrait Series." *Southern Literary Messenger* April 1842: 341–49. Reprinted in *New World* November 25, 1843: 718–29.

Lee, Kenneth R. "Famed Local Poet Snubbed." *Shore Line Times* [Guilford, Conn.] November 16, 1988.

Lee, Kenneth R. Letter. *Shore Line Times* [Guilford, Conn.] December 4, 1980.

Lee, Kenneth R. "150 Years Ago—Fitz-Greene Halleck." *Shore Line Times* [Guilford, Conn.] November 8, 1977: 1–3.

Leggett, William. "Fitz-Greene Halleck." *Critic* December 30, 1828: 129–32.

Leitch, Vincent B. *American Literary Criticism: From the 30s to the 80s.* New York: Columbia University Press, 1988.

Lentricchia, Frank, and Thomas McLaughlin, eds. *Critical Terms for Literary Study.* Chicago: University of Chicago Press, 1990.

Leonard, William Ellery. *Byron and Byronism in America.* 1905. New York: Haskell House, 1964.

Letter. *Brooklyn Eagle.* Folder 1, Halleck Papers. New York Public Library Rare Manuscripts Department.

Leverenz, David. *Manhood and the American Renaissance.* Ithaca, N.Y.: Cornell University Press, 1989.

Levin, James. *The Gay Novel.* New York: Irvington, 1983.

Lewisohn, Ludwig. *Expression in America.* New York: Harper and Brothers, 1932. Reprinted as *The Story of American Literature.* New York: Kraus, 1972.

Licata, Salvatore J., and Robert R. Peterson, eds. *The Gay Past: A Collection of Historical Essays.* New York: Harrington Park Press, 1985.

Lilly, Mark, ed. *Lesbian and Gay Writing: An Anthology of Critical Essays.* Philadelphia: Temple University Press, 1990.

"Literary Report." *New York Mirror* August 2, 1834: 39.

Mabbott, Thomas O. *Notes and Queries* March 1926.

Maccubbin, Robert, ed. *Unauthorized Sexual Behavior during the Enlightenment: 18 Essays.* Williamsburg, Va.: College of William and Mary, 1985.

Bibliography

Magnusson, Magnus, ed. *Larousse Biographical Dictionary*. 1897. 5th ed. New York: Larousse, 1995.

Malinowski, Bronislaw. *The Sexual Life of Savages*. Preface Havelock Ellis. New York: Halcyon House, 1929.

Martin, Robert Bernard. *Gerard Manley Hopkins: A Very Private Life*. New York: G. P. Putnam's Sons, 1991.

Martin, Robert K. *Hero, Captain, and Stranger: Male Friendship, Social Critique, and Literary Form in the Sea Novels of Herman Melville*. Chapel Hill: University of North Carolina Press, 1986.

Martin, Robert K. *The Homosexual Tradition in American Poetry*. Austin: University of Texas Press, 1979.

Martin, Robert K. "Knights-Errant and Gothic Seducers: The Representation of Male Friendship in Mid-Nineteenth-Century America." Duberman, Vicinus, and Chauncey 169–82.

Martin, Robert K., ed. *The Continuing Presence of Walt Whitman: The Life after the Life*. Iowa City: University of Iowa Press, 1992.

Maslan, Mark. "Whitman and His Doubles: Division and Union in *Leaves of Grass* and Its Critics." *American Literary History* 6.1 (1994): 119–39.

Mason, Michael. *The Making of Victorian Sexuality*. New York: Oxford University Press, 1995.

Mather, Cotton. *Magnalia Christi Americana*. Ed. Raymond Cunningham. New York: Fredrick Ungar, 1970.

Matthiessen, F. O., ed. *Oxford Book of American Poetry*. New York: Oxford University Press, 1950.

McCormick, Ian, ed. *Secret Sexualities: A Sourcebook of Seventeenth and Eighteenth Century Writing*. New York: Routledge, 1997.

McGovern, Jimmy. Screen play. *Priest*. Dir. Antonio Bird. Miramax, 1995.

McIlwain, Charles Howard, ed. *Political Works*. Cambridge, Mass.: Harvard University Press, 1918.

McMullen, Richie J. *Male Rape: Breaking the Silence on the Last Taboo*. London: Gay Men's Press, 1990.

Meeker, Richard. *Better Angel*. 1933. Introd. Hubert Kennedy. Boston: Alyson Press, 1987.

Melville, Herman. *Mardi and a Voyage Thither*. 1849. Evanston, Ill.: Northwestern University Press, 1970.

Memorial of Fitz-Greene Halleck: A Description of the Dedication of the Monument Erected to His Memory at Guilford, Connecticut; and of the Proceedings Connected with the Unveiling of the Poet's Statue in the Central Park, New York. New York: Amerman and Wilson, 1877. Section on Guilford Monument reprint, of *A Memorial of Fitz-Greene Halleck: A Description of the Monument Erected in Guilford, CT*. New York: D. Appleton, 1869. 1–72.

Meyer, Moe, ed. *The Politics and Poetics of Camp*. New York: Routledge, 1994.

Miller, Edwin Haviland. *Walt Whitman's Poetry: A Psychological Journey*. Boston: Houghton Mifflin, 1968.

Miller, Edwin Haviland. *Walt Whitman's "Song of Myself": A Mosaic of Interpretations*. Iowa City: University of Iowa Press, 1989.

Miller, Edwin Haviland, ed. *Selected Letters of Walt Whitman.* Iowa City: University of Iowa Press, 1990.

Miller, Neil. *Out of the Past: Gay and Lesbian History from 1869 to the Present.* New York: Vintage, 1995.

Mitchell, Mary Hewitt. *History of New Haven County.* Vol. 1. Boston: Pioneer Historical Press, 1930.

Moon, Michael. "Disseminating Whitman." Butters, Clum, and Moon 235–53.

Moon, Michael. *Disseminating Whitman: Revision and Corporeality in* Leaves of Grass. Cambridge, Mass.: Harvard University Press, 1991.

Moore, Frank, comp. *The Civil War in Song and Story.* New York: Collier, 1882.

Morris, Timothy. *Becoming Canonical in American Poetry.* Champaign: University of Illinois Press, 1995.

Morton, Nathaniel. *The New-England Memorial: or, a Brief Relation of the Most Memorable and Remarkable Passages of the Providence of God Manifested to the Planters of New-England, in America: With Special Reference to the First Colony Thereof, Called New Plimouth* . . . 1699. Boston: D. Henchman, 1721; Plymouth: Allen Danforth, 1826.

Moss, Sidney P. *Poe's Literary Battles: The Critic in the Context of His Literary Milieu.* Durham, N.C.: Duke University Press, 1963.

Murphy, Francis, ed. *Walt Whitman — A Critical Anthology.* Middlesex: Penguin, 1969.

Myerson, Joel, ed. *The American Renaissance in New England.* Detroit: Gale Research, 1978.

Nakamura, Junichi. *Edgar Allan Poe's Relations with New England.* Tokyo: Hokuseido Press, 1957.

Nardi, Peter M., David Sanders, and Judd Marmor. *Growing Up before Stonewall.* New York: Routledge, 1994.

National Portrait Gallery: Permanent Collection Illustrated Checklist. Washington, D.C.: National Portrait Gallery with the Smithsonian Institution Press, 1987.

"New Publications: Life of Fitz-Greene Halleck." Review of *Life and Letters,* by James Grant Wilson. Folder 1, Halleck Papers. New York Public Library Rare Manuscripts Department.

New York Mirror. July 11, 1835: 12. Call for Halleck to edit Drake's collected works.

New York Mirror. May 6, 1837: 359. Samuel Rodgers's letter to Irving.

Norton, Rictor. *Mother Clap's Molly House: The Gay Subculture in England 1700–1830.* London: Gay Men's Press, 1992.

Norton, Rictor. *The Myth of the Modern Homosexual: Queer History and the Search for Cultural Unity.* Washington, D.C.: Cassell, 1997.

Norton, Rictor, ed. *My Dear Boy: Gay Love Letters through the Centuries.* San Francisco: LeyLand Press, 1998.

"Not to Them" from "Ode to Sickness." *Churchmaus Monthly Magazine of New Haven* December 1807: 477.

Olsen, Donald S. *The Confessions of Aubrey Beardsley.* New York: Bantam Press, 1993.

Orgel, Stephen. "Nobody's Perfect: Or Why Did the English Stage Take Boys for Women?" Butters, Clum, and Moon 7–29.

Ostrom, John, ed. *The Letters of Edgar Allan Poe.* 2 vols. New York: Gordian sPress, 1966.

Paglia, Camille. *Vamps and Tramps.* New York: Vintage, 1994.

Panati, Charles. *Sexy Origins and Intimate Things: The Rites and Rituals of Straights, Gays, Bi's, Drags, Trans, Virgins, and Others.* New York: Penguin Books, 1998.

Parker, Hershel. *Herman Melville: A Biography.* Vol. 1: *1819–1851.* Baltimore: Johns Hopkins University Press, 1996.

Parks, Edd Winfield. *Edgar Allan Poe as Literary Critic.* Athens: University of Georgia Press, 1964.

Parton, James. *Famous Americans of Recent Times.* Boston: Ticknor and Fields, 1867.

Parton, James. *Life of John Jacob Astor to Which Is Appended a Copy of His Last Will.* New York: American News, 1865.

Pattee, Fred Lewis. *The First Century of American Literature 1770–1870: Student's Edition.* New York: D. Appleton-Century, 1935.

Percy, William A. *Greek Pederasty.* New York: Garland, 1990.

Percy, William A. *Pederasty and Pedagogy in Archaic Greece.* Chicago: University of Illinois Press, 1996.

Perkins, George, et al., eds. *The American Tradition in Literature: Colonial Period through Whitman.* 7th ed. New York: McGraw-Hill, 1990.

Plant, Richard. *The Pink Triangle: The Nazi War against Homosexuals.* New York: Henry Holt, 1986.

Pleadwell, Frank Lester. *The Life and Works of Joseph Rodman Drake: A Memoir.* Boston: Merrymount Press, 1935.

Poe, Edgar Allan. "Critical Notices, Drake-Halleck." *Southern Literary Messenger* April 1836: 326–36. Reprinted in *Southern Literary Messenger* June 2, 1877.

Poe, Edgar Allan. "Fitz-Greene Halleck: With a Portrait by Henry Inman." *Graham's* September 1843: 160–63.

Poe, Edgar Allan. "The Literati of New York City—No. III: Some Honest Opinions at Random Respecting Their Auctorial Merits, with Occasional Words of Personality. Fitz-Greene Halleck." *Godey's Magazine and Lady's Book* July 1846: 13–15.

Poe, Edgar Allan. *The Poets and Poetry of America; a Satire.* 1847. New York: Benjamin and Bell, 1887.

"Poet Halleck's Great Scrap Book: A Hitherto Unpublished Poem and Many Reminiscences. Gloomy Letter from Poet Poe. Halleck's Views on the Cost of Bachelor Life—A Veiled Romance." *The Sheet.* N.p.: n.d. Folder 1, Halleck Papers. New York Public Library Rare Manuscripts Department.

"Poetry of Fitz-Greene Halleck." *Knickerbocker* December 1845: 553–59.

Porter, Roy. *A Social History of Madness: The World through the Eyes of the Insane.* New York: Weidenfeld and Nicolson, 1987.

Porter, Roy, and Mikulas Teich, eds. *Sexual Knowledge, Sexual Science: The History of Attitudes to Sexuality.* New York: Cambridge University Press, 1994.

Poussaint, Alvin F. "An Honest Look at Black Gays and Lesbians." *Ebony* September 1990: 124–31.

Powell, Thomas. *The Living Writers of America*. New York: Stringer and Townsend, 1850.

Powers, Edwin. *Crime and Punishment in Early Massachusetts: 1620–1692*. Boston: Beacon Press, 1966.

Preminger, Alex, and T.V.F. Brogan, eds. *The New Princeton Encyclopedia of Poetry and Poetics*. Princeton, N.J.: Princeton University Press, 1993.

Programme of the Amateur Entertainment in Aid of the Halleck Statue Fund. New York: n. p., 1869.

Pulsifer, David, ed. *Records of the Colony of Plymouth in New England*. Boston: William White, 1855.

Quennell, Peter. *Byron: The Years of Fame*. New York: Viking Press, 1935.

Quiller-Couch, Arthur, ed. *The Oxford Book of Victorian Verse*. New York: Oxford University Press, 1925.

Quinn, Arthur Hobson, ed. *The Literature of the American People: An Historical and Critical Survey*. New York: Appleton-Century-Crofts, 1951.

Quinn, D. Michael. *Same-Sex Dynamics among Nineteenth-Century Americans: A Mormon Example*. Chicago: University of Illinois Press, 1996.

Rajasekharaiah, T. R. *Roots of Whitman's Grass*. Cranbury, N.J.: Associated University Presses, 1970.

Reiss, Warren P. "An Ode to Fitz." Letter to the editor. *New York Times Magazine* July 13, 1997: 8.

"Remembering Pain and Pleasure: Roger Casement's Diaries." *Perversions: The International Journal of Gay and Lesbian Studies* 2 (1994).

Review of *Alnwick Castle and Other Poems*, by Fitz-Greene Halleck. *Broadway Journal* April 5, 1845: 211.

Review of *Alnwick Castle and Other Poems*, by Fitz-Greene Halleck. *Knickerbocker* January 1836: 88.

Review of *Alnwick Castle and Other Poems*, by Fitz-Greene Halleck. *Literary Gazette* February 24, 1827.

Review of *Fanny*, by Fitz-Greene Halleck. *Literary Gazette* April 7, 1821: 209.

Review of *Fanny with Other Poems*, by Fitz-Greene Halleck. *Knickerbocker* September 1839: 283.

Review of *Poetical Works of Fitz-Greene Halleck*, by Fitz-Greene Halleck. *Knickerbocker* August 1852: 164.

Review of *Poetical Works of Fitz-Greene Halleck*, by Fitz-Greene Halleck. *New York Times* December 15, 1868: 2.

Review of *Poetical Works of Fitz-Greene Halleck*, by Fitz-Greene Halleck. *Southern Literary Messenger* August 1852: 511.

Review of *Sukey*, by William B. Walter. *Literary Gazette* April 28, 1821: 257–59.

Reynolds, David S. *Walt Whitman's America: A Cultural Biography*. New York: Knopf, 1995.

Ringer, Jeffrey R., ed. *Queer Words, Queer Images: Communication and the Construction of Homosexuality*. New York: New York University Press, 1994.

Rood, Karen L., ed. *American Literary Almanac: From 1608 to the Present*. New York: Facts on File, 1988.

Rosario, Vernon A., ed. *Science and Homosexualities*. New York: Routledge, 1996.

Roscoe, Will. *The Zuni Man-Woman*. Albuquerque: University of New Mexico Press, 1991.

Roscoe, Will, ed. *Living the Spirit: A Gay American Indian Anthology*. New York: St. Martin's Press, 1988.

Rossetti, William Michael, ed. *American Poems*. [London]: 1872; New York: AMS Press, n.d.

Rousseau, G. S. "An Introduction to the *Love-Letters:* Circumstances of Publication, Context, and Cultural Commentary." Kimmel 47–91.

Rousseau, G. S. "The Pursuit of Homosexuality in the Eighteenth Century: 'Utterly Confused Category' and/or Rich Repository?" Maccubbin 132–68.

Rowse, A. L. *Homosexuals in History*. New York: Carroll and Graf, 1977.

Rutherford, Mildred. *American Authors*. Atlanta: Franklin Press, 1894.

Salholz, Eloise, et al. "The Future of Gay America." *Newsweek* March 12, 1990: 20–25+.

Santagati, Salvatore, ed. *The European Gay Review*. Vol. 4. London: Verlaine-Rimbaud, 1989.

Saslow, James M. "Homosexuality in the Renaissance: Behavior, Identity and Artistic Expression." Duberman, Vicinus, and Chauncey 90–105.

Schlesser, Karl H. *The Wolves of Heaven*. Norman: University of Oklahoma Press, 1987.

Schmitz, Neil. "Refiguring Lincoln: Speeches and Writings, 1832–1865." *American Literary History* 6.1 (spring 1994): 103–18.

Sedgwick, Eve Kosofsky. *Between Men: English Literature and Male Homosocial Desire*. New York: Columbia University Press, 1985.

Sedgwick, Eve Kosofsky. *Epistemology of the Closet*. Berkeley: University of California Press, 1990.

Selections from the British Poets, Chronologically Arranged from Chaucer to the Present Time, under Separate Divisions, with Introductions Explaining the Different Species of Poetry. Vol. 1. Dublin: n. p., 1851.

Sergent, Bernard. *Homosexuality in Greek Myth*. Boston: Beacon Press, 1986.

Sewall, Samuel. *The Diary of Samuel Sewall*. Ed. Harvey Wish. New York: Putnam, 1967.

Sherwood, Dolly. *Harriet Hosmer, American Sculptor, 1830–1908*. Columbia: University of Missouri Press, 1991.

Shively, Charley. *Calamus Lovers: Walt Whitman's Working-Class Camerados*. San Francisco: Gay Sunshine Press, 1987.

Shively, Charley, ed. *Drum Beats: Walt Whitman's Civil War Boy Lovers*. San Francisco: Gay Sunshine Press, 1989.

Showalter, Elaine. *Sexual Anarchy: Gender and Culture at the Fin de Siècle*. New York: Viking-Penguin, 1990.

Shucard, Alan. *American Poetry: The Puritans through Whitman*. Amherst: University of Massachusetts Press, 1990.

Simons, Laird R., ed. *Cyclopaedia of American Literature*. Philadelphia: W. M. Rutter, 1875.

Sinfield, Alan. *The Wilde Century: Effeminacy, Oscar Wilde, and the Queer Movement*. New York: Columbia University Press, 1994.

Bibliography

Singer, Bennett. *Growing Up Gay: A Literary Anthology.* New York: New Press, 1993.

Smith, Bruce R. *Homosexual Desire in Shakespeare's England: A Cultural Poetics.* Chicago: University of Chicago Press, 1991.

Smith, Herbert F., ed. *Literary Criticism of James Russell Lowell.* Lincoln: University of Nebraska Press, 1969.

Smith-Rosenberg, Carroll. *Disorderly Conduct: Visions of Gender in Victorian America.* New York: Knopf, 1985.

Smollett, Tobias. *The Adventures of Roderick Random.* New York: Oxford University Press, 1981.

Snelling, William, ed. *Truth, A New Year's Gift Book for Scribblers.* Boston: n. p., 1831.

Specimens of the American Poets. 1822. New York: Scholar's Facsimiles and Reprints, 1972.

Spiller, Robert E., ed. *The Roots of National Culture: American Literature to 1830.* New York: Macmillan, 1933.

Spiller, Robert E., Willard Thorp, and Thomas H. Johnson, eds. *Literary History of the United States.* 3d ed. New York: Macmillan, 1963.

Stanley, Jo, ed. *Bold in Her Breeches: Women Pirates across the Ages.* San Francisco: HarperCollins, 1995.

"Statue of Fitz-Greene Halleck." *New York Times* January 22, 1869: 2.

Stedman, Edmund Clarence. *Poets of America.* 1885. Grosse Pointe, Mich.: Scholarly Press, 1968.

Steiner, Bernard Christian. *History of Guilford and Madison, Connecticut.* 1897. [Guilford, Conn.]: Guilford Free Library, 1975.

Stevens, Abel, ed. "Fitz-Greene Halleck." *National Magazine* December 1852: 481–87.

Stoddard, Richard Henry. "Fitz-Greene Halleck." *Lippincott's* June 1889: 886–97.

Stowe, Harriet Beecher. *Uncle Tom's Cabin.* 1852. Introd. Langston Hughes. New York: Dodd, Mead, 1952.

Straub, Kristina. *Sexual Suspects: Eighteenth-Century Players and Sexual Ideology.* Princeton, N.J.: Princeton University Press, 1992.

Stubbes, Philip. *Anatomie of Abuses.* Ed. W. Turnbull. London: n. p., 1836.

Sullivan, Catherine. "Poet Was a Figure Who Couldn't Be Ignored." *New Haven Register* June 29, 1989: G35.

Summers, Claude J., ed. *The Gay and Lesbian Literary Heritage.* New York: Henry Holt, 1995.

Summers, Claude J., ed. *Homosexuality in Renaissance and Enlightenment England: Literary Representations in Historical Context.* New York: Harrington Park Press, 1992.

Swerdlow, Joel L. "Central Park." *National Geographic* May 1993: 6–37.

Symington, Andrew James. "The First Statue to an American Poet." *Glasgow Herald* April 14, 1877.

Symonds, John Addington. *The Memoirs of John Addington Symonds.* Ed. Phyllis Grosskurth. London: Hutchinson, 1984.

Symonds, John Addington. *Walt Whitman: A Study.* New York: AMS Press, 1968.

Taft, Kendall B. "The First Printing of Halleck's 'The Winds of March Are Humming.'" *New-York Historical Society Quarterly* April 1943: 35–36.

"Talk of the Town." *New Yorker* September 3, 1990: 29–33.

Taylor, Bayard. "Fitz-Greene Halleck." *New York Tribune* May 15, 1877: 20–21.

Taylor, Bayard. "Fitz-Greene Halleck." *North American Review* July 1877: 60–67.

Taylor, Bayard. *Joseph and His Friend: A Story of Pennsylvania.* New York: Putnam, 1903.

Taylor, Bayard. *The Lands of the Saracens: Or, Pictures of Palestine, Asia Minor, Sicily and Spain.* 1855. New York: Putnam's Sons, 1881.

Thomas, Dwight, and David K. Jackson. *The Poe Log: A Documentary Life of Edgar Allan Poe 1809–1849.* Boston: G. K. Hall, 1987.

Thompson, Roger. "Attitudes towards Homosexuality in the Seventeenth-Century New England Colonies." *Journal of American Studies* 23 (1989): 27–40.

Tierney, John. "An Ode to Fitz." *New York Times Magazine* June 22, 1997.

Travelli, J. S. "Halleck's 'Ellen': The Complete Story of the Poet's Romance." *Press* December 1874. Reprinted in *New York Times* December 27, 1874: 4.

Trent, William Peterford, et al., eds. *The Cambridge History of American Literature.* New York: Macmillan, 1960.

Trevisan, João. *Perverts in Paradise.* London: Gay Men's Press, 1986.

Trumbach, Randolph. "The Birth of the Queen: Sodomy and the Emergence of Gender Equality in Modern Culture, 1660–1750." Duberman, Vicinus, and Chauncey 129–40.

Trumbach, Randolph. "Sodomy Transformed: Aristocratic Libertinage, Public Reputation and the Gender Revolution of the 18th Century." Kimmel 105–24.

Tuckerman, Henry T. "Reminiscences of Fitz-Greene Halleck." *Lippincott's* February 1868: 208–17.

Tyler, Royall. *The Contrast. Prose and Poetry of the Revolution.* Eds. Frederick C. Prescott and John H. Nelson. Port Washington, N.Y.: Kennikate Press, 1969. 245–58.

Van Leer, David. *The Queening of America: Gay Culture in Straight Society.* New York: Routledge, 1995.

Vidal, Gore. *Burr: A Novel.* New York: Random House, 1973.

Vidal, Gore. *1876.* New York: Random House, 1976.

Ward, Stanley M. "A Romantic Episode in the Life of the Poet, Fitz-Greene Halleck." *Bookman* 47 (1918): 499–502.

Weeks, Jeffrey. "Inverts, Perverts, and Mary-Annes: Male Prostitution and the Regulation of Homosexuality in England in the Nineteenth and Early Twentieth Centuries." Licata and Peterson 113–34.

Weeks, Jeffrey. "Uses and Abuses of Michel Foucault." *Against Nature: Essays on History, Sexuality and Identity.* 1991. London: Rivers Oram Press, 1992.

Weidenfeld, George. *The Pen and the Sword.* New York: Nicolson, 1974.

Wendell, Barrett. *A Literary History of America.* New York: Charles Scribner's Sons, 1920.

West, Paul. *Lord Byron's Doctor: A Novel.* Chicago: University of Chicago Press, 1989.

Wetmore, Prosper M. *Lexington with Other Fugitive Poems.* New York: G., C., and H. Carvill, 1830.

Wharton, Edith. *Summer.* Introd. Marilyn French. New York: Macmillan, 1981.

Whitman, Walt. *Leaves of Grass.* Eds. Sculley Bradley and Harold W. Blodgett. New York: Norton, 1973.

Whitmore, William H., ed. *The Colonial Laws of Massachusetts.* Boston: Rockwell and Churchill, 1890.

Wienandt, Elwyn A., and Robert H. Young. *The Anthem in England and America.* New York: Free Press, 1970.

Wilkins, William Glyde, ed. *Charles Dickens in America.* New York: Charles Scribner's Sons, 1911.

Williams, Stanley T., and Nelson F. Adkins, eds. *Courses of Reading in American Literature with Bibliographies.* New York: Harcourt, Brace, 1930.

Williams, Walter L. *The Spirit and the Flesh: Sexual Diversity in American Indian Culture.* Boston: Beacon Press, 1986.

Willson, Marcius. *The Fifth Reader of the School and Family Series.* Part I. New York: Harper Brothers, 1861.

Wilson, Edmund. *To the Finland Station: A Study in the Writing and Acting of History.* New York: Doubleday, 1940.

Wilson, James Grant. *Bryant and His Friends: Some Reminiscences of the Knickerbocker Writers.* New York: Fords, Howard and Hulbert, 1886.

Wilson, James Grant. "Fitz-Greene Halleck." *New York Ledger* January 25, 1868.

Wilson, James Grant. "Halleck and His Theatrical Friends." *Potter's American Monthly* March 1875: 217–22.

Wilson, James Grant. "Halleckiana." *Independent* February 1872.

Wilson, James Grant. "Joseph Rodman Drake." *Harper's New Monthly* June 1874: 65–71.

Wilson, James Grant. *Life and Letters of Fitz-Greene Halleck.* New York: D. Appleton, 1869.

Wilson, James Grant. "Poet Halleck." *Littell's Living Age* December 12, 1868: 701–3.

Wilson, James Grant. "Recollections of American Authors, No. 5. Fitz-Greene Halleck." *Book News Monthly* November 1911: 170–76.

Wilson, James Grant, and John Fiske. *Appleton's Cyclopaedia of American Biography.* Vol. 3. New York: D. Appleton, 1888.

Winthrop, John. *The History of New England from 1630 to 1649.* Ed. James Savage. Vol. 2. Boston: Little and Brown, 1853.

Woods, Gregory. *Articulate Flesh: Male Homo-Eroticism and Modern Poetry.* New Haven, Conn.: Yale University Press, 1987.

Woods, Gregory. "Walt Whitman's Boys." Review of *Calamus Lovers,* by Charles Shively. Santagati 122–27.

Wordsworth, William. *Selected Poems and Prefaces by William Wordsworth.* Ed. Jack Stillinger. Boston: Houghton Mifflin, 1965.

Wynne, James. "Fitz-Greene Halleck." *Harper's New Monthly* April 1862: 634–39.

Yarbrough, Jeff, ed. *The Advocate* October 17, 1995.

Zeeland, Steven. *Sailors and Sexual Identity: Crossing the Line between "Straight" and "Gay" in the U.S. Navy.* New York: Harrington Park Press, 1995.

INDEX